Easy

2025

MEDITERRANEAN

DIET *COOKBOOK* for Beginners

Setiuysilma Nissenuilo

1900

Days of Delicious and Wholesome Recipes Book to Help You Eat Well and Live Better | No-Stress 30-Day Meal Plan

D1709530

TABLE OF CONTENTS

Introduction

Chapter 1   The Mediterranean Pantry   / 4

Chapter 2   Breakfasts   / 10

Chapter 3   Beans and Grains   / 18

Chapter 4   Vegetables and Sides   / 28

Chapter 5   Vegetarian Mains   / 37

Chapter 6   Fish and Seafood   / 43

Chapter 7   Beef, Pork, and Lamb   / 52

Chapter 8   Poultry   / 58

Chapter 9   Snacks and Appetizers   / 65

Chapter 10   Salads   / 71

Chapter 11   Pizzas, Wraps, and Sandwiches   / 78

Chapter 12   Desserts   / 83

Chapter 13   Pasta   / 89

Chapter 14   Staples, Sauces, Dips, and Dressings   / 93

Appendix 1:   Measurement Conversion Chart   / 97

Appendix 2:   The Dirty Dozen and Clean Fifteen   / 98

Appendix 3:   Recipes Index   / 99

INTRODUCTION

The Mediterranean diet is more than just a diet; it is a way of life, a cultural celebration that encompasses healthy eating habits, vibrant flavors, and the joy of sharing meals with loved ones. Rooted in the culinary traditions of countries surrounding the Mediterranean Sea, this diet has gained recognition worldwide not only for its delicious diversity of dishes but also for its scientifically-proven health benefits. From the sun-drenched olive groves of Greece to the vibrant marketplaces of Morocco, the Mediterranean diet brings together flavors that are both nutritious and soul-satisfying.

In this cookbook, we embark on a journey through this remarkable cuisine. Whether you are seeking a healthier lifestyle, new cooking inspirations, or simply want to reconnect with the pleasure of eating, the Mediterranean Diet Cookbook offers something for everyone. Let's explore the principles behind this lifestyle, its profound impact on health, and how you can easily adopt it in your everyday life.

The Core of the Mediterranean Diet

At the heart of the Mediterranean diet are its core principles, which revolve around wholesome ingredients, balanced meals, and an emphasis on plant-based eating. Unlike many restrictive diets, the Mediterranean way of eating focuses on abundance—an abundance of vegetables, fruits, legumes, whole grains, and healthy fats like olive oil. Fish and seafood are central sources of protein, while dairy, poultry, and eggs are consumed in moderation. Red meat, while not excluded, plays only a minor role, reserved for occasional indulgence.

A key element that sets the Mediterranean diet apart is its reliance on fresh, seasonal, and minimally processed foods. Whether it is freshly harvested tomatoes, handpicked olives, or aromatic herbs, the ingredients used in Mediterranean cooking reflect an appreciation for nature's bounty. By prioritizing quality over quantity, this diet provides ample nutrients, antioxidants, and essential vitamins that contribute to a healthy lifestyle.

Another essential part of this dietary pattern is the use of healthy fats, primarily from olive oil. Olive oil is rich in monounsaturated fatty acids, which are beneficial for cardiovascular health. It also adds flavor and richness to Mediterranean dishes, turning simple ingredients into comforting, satisfying meals. Additionally, nuts and seeds provide another layer of healthy fats and texture to many dishes, making them staples in the Mediterranean kitchen.

Health Benefits Backed by Science

The Mediterranean diet has long been associated with numerous health benefits, and scientific research continues to support its role in promoting longevity and reducing the risk of chronic diseases. The diet's emphasis on whole foods, healthy fats, and lean protein sources makes it a powerful ally against heart disease, diabetes, and obesity. Studies have shown that individuals who adhere to a Mediterranean diet tend to have lower cholesterol levels, better blood sugar regulation, and reduced inflammation— all of which are critical for overall health.

Perhaps one of the most notable aspects of the Mediterranean diet is its effect on heart health. The combination of omega-3 fatty acids from fish, antioxidants from fruits and vegetables, and the heart-healthy fats from olive oil work synergistically to support cardiovascular function. Research has indicated that following a Mediterranean diet can significantly reduce the risk of heart attack and stroke, making it an excellent choice for those looking to maintain a healthy heart.

In addition to its cardiovascular benefits, the Mediterranean diet has been linked to improved brain health. The inclusion of omega-3-rich foods, such as salmon and walnuts, along with antioxidant-packed produce like berries and leafy greens, helps protect against cognitive decline. Moreover, the balanced nature of this diet promotes stable energy levels and better mood regulation, contributing to overall mental well-being.

Embracing the Mediterranean Lifestyle

One of the defining characteristics of the Mediterranean diet is that it is not merely about the food you eat—it is about how you eat it. In Mediterranean cultures, mealtimes are sacred moments for socializing, relaxing, and connecting with others. Instead of eating on the go or in front of a screen, meals are enjoyed slowly, often in the company of family and friends. This approach fosters a deeper relationship with food, allowing individuals to savor each bite, practice mindful eating, and experience a greater sense of satisfaction.

The Mediterranean lifestyle also encourages physical activity and a connection to nature. Long walks, gardening, and other forms of light physical activity are incorporated into daily

routines, supporting both physical and mental health. By combining a nutrient-rich diet with regular physical movement, this way of living promotes a holistic sense of wellness that goes beyond simply losing weight or counting calories.

For those who are new to the Mediterranean diet, the idea of changing long-established eating habits may seem daunting. However, adopting this lifestyle does not require a drastic overhaul. Simple changes, such as using olive oil instead of butter, adding more vegetables to your meals, or choosing fruit as a dessert, can make a big difference over time. The Mediterranean Diet Cookbook will guide you through these small, achievable steps, helping you integrate the principles of this diet into your daily routine.

A Culinary Journey

The Mediterranean region is home to an incredibly diverse range of flavors and culinary traditions. This cookbook aims to capture that diversity, offering a variety of recipes that reflect the unique ingredients, techniques, and tastes of different Mediterranean countries. From the comforting flavors of a hearty Italian minestrone to the zesty tang of a Greek tzatziki, each recipe is designed to bring the essence of the Mediterranean into your kitchen.

You will find recipes for every occasion—light and vibrant salads perfect for a summer picnic, nourishing stews that warm the soul on a chilly evening, and delectable desserts that showcase the natural sweetness of fruits and honey. Whether you are an experienced home cook or a beginner, these recipes are straightforward and accessible, encouraging you to explore new ingredients, experiment with different flavors, and most importantly, enjoy the process of cooking.

As you embark on this culinary journey, remember that the Mediterranean diet is not about perfection. It is about celebrating the pleasures of good food, embracing a healthier lifestyle, and finding joy in every meal. The recipes in this book are designed to inspire you, to help you discover the beauty of Mediterranean cooking, and to support your journey toward a healthier, more fulfilling way of eating.

The Mediterranean Diet Cookbook invites you to explore the vibrant world of Mediterranean cuisine. With every recipe, you will not only nourish your body but also connect with a rich culinary tradition that values simplicity, balance, and the joy of sharing. Let's dive into the kitchen and start creating dishes that are as wholesome as they are delicious—and, in true Mediterranean fashion, let's share them with the ones we love.

Chapter 1
The Mediterranean Pantry

Chapter 1 The Mediterranean Pantry

To truly embrace the Mediterranean way of eating, it all starts with a well-stocked pantry. The Mediterranean pantry is a treasure trove of ingredients that bring flavor, nutrition, and versatility to your cooking. Unlike some specialized diets that require hard-to-find or overly processed foods, the Mediterranean pantry is composed of everyday staples that are easy to source and naturally wholesome. This chapter will introduce you to the essential ingredients that define Mediterranean cuisine, helping you lay a strong foundation for your culinary journey.

1. Olive Oil: The Golden Elixir

Olive oil is, without question, the cornerstone of Mediterranean cooking. This golden elixir is used for everything—from sautéing vegetables to dressing salads, and even as a drizzle over finished dishes. Rich in healthy monounsaturated fats and antioxidants, olive oil imparts a richness to dishes while also contributing to heart health. Extra virgin olive oil is the highest quality, with a fruity aroma and distinct flavor that enhances both savory and sweet recipes.

When choosing olive oil for your kitchen, opt for cold-pressed extra virgin varieties for their purity and nutritional benefits. Keep it in a cool, dark place to preserve its quality, and always taste it before use—good olive oil should have a fresh, grassy flavor that brings vibrancy to your dishes.

2. Fresh and Dried Herbs: Nature's Flavor Boosters

Herbs are at the core of Mediterranean cooking, bringing layers of flavor to even the simplest ingredients. Fresh herbs such as basil, oregano, rosemary, thyme, and parsley are used generously to add freshness, while dried herbs are often mixed into marinades, soups, and stews. Herbs are not just about taste—they also offer a host of health benefits. Oregano, for example, is rich in antioxidants, while rosemary contains compounds that can support digestion.

Dried herbs are particularly important for building complex flavors in slow-cooked dishes. You may wish to create your own blend of "herbes de Provence," a mixture that often includes thyme, rosemary, marjoram, and lavender—perfect for adding a

Mediterranean flair to your cooking.

3. Legumes and Grains: The Heart of Mediterranean Meals

Legumes such as lentils, chickpeas, and beans are key players in the Mediterranean diet. These plant-based proteins are incredibly versatile, featuring in dishes ranging from hearty stews to simple salads. Legumes are also a great source of fiber, helping to keep you full and satisfied, while supporting healthy digestion.

Whole grains are another staple of the Mediterranean pantry. Farro, bulgur, quinoa, and brown rice are used to create nourishing dishes with varied textures and flavors. Whole grains are not only rich in complex carbohydrates that provide sustained energy, but they are also packed with vitamins, minerals, and fiber—making them a nutritious choice for any meal.

4. Fresh Vegetables and Fruits: The Vibrant Core

The Mediterranean diet is a celebration of fresh produce, and for good reason. Seasonal vegetables and fruits are the vibrant core of nearly every meal, providing an array of colors, flavors, and textures. Tomatoes, bell peppers, zucchini, eggplant, leafy greens, and artichokes are commonly used, often roasted, grilled, or served raw to preserve their natural flavor.

Fruits are also an integral part of the Mediterranean table, serving as a natural sweetener or a light dessert. Figs, grapes, pomegranates, and citrus fruits like lemons and oranges are enjoyed fresh, dried, or incorporated into savory dishes. The emphasis on fresh, colorful produce ensures that every meal is packed with nutrients and antioxidants that support overall health.

5. Seafood: The Protein of Choice

The Mediterranean diet places a strong emphasis on fish and seafood as the primary source of animal protein. Rich in omega-3 fatty acids, fish such as salmon, mackerel, sardines, and anchovies are not only delicious but also essential for maintaining heart and brain health. Shellfish, including shrimp, mussels, and clams, are also widely used, bringing briny flavors and a touch of elegance to Mediterranean dishes.

To get the most out of your seafood, aim to include a variety of fish in your diet, and try to source sustainably caught options whenever possible. Simple preparations like grilling, baking, or poaching allow the natural flavors of the fish to shine, enhanced by just a touch of olive oil, lemon, and fresh herbs.

6. Nuts and Seeds: The Crunchy Companions

Nuts and seeds are an important element of the Mediterranean pantry, providing crunch, flavor, and nutrition. Almonds, walnuts, pine nuts, and sesame seeds are frequently used to add texture to salads, dips, and baked goods. Rich in healthy fats, protein, and essential nutrients, nuts and seeds make an excellent addition to both sweet and savory dishes.

Tahini, a paste made from ground sesame seeds, is a popular ingredient in Mediterranean cooking, adding creaminess to sauces, dips like hummus, and even desserts. Similarly, toasted nuts can elevate a simple dish to something extraordinary, offering depth of flavor and a satisfying crunch.

7. Cheese and Dairy: The Finishing Touch

Dairy products, particularly cheese, are used sparingly in the Mediterranean diet but play an important role in adding flavor and richness. Feta, halloumi, ricotta, and yogurt are commonly enjoyed in a variety of dishes—from salads to baked goods. Greek yogurt, in particular, is a staple, used as a base for dips, a topping for

savory dishes, or a simple, creamy dessert with a drizzle of honey.

The key to enjoying dairy in the Mediterranean way is moderation. Rather than making cheese the focus of a dish, it is often used as a garnish or a complementary ingredient that adds a layer of flavor without overwhelming the other components.

8. Aromatics and Spices: Building Layers of Flavor

Aromatics such as garlic, onions, and shallots are fundamental to Mediterranean cooking, forming the flavor base for countless dishes. These ingredients, often sautéed in olive oil, release their natural sweetness and richness, infusing the entire dish with depth of flavor. Spices like cumin, coriander, paprika, and saffron are also used to add warmth and complexity.

The careful use of spices and aromatics allows Mediterranean dishes to be both deeply flavorful and well-balanced. The flavors are layered thoughtfully, with each ingredient contributing to the overall harmony of the dish.

Bringing It All Together

The Mediterranean pantry is more than just a collection of ingredients—it is a philosophy that emphasizes freshness, simplicity, and quality. By stocking your kitchen with these essential ingredients, you will be well-prepared to create a variety of delicious, wholesome dishes that embody the spirit of the Mediterranean diet. Each ingredient has its own story, a unique role in enhancing both the flavor and the health benefits of your meals.

In the following chapters, we will explore how to bring these ingredients to life through simple, flavorful recipes that are as nourishing as they are enjoyable to make. Whether you are crafting a vibrant salad, a comforting stew, or a light seafood dish, the key to Mediterranean cooking is to let the ingredients shine—celebrating their natural beauty and the joy of sharing good food with the people you love.

Mediterranean Diet Pyramid

A contemporary approach to delicious, healthy eating

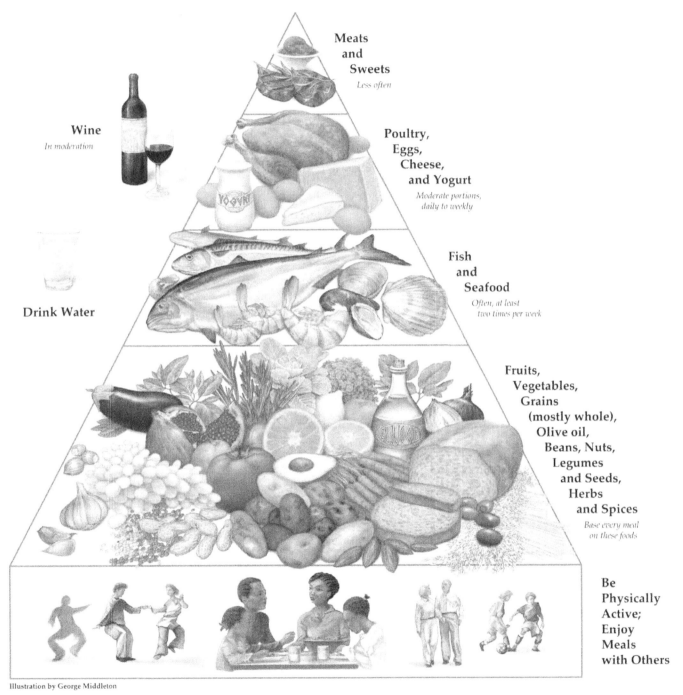

Meats and Sweets
Less often

Wine
In moderation

Poultry, Eggs, Cheese, and Yogurt
Moderate portions, daily to weekly

Fish and Seafood
Often, at least two times per week

Drink Water

Fruits, Vegetables, Grains (mostly whole), Olive oil, Beans, Nuts, Legumes and Seeds, Herbs and Spices
Base every meal on these foods

Be Physically Active; Enjoy Meals with Others

Illustration by George Middleton

30-Day Meal Plan

DAYS	BREAKFAST	LUNCH	DINNER	SNACK/DESSERT
1	Bell Pepper Egg Rings with Avocado Salsa 11	Farro Salad with Tomatoes and Olives 20	Lemon Pesto Salmon 46	Mascarpone-Stuffed Dates with Toasted Pecans 69
2	Mediterranean Fruit Bulgur Breakfast Bowl 12	Chili-Spiced Beans 22	Balsamic Pork Tenderloin 57	Greens Chips with Curried Yogurt Sauce 67
3	Almond Butter Banana Blueberry Smoothie 14	Herbed Lima Beans 24	Moroccan-Spiced Sea Bass with Chickpeas and Artichokes 51	Citrus-Infused Melon Salad 66
4	Warm Fava Beans with Whole-Wheat Pita 14	Mediterranean Tomato Rice with Fresh Herbs 19	Braised Turkey Thighs with Fig Balsamic Sauce 59	Heart-Healthy Nut and Fruit Trail Mix 69
5	Greek Yogurt Parfait with Granola 16	French Green Lentils with Swiss Chard and Almonds 25	Air-Fried Salmon Spring Rolls with Fresh Herbs 45	Tirokafteri (Spicy Feta and Yogurt Dip) 68
6	Spinach and Feta Frittata 15	Simple Tri-Color Lentil Salad 21	Lamb Stew 54	Stuffed Cucumber Cups 70
7	Spanish Tortilla with Potatoes and Peppers 11	Za'atar Chickpeas and Chicken 25	Cod with Lemon Parsley Pistou 44	Crispy Five-Spice Air-Fried Chicken Wings 68
8	Breakfast Quinoa with Figs and Walnuts 16	Moroccan Lamb with White Beans and Spices 24	Parchment-Baked Halibut with Fennel and Carrot Medley 49	Mediterranean Pita Pizza with Feta and Olives 70
9	Greek Egg and Tomato Scramble 12	Lentils with Cilantro and Lime 21	Red Wine Braised Short Ribs 54	Herb-Infused Steamed Artichokes with Lemon Garlic Dip 67
10	Pumpkin Spice Greek Yogurt Parfait 17	Chickpea Hash with Eggs 12	Grilled Kefta 53	Herb-Infused Steamed Artichokes 67
11	Almond Date Oatmeal 14	Slow Cooker White Beans with Kale 23	Roast Pork Tenderloin with Cherry Balsamic Reduction 53	Radish Chips 31
12	Smoky Sausage Patties 14	Asparagus-Spinach Farro 20	Southern Italian Seafood Stew in Tomato Broth 50	Spanish Home Fries with Spicy Tomato Sauce 70
13	Warm Bulgur Wheat Breakfast with Apples 13	Skillet Bulgur with Kale and Tomatoes 25	Moroccan Chicken Stew with Green Olives and Couscous 62	Spicy Roasted Potatoes 66
14	Mediterranean Muesli and Breakfast Bowl 13	Chili Lime Cauliflower with Cilantro 29	Pistachio-Crusted Whitefish 47	Tuna Croquettes 67
15	Spinach, Sun-Dried Tomato, and Feta Egg Wraps 17	Pasta E Fagioli with Rosemary and Parmesan 22	Air-Fried Mushroom Zucchini Veggie Burgers 39	Dijon Salmon Niçoise with Chive Vinaigrette 66
16	Cauliflower Baklava Breakfast Bowl 13	Chickpea and Green Bean Salad with Herbs 22	Herb-Crusted Parmesan Filet Mignon 55	Citrus Shrimp Ceviche Salad 49

DAYS	BREAKFAST	LUNCH	DINNER	SNACK/DESSERT
17	Instant Pot Farro Breakfast Bowl with Maple 14	Hearty Three-Bean Vegan Chili 23	Cod and Cauliflower Chowder 45	Fresh Stuffed Cucumbers with Avocado 31
18	Power Peach Smoothie Bowl 13	Mediterranean Roasted Chickpeas with Tomatoes 38	One-Pot Pork Loin Dinner 54	Spicy Buffalo Chicken Cheese Bites 59
19	Air Fryer Butternut Squash and Ricotta Frittata 16	Mediterranean Fish Stew 49	Balsamic Marinated Tofu with Basil and Oregano 39	Greek Street Tacos 68
20	Turkish Poached Eggs with Spiced Yogurt 16	Slow Cooker Root Vegetable Hash 29	Wild Cod Oreganata 51	Crispy Lemon-Pepper Air-Fried Drumsticks 68
21	Iced Coffee with Almond and Cinnamon Twist 15	Buckwheat and Halloumi Bowl with Mint Dressing 23	Braised Eggplant and Tomatoes 29	Caponata (Sicilian Eggplant) 34
22	Black Olive Toast with Herbed Hummus 15	Roasted Fennel with Za'atar 32	Chicken Avgolemono 59	Quick Garlic Mushrooms 67
23	Instant Pot Buckwheat Porridge with Balsamic Berries 12	Moroccan Red Lentil and Pumpkin Stew 42	Almond-Crusted Salmon with Honey Thyme Glaze 47	Sumac-Spiced Red Lentil Dip 66
24	Strawberry Vanilla Collagen Smoothie 17	Quinoa with Kale, Carrots, and Walnuts 26	Zucchini Ribbons with Lemon Ricotta and Fresh Herbs 34	Crispy Green Beans 34
25	Air-Fried Crustless Spinach and Cheddar Pie 41	Instant Pot Polenta with Arugula, Figs, and Blue Cheese 19	Asian Swordfish 50	No-Mayo Tuna Salad Cucumber Bites 70
26	Spinach Puff Pastry Pie 15	Black Bean Salad with Corn and Tomato Relish 27	Roast Pork Tenderloin 55	Honey Roasted Plums with Nutty Crumble and Yogurt 86
27	South of the Coast Sweet Potato Toast 11	Warm Mediterranean Farro Bowl 40	Cod with Tomatoes and Garlic 47	Refreshing Cucumber Lime Popsicles 85
28	Cauliflower Steaks with Olive Citrus Sauce 42	Instant Pot Farro Mushroom Risotto 20	Three-Cheese Zucchini Boats 38	Pesto-Stuffed Cucumber Boats 70
29	Baked Harissa Shakshuka with Fresh Basil 17	Air-Fried Eggplant Parmesan 41	Chicken Skewers 64	Manchego Crackers 68
30	Savory Cottage Cheese Breakfast Bowl 17	Creamy Chickpea Sauce with Whole-Wheat Fusilli 39	Air-Fried Caprese Eggplant Stacks 40	Baked Spinach Ricotta Bites with Basil 69

Chapter 2

Breakfasts

Chapter 2 Breakfasts

Bell Pepper Egg Rings with Avocado Salsa

Prep time: 15 minutes | Cook time: 5 minutes | Serves 4

- 4 bell peppers, any color
- 1 tablespoon extra-virgin olive oil
- 8 large eggs
- ¾ teaspoon kosher salt, divided
- ¼ teaspoon freshly ground
- black pepper, divided
- 1 avocado, peeled, pitted, and diced
- ¼ cup red onion, diced
- ¼ cup fresh basil, chopped
- Juice of ½ lime

1. Stem and seed the bell peppers. Cut 2 (2-inch-thick) rings from each pepper. Chop the remaining bell pepper into small dice, and set aside. 2. Heat the olive oil in a large skillet over medium heat. Add 4 bell pepper rings, then crack 1 egg in the middle of each ring. Season with ¼ teaspoon of the salt and ⅛ teaspoon of the black pepper. Cook until the egg whites are mostly set but the yolks are still runny, 2 to 3 minutes. Gently flip and cook 1 additional minute for over easy. Move the egg-bell pepper rings to a platter or onto plates, and repeat with the remaining 4 bell pepper rings. 3. In a medium bowl, combine the avocado, onion, basil, lime juice, reserved diced bell pepper, the remaining ¼ teaspoon kosher salt, and the remaining ⅛ teaspoon black pepper. Divide among the 4 plates.

Per Serving:
2 egg-pepper rings: calories: 270 | fat: 19g | protein: 15g | carbs: 12g | fiber: 5g | sodium: 360mg

South of the Coast Sweet Potato Toast

Prep time: 5 minutes | Cook time: 15 minutes | Serves 4

- 2 plum tomatoes, halved
- 6 tablespoons extra-virgin olive oil, divided
- Salt
- Freshly ground black pepper
- 2 large sweet potatoes, sliced lengthwise
- 1 cup fresh spinach
- 8 medium asparagus,
- trimmed
- 4 large cooked eggs or egg substitute (poached, scrambled, or fried)
- 1 cup arugula
- 4 tablespoons pesto
- 4 tablespoons shredded Asiago cheese

1. Set your oven to 450°F (235°C) to preheat. 2. Arrange the plum tomato halves on a baking sheet, brush them with 2 tablespoons of olive oil, and season with salt and pepper. Roast the tomatoes for about 15 minutes until they are tender, then remove them from the oven to rest. 3. On a separate baking sheet, place the sweet potato slices. Brush each side with about 2 tablespoons of olive oil, and sprinkle with salt and pepper. Bake the sweet potatoes for around 15 minutes, flipping them halfway through after 5 to 7 minutes, until they are tender but not too soft. Remove them from the oven

and set aside. 4. In a skillet, heat the remaining 2 tablespoons of olive oil over medium heat. Sauté the fresh spinach briefly until it just begins to wilt, then transfer it to a plate lined with paper towels. In the same skillet, add the asparagus and cook until slightly tender, making sure to turn them regularly. Transfer the asparagus to a paper-towel-lined plate as well. 5. Arrange the baked sweet potato slices on serving plates. Evenly distribute the sautéed spinach and asparagus over the potato slices. Place a prepared egg on top of each, then add ¼ cup of fresh arugula to each serving. 6. To finish, drizzle each dish with 1 tablespoon of pesto and sprinkle 1 tablespoon of cheese over the top. Serve with one roasted plum tomato on the side.

Per Serving:
calories: 441 | fat: 35g | protein: 13g | carbs: 23g | fiber: 4g | sodium: 481mg

Spanish Tortilla with Potatoes and Peppers

Prep time : 5 minutes | Cook time: 50 minutes | Serves 6

- ½ cup olive oil, plus 2 tablespoons, divided
- 2 pounds (907 g) baking potatoes, peeled and cut into ¼-inch slices
- 2 onions, thinly sliced
- 1 roasted red pepper, drained and cut into strips
- 6 eggs
- 2 teaspoons salt
- 1 teaspoon freshly ground black pepper

1. In a large skillet, heat ½ cup of olive oil over medium heat. Once hot, add the potatoes and cook, stirring occasionally, for about 20 minutes until they are tender. Remove the potatoes using a slotted spoon and discard any excess oil remaining in the skillet. 2. In a medium skillet over medium heat, warm the remaining 2 tablespoons of olive oil. Add the onions and cook, stirring frequently, until they become soft and golden brown, roughly 10 minutes. Remove the onions with a slotted spoon, keeping the oil in the pan, and add them to the cooked potatoes. Add the sliced bell peppers to the potatoes as well. 3. In a large mixing bowl, whisk together the eggs, salt, and black pepper. Gently fold in the cooked vegetables, ensuring they are evenly coated with the egg mixture. 4. Heat the medium skillet over low heat. Pour the egg and vegetable mixture into the skillet, cooking for about 10 minutes until the bottom is lightly browned and set. Carefully use a spatula to loosen the tortilla around the edges. Transfer it to a large plate by sliding it out of the skillet, browned side down. Invert the skillet over the plate and then flip the tortilla back into the skillet so that the browned side is now on top. Continue to cook over low heat until the tortilla is fully set in the center, about 5 additional minutes. 5. Serve the tortilla warm or at room temperature. This dish is versatile and can be enjoyed on its own or paired with a fresh salad for a hearty meal.

Per Serving:
calories: 370 | fat: 26g | protein: 9g | carbs: 29g | fiber: 5g | sodium: 876mg

Greek Egg and Tomato Scramble

Prep time: 10 minutes | Cook time: 25 minutes | Serves 4

- ¼ cup extra-virgin olive oil, divided
- 1½ cups chopped fresh tomatoes
- ¼ cup finely minced red onion
- 2 garlic cloves, minced
- ½ teaspoon dried oregano or 1 to 2 teaspoons chopped fresh oregano
- ½ teaspoon dried thyme or 1 to 2 teaspoons chopped fresh thyme
- 8 large eggs
- ½ teaspoon salt
- ¼ teaspoon freshly ground black pepper
- ¾ cup crumbled feta cheese
- ¼ cup chopped fresh mint leaves

1. In a large skillet, heat the olive oil over medium heat. Add the chopped tomatoes and red onion, and sauté for about 10 to 12 minutes, until the tomatoes are soft and cooked through. 2. Stir in the minced garlic, dried oregano, and dried thyme, and continue to sauté for another 2 to 4 minutes until the mixture becomes fragrant and the excess liquid has reduced. 3. In a medium mixing bowl, whisk the eggs together with salt and black pepper until well blended. 4. Pour the eggs into the skillet, reduce the heat to low, and cook them gently, scrambling until they are just set and creamy. Use a spatula to move the eggs constantly for 3 to 4 minutes, ensuring they don't overcook. Remove the skillet from the heat, fold in the crumbled feta cheese and fresh mint, and serve the dish warm.

Per Serving:
calories: 355 | fat: 29g | protein: 17g | carbs: 6g | fiber: 1g | sodium: 695mg

Mediterranean Fruit Bulgur Breakfast Bowl

Prep time: 5 minutes | Cook time: 15 minutes | Serves: 6

- 1½ cups uncooked bulgur
- 2 cups 2% milk
- 1 cup water
- ½ teaspoon ground cinnamon
- 2 cups frozen (or fresh, pitted) dark sweet cherries
- 8 dried (or fresh) figs, chopped
- ½ cup chopped almonds
- ¼ cup loosely packed fresh mint, chopped
- Warm 2% milk, for serving (optional)

1. In a medium saucepan, mix together the bulgur, milk, water, and cinnamon. Stir briefly, then bring the mixture to a boil. Once boiling, cover the pan, lower the heat to medium-low, and let it simmer for about 10 minutes until all the liquid is absorbed. 2. Once the bulgur is ready, turn off the heat but keep the saucepan on the stove. Add the frozen cherries (no need to thaw), figs, and almonds to the hot bulgur. Stir everything thoroughly, cover the pan again, and let it sit for 1 minute, allowing the bulgur to thaw the cherries and slightly rehydrate the figs. Stir in the chopped mint to finish. 3. Spoon the mixture into serving bowls. You can serve it with warm milk on the side for extra creaminess, or let it cool down and enjoy it chilled.

Per Serving:
calories: 273 | fat: 7g | protein: 10g | carbs: 48g | fiber: 8g | sodium: 46mg

Chickpea Hash with Eggs

Prep time: 20 minutes | Cook time: 35 minutes | Serves 4

- 1 cup dried chickpeas
- 4 cups water
- 2 tablespoons extra-virgin olive oil, divided
- 1 medium onion, peeled and chopped
- 1 medium zucchini, trimmed and sliced
- 1 large red bell pepper,
- seeded and chopped
- 1 teaspoon minced garlic
- ½ teaspoon ground cumin
- ½ teaspoon ground black pepper
- ¼ teaspoon salt
- 4 large hard-cooked eggs, peeled and halved
- ½ teaspoon smoked paprika

1. Add chickpeas, water, and 1 tablespoon of oil to the Instant Pot®. Close the lid, set the steam release to Sealing, press the Manual button, and set the cooking time to 30 minutes. 2. Once the timer goes off, carefully perform a quick-release until the float valve drops. Press the Cancel button, open the lid, and drain the chickpeas thoroughly. Transfer them to a medium bowl and set aside. 3. Clean and dry the pot. Return it to the Instant Pot machine, press the Sauté button, and heat the remaining 1 tablespoon of oil. Add the onion, zucchini, and bell pepper, and cook for about 5 minutes until the vegetables are tender. Add the minced garlic, cumin, black pepper, and salt, cooking for an additional 30 seconds. Stir in the cooked chickpeas, ensuring they are evenly coated with the seasoning. 4. Transfer the chickpea and vegetable mixture to a serving platter. Arrange eggs on top, sprinkle with paprika, and serve immediately while still warm.

Per Serving:
calories: 274 | fat: 14g | protein: 15g | carbs: 36g | fiber: 16g | sodium: 242mg

Instant Pot Buckwheat Porridge with Balsamic Berries

Prep time: 10 minutes | Cook time: 6 minutes | Serves 4

- 1 cup buckwheat groats, rinsed and drained
- 3 cups water
- ½ cup chopped pitted dates
- 1 tablespoon light olive oil
- ¼ teaspoon ground cinnamon
- ¼ teaspoon salt
- ½ teaspoon vanilla extract
- 1 cup blueberries
- 1 cup raspberries
- 1 cup hulled and quartered strawberries
- 2 tablespoons balsamic vinegar

1. Place buckwheat, water, dates, oil, cinnamon, and salt in the Instant Pot® and stir well. Close lid and set steam release to Sealing. Press the Manual button and set time to 6 minutes. 2. When the timer beeps, let pressure release naturally, about 20 minutes. Open lid and stir in vanilla. 3. While buckwheat cooks, combine blueberries, raspberries, strawberries, and vinegar in a medium bowl. Stir well. Top porridge with berry mixture. Serve hot.

Per Serving:
calories: 318 | fat: 5g | protein: 6g | carbs: 64g | fiber: 9g | sodium: 151mg

Cauliflower Baklava Breakfast Bowl

Prep time: 5 minutes | Cook time: 5 minutes | Serves 2

- 2 cups riced cauliflower
- ¾ cup unsweetened almond, flax, or hemp milk
- 4 tablespoons extra-virgin olive oil, divided
- 2 teaspoons grated fresh orange peel (from ½ orange)
- ½ teaspoon ground cinnamon
- ½ teaspoon almond extract or vanilla extract
- ⅛ teaspoon salt
- 4 tablespoons chopped walnuts, divided
- 1 to 2 teaspoons liquid stevia, monk fruit, or other sweetener of choice (optional)

1. In medium saucepan, combine the riced cauliflower, almond milk, 2 tablespoons olive oil, grated orange peel, cinnamon, almond extract, and salt. Stir to combine and bring just to a boil over medium-high heat, stirring constantly. 2. Remove from heat and stir in 2 tablespoons chopped walnuts and sweetener (if using). Stir to combine. 3. Divide into bowls, topping each with 1 tablespoon of chopped walnuts and 1 tablespoon of the remaining olive oil.

Per Serving:
calories: 414 | fat: 38g | protein: 6g | carbs: 16g | fiber: 4g | sodium: 252mg

Air Fryer Pepper Egg Rings with Salsa

Prep time: 5 minutes | Cook time: 10 minutes | Serves 4

- Olive oil
- 1 large red, yellow, or orange bell pepper, cut into four ¾-inch rings
- 4 eggs
- Salt and freshly ground black pepper, to taste
- 2 teaspoons salsa

1. Preheat the air fryer to 350ºF (177ºC). Lightly spray a baking pan with olive oil. 2. Place 2 bell pepper rings on the pan. Crack one egg into each bell pepper ring. Season with salt and black pepper. 3. Spoon ½ teaspoon of salsa on top of each egg. 4. Place the pan in the air fryer basket. Air fry until the yolk is slightly runny, 5 to 6 minutes or until the yolk is fully cooked, 8 to 10 minutes. 5. Repeat with the remaining 2 pepper rings. Serve hot.

Per Serving:
calories: 76 | fat: 4g | protein: 6g | carbs: 3g | fiber: 1g | sodium: 83mg

Warm Bulgur Wheat Breakfast with Apples and Almonds

Prep time: 2 minutes | Cook time: 23 minutes | Serves 1

- ½ teaspoon extra virgin olive oil
- ¼ cup medium-grain uncooked bulgur wheat
- ½ medium apple (any variety), chopped
- 1 tablespoon raisins
- ¾ cup hot water
- 1 teaspoon honey
- 1 tablespoon slivered or finely chopped almonds
- Pinch of ground cinnamon

1. Add the olive oil to a small pan placed over medium heat. When the oil becomes hot, add the bulgur and sauté for 2–3 minutes, stirring frequently with a wooden spoon. 2. Add the apple, raisins, and hot water. When the mixture begins to boil, promptly remove the pan from the heat, cover, and set it aside for 10 minutes. After 10 minutes, add the honey and stir. 3. Top the cereal with the almonds and then sprinkle the cinnamon over the top. Serve warm.

Per Serving:
calories: 297 | fat: 8g | protein: 7g | carbs: 56g | fiber: 8g | sodium: 14mg

Power Peach Smoothie Bowl

Prep time: 15 minutes | Cook time: 0 minutes | Serves 2

- 2 cups packed partially thawed frozen peaches
- ½ cup plain or vanilla Greek yogurt
- ½ ripe avocado
- 2 tablespoons flax meal
- 1 teaspoon vanilla extract
- 1 teaspoon orange extract
- 1 tablespoon honey (optional)

1. Add all of the ingredients to a blender and blend until the mixture is completely smooth and creamy. 2. Divide the blended mixture evenly between two bowls. If you like, sprinkle some extra toppings of your choice over each bowl before serving. Enjoy immediately for a fresh and vibrant treat.

Per Serving:
calories: 213 | fat: 13g | protein: 6g | carbs: 23g | fiber: 7g | sodium: 41mg

Mediterranean Muesli and Breakfast Bowl

Prep time: 10 minutes | Cook time: 0 minutes | Serves 12

Muesli:
- 3 cups old-fashioned rolled oats
- 1 cup wheat or rye flakes
- 1 cup pistachios or almonds, coarsely chopped
- ½ cup oat bran
- 8 dried apricots, chopped
- 8 dates, chopped
- 8 dried figs, chopped

Breakfast Bowl:
- ½ cup Mediterranean Muesli (above)
- 1 cup low-fat plain Greek yogurt or milk
- 2 tablespoons pomegranate seeds (optional)
- ½ teaspoon black or white sesame seeds

1. For the muesli: In a medium mixing bowl, combine the oats, wheat or rye flakes, pistachios or almonds, oat bran, dried apricots, dates, and figs. Mix well and transfer to an airtight container. You can store the muesli for up to one month, making it a convenient and healthy breakfast option. 2. To prepare the breakfast bowl: In a serving bowl, add your desired portion of muesli and mix with either yogurt or milk, depending on your preference. Sprinkle with pomegranate seeds, if you're using them, and finish with a topping of sesame seeds. Enjoy a nutritious and easy breakfast!

Per Serving:
calories: 234 | fat: 6g | protein: 8g | carbs: 40g | fiber: 6g | sodium: 54mg

Instant Pot Farro Breakfast Bowl with Maple and Mixed Fruit

Prep time: 10 minutes | Cook time: 20 minutes | Serves 8

- 16 ounces (454 g) farro, rinsed and drained
- 4½ cups water
- ¼ cup maple syrup
- ¼ teaspoon salt
- 1 cup dried mixed fruit
- ½ cup chopped toasted mixed nuts
- 2 cups almond milk

1. Place farro, water, maple syrup, and salt in the Instant Pot® and stir to combine. Close lid, set steam release to Sealing, press the Multigrain button, and set time to 20 minutes. When the timer beeps, let pressure release naturally, about 30 minutes. 2. Press the Cancel button, open lid, and add dried fruit. Close lid and let stand on the Keep Warm setting for 20 minutes. Serve warm with nuts and almond milk.

Per Serving:
calories: 347 | fat: 7g | protein: 9g | carbs: 65g | fiber: 9g | sodium: 145mg

Almond Butter Banana Blueberry Smoothie

Prep time: 5 minutes | Cook time: 0 minutes | Serves 1

- ¾ cup almond milk
- ½ medium banana, preferably frozen
- ¼ cup frozen blueberries
- 1 tablespoon almond butter
- 1 tablespoon unsweetened cocoa powder
- 1 tablespoon chia seeds

1. In a blender or Vitamix, add all the ingredients. Blend to combine.

Per Serving:
calories: 300 | fat: 16g | protein: 8g | carbs: 37g | fiber: 10g | sodium: 125mg

Warm Fava Beans with Whole-Wheat Pita

Prep time: 5 minutes | Cook time: 10 minutes | Serves 4

- 1½ tablespoons olive oil
- 1 large onion, diced
- 1 large tomato, diced
- 1 clove garlic, crushed
- 1 (15-ounce / 425-g) can fava beans, not drained
- 1 teaspoon ground cumin
- ¼ cup chopped fresh parsley
- ¼ cup lemon juice
- Salt
- Freshly ground black pepper
- Crushed red pepper flakes
- 4 whole-grain pita bread pockets

1. Warm the olive oil in a large skillet over medium-high heat. Add the chopped onion, diced tomato, and minced garlic, and cook, stirring occasionally, for about 3 minutes until the vegetables have softened. 2. Stir in the fava beans, including the liquid from the can, and allow the mixture to come to a boil. 3. Reduce the heat to medium and add the ground cumin, chopped parsley, and fresh lemon juice. Season with salt, black pepper, and crushed red pepper flakes for a touch of spice. Let the mixture simmer, stirring occasionally, for about 5 minutes until the flavors meld together. 4. While the beans are simmering, warm the pita bread in a toaster oven or a cast-iron skillet over medium heat. To serve, cut the pitas into triangles for easy dipping or fill each pita half with the fava bean mixture for a delicious handheld option. Enjoy warm.

Per Serving:
calories: 524 | fat: 8g | protein: 32g | carbs: 86g | fiber: 31g | sodium: 394mg

Smoky Sausage Patties

Prep time: 30 minutes | Cook time: 9 minutes | Serves 8

- 1 pound (454 g) ground pork
- 1 tablespoon coconut aminos
- 2 teaspoons liquid smoke
- 1 teaspoon dried sage
- 1 teaspoon sea salt
- ½ teaspoon fennel seeds
- ½ teaspoon dried thyme
- ½ teaspoon freshly ground black pepper
- ¼ teaspoon cayenne pepper

1. In a large mixing bowl, combine the ground pork, coconut aminos, liquid smoke, dried sage, salt, fennel seeds, thyme, black pepper, and cayenne pepper. Use your hands to thoroughly mix the meat until the seasonings are evenly distributed throughout. 2. Form the seasoned pork mixture into 8 equal-sized patties. Press your thumb gently into the center of each patty to create a small indentation, which helps them cook evenly. Arrange the patties on a plate, cover with plastic wrap, and refrigerate for at least 30 minutes to allow the flavors to meld. 3. When ready to cook, arrange the patties in a single layer in the air fryer basket, working in batches if necessary to avoid overcrowding. 4. Set the air fryer to 400°F (204°C) and cook the patties for 5 minutes. Carefully flip each patty and continue cooking for an additional 4 minutes, or until the patties are fully cooked through and golden brown. Serve hot.

Per Serving:
calories: 70 | fat: 2g | protein: 12g | carbs: 0g | fiber: 0g | sodium: 329mg

Instant Pot Almond Date Oatmeal

Prep time: 5 minutes | Cook time: 12 minutes | Serves 4

- 1 cup sliced almonds
- 4 cups water
- 2 cups rolled oats
- 1 tablespoon extra-virgin
- olive oil
- ¼ teaspoon salt
- ½ cup chopped pitted dates

1. Press the Sauté button on the Instant Pot® and add almonds. Toast, stirring constantly, until almonds are golden brown, about 8 minutes. Press the Cancel button and add water, oats, oil, salt, and dates to the pot. Stir well. Close lid and set steam release to Sealing. Press the Manual button and set time to 4 minutes. 2. When the timer beeps, quick-release the pressure until the float valve drops, open lid, and stir well. Serve hot.

Per Serving:
calories: 451 | fat: 25g | protein: 14g | carbs: 52g | fiber: 9g | sodium: 320mg

Spinach and Feta Frittata

Prep time: 10 minutes | Cook time: 26 minutes | Serves 4

- 1 tablespoon olive oil
- ½ medium onion, peeled and chopped
- ½ medium red bell pepper, seeded and chopped
- 2 cups chopped fresh baby spinach
- 1 cup water
- 1 cup crumbled feta cheese
- 6 large eggs, beaten
- ¼ cup low-fat plain Greek yogurt
- ½ teaspoon salt
- ½ teaspoon ground black pepper

1. Press the Sauté button on the Instant Pot® and add the oil. Once hot, add the chopped onion and bell pepper, cooking for about 8 minutes until they are tender. Add the fresh spinach, stirring for about 3 minutes until it wilts. Press the Cancel button, transfer the vegetables to a medium bowl, and allow them to cool. Wipe out the inner pot of the Instant Pot® to prepare for the next steps. 2. Place the metal rack inside the Instant Pot® and pour in the water. Spray a 1.5-liter baking dish with nonstick cooking spray to prevent sticking. Drain any excess liquid from the spinach mixture, then add the vegetables to the baking dish along with the cheese. 3. In a separate medium bowl, whisk together the eggs, yogurt, salt, and black pepper until fully combined. Pour the egg mixture over the vegetables and cheese in the baking dish, ensuring everything is evenly distributed. Cover the dish tightly with aluminum foil, then carefully lower it into the Instant Pot®. 4. Close the lid of the Instant Pot®, set the steam release valve to Sealing, press the Manual button, and set the cooking time to 15 minutes. Once the timer beeps, allow the pressure to release naturally for 10 minutes, then perform a quick-release to let out any remaining pressure until the float valve drops. Press the Cancel button and open the lid. Let the frittata stand for 10 to 15 minutes before carefully removing the dish from the Instant Pot®. 5. Use a thin knife to run along the edge of the frittata to help release it, then turn it out onto a serving platter. Serve warm for a comforting and flavorful dish.

Per Serving:
calories: 259 | fat: 19g | protein: 16g | carbs: 6g | fiber: 1g | sodium: 766mg

Iced Coffee with Almond and Cinnamon Twist

Prep time: 10 minutes | Cook time: 0 minutes | Serves 1

- 1 cup freshly brewed strong black coffee, cooled slightly
- 1 tablespoon extra-virgin olive oil
- 1 tablespoon half-and-half or heavy cream (optional)
- 1 teaspoon MCT oil (optional)
- ⅛ teaspoon almond extract
- ⅛ teaspoon ground cinnamon

1. Pour the slightly cooled coffee into a blender or large glass (if using an immersion blender). 2. Add the olive oil, half-and-half (if using), MCT oil (if using), almond extract, and cinnamon. 3. Blend well until smooth and creamy. Drink warm and enjoy.

Per Serving:
calories: 124 | fat: 14g | protein: 0g | carbs: 0g | fiber: 0g | sodium: 5mg

Black Olive Toast with Herbed Hummus

Prep time: 5 minutes | Cook time: 5 minutes | Serves 2

- ¼ cup store-bought plain hummus
- 2 tablespoons finely chopped fresh flat-leaf parsley
- 1 tablespoon finely chopped fresh dill
- 1 tablespoon finely chopped
- fresh mint
- 1 teaspoon finely grated lemon peel
- 2 slices (½" thick) black olive bread
- 1 clove garlic, halved
- 1 tablespoon extra-virgin olive oil

1. In a small bowl, mix the hummus with the fresh herbs and grated lemon peel until everything is well combined. This will add a burst of freshness to the spread. 2. Toast the slices of bread until they are golden and crispy. While still warm, rub each slice with a clove of garlic to infuse them with a subtle garlic flavor. 3. Spread half of the herbed hummus mixture evenly over each slice of bread. Drizzle each slice with a bit of olive oil for a finishing touch. Serve immediately for a simple yet flavorful snack or appetizer.

Per Serving:
calories: 197 | fat: 11g | protein: 6g | carbs: 20g | fiber: 4g | sodium: 177mg

Golden Spinach Puff Pastry Pie

Prep time: 10 minutes | Cook time: 25 minutes | Serves 8

- Nonstick cooking spray
- 2 tablespoons extra-virgin olive oil
- 1 onion, chopped
- 1 pound (454 g) frozen spinach, thawed
- ¼ teaspoon garlic salt
- ¼ teaspoon freshly ground black pepper
- ¼ teaspoon ground nutmeg
- 4 large eggs, divided
- 1 cup grated Parmesan cheese, divided
- 2 puff pastry doughs, (organic, if available), at room temperature
- 4 hard-boiled eggs, halved

1. Preheat the oven to 350°F(180ºC). Spray a baking sheet with nonstick cooking spray and set aside. 2. Heat a large sauté pan or skillet over medium-high heat. Put in the oil and onion and cook for about 5 minutes, until translucent. 3. Squeeze the excess water from the spinach, then add to the pan and cook, uncovered, so that any excess water from the spinach can evaporate. Add the garlic salt, pepper, and nutmeg. Remove from heat and set aside to cool. 4. In a small bowl, crack 3 eggs and mix well. Add the eggs and ½ cup Parmesan cheese to the cooled spinach mix. 5. On the prepared baking sheet, roll out the pastry dough. Layer the spinach mix on top of dough, leaving 2 inches around each edge. 6. Once the spinach is spread onto the pastry dough, place hard-boiled egg halves evenly throughout the pie, then cover with the second pastry dough. Pinch the edges closed. 7. Crack the remaining egg in a small bowl and mix well. Brush the egg wash over the pastry dough. 8. Bake for 15 to 20 minutes, until golden brown and warmed through.

Per Serving:
calories: 417 | fat: 28g | protein: 17g | carbs: 25g | fiber: 3g | sodium: 490mg

Greek Yogurt Parfait with Granola

Prep time: 10 minutes | Cook time: 30 minutes | Serves 4

For the Granola:
- ¼ cup honey or maple syrup
- 2 tablespoons vegetable oil
- 2 teaspoons vanilla extract
- ½ teaspoon kosher salt
- 3 cups gluten-free rolled oats
- 1 cup mixed raw and unsalted nuts, chopped
- ¼ cup sunflower seeds
- 1 cup unsweetened dried cherries

For the Parfait:
- 2 cups plain Greek yogurt
- 1 cup fresh fruit, chopped
- (optional)

1. Set your oven to 325°F (163°C) to preheat. Line a baking sheet with parchment paper or foil to prevent sticking. 2. In a small saucepan over medium heat, combine the honey, oil, vanilla extract, and salt. Let the mixture simmer for about 2 minutes, stirring to combine well. 3. In a large mixing bowl, add the oats, nuts, and seeds. Pour the warm honey-oil mixture over the dry ingredients and mix thoroughly to ensure everything is coated. Spread the granola mixture evenly on the prepared baking sheet in a single layer. Bake for about 30 minutes, stirring halfway through to achieve an even golden color. 4. Once baked, remove from the oven and immediately mix in the dried cherries. Allow the granola to cool completely before storing it in an airtight container at room temperature for up to 3 months. 5. To make a parfait: For one serving, layer ½ cup of yogurt, ½ cup of granola, and ¼ cup of fruit, if desired, in a bowl or a lowball glass. You can create layers in any pattern you like for an appealing presentation. Enjoy your fresh and crunchy parfait!

Per Serving:
calories: 370 | fat: 144g | protein: 19g | carbs: 44g | fiber: 6g | sodium: 100mg

Turkish Poached Eggs with Spiced Yogurt

Prep time: 10 minutes | Cook time: 15 minutes | Serves 2

- 2 tablespoons ghee
- ½–1 teaspoon red chile flakes
- 2 tablespoons extra-virgin olive oil
- 1 cup full-fat goat's or sheep's milk yogurt
- 1 clove garlic, minced
- 1 tablespoon fresh lemon
- juice
- Salt and black pepper, to taste
- Dash of vinegar
- 4 large eggs
- Optional: pinch of sumac
- 2 tablespoons chopped fresh cilantro or parsley

1. In a skillet, melt the ghee over low heat. Add the chile flakes and let it infuse while you prepare the eggs. Remove from the heat and mix with the extra-virgin olive oil. Set aside. Combine the yogurt, garlic, lemon juice, salt, and pepper. 2. Poach the eggs. Fill a medium saucepan with water and a dash of vinegar. Bring to a boil over high heat. Crack each egg individually into a ramekin or a cup. Using a spoon, create a gentle whirlpool in the water; this will help the egg white wrap around the egg yolk. Slowly lower the egg into the water in the center of the whirlpool. Turn off the heat and cook for 3 to 4 minutes. Use a slotted spoon to remove the egg from the water and place it on a plate. Repeat for all remaining eggs. 3. To assemble, place the yogurt mixture in a bowl and add the poached eggs. Drizzle with the infused oil, and garnish with cilantro. Add a pinch of sumac, if using. Eat warm.

Per Serving:
calories: 576 | fat: 46g | protein: 27g | carbs: 17g | fiber: 4g | sodium: 150mg

Air Fryer Butternut Squash and Ricotta Frittata

Prep time: 10 minutes | Cook time: 33 minutes | Serves 2 to 3

- 1 cup cubed (½-inch) butternut squash (5½ ounces / 156 g)
- 2 tablespoons olive oil
- Kosher salt and freshly ground black pepper, to
- taste
- 4 fresh sage leaves, thinly sliced
- 6 large eggs, lightly beaten
- ½ cup ricotta cheese
- Cayenne pepper

1. In a bowl, toss the squash with the olive oil and season with salt and black pepper until evenly coated. Sprinkle the sage on the bottom of a cake pan and place the squash on top. Place the pan in the air fryer and bake at 400°F (204°C) for 10 minutes. Stir to incorporate the sage, then cook until the squash is tender and lightly caramelized at the edges, about 3 minutes more. 2. Pour the eggs over the squash, dollop the ricotta all over, and sprinkle with cayenne. Bake at 300°F (149°C) until the eggs are set and the frittata is golden brown on top, about 20 minutes. Remove the pan from the air fryer and cut the frittata into wedges to serve.

Per Serving:
calories: 289 | fat: 22g | protein: 18g | carbs: 5g | fiber: 1g | sodium: 184mg

Breakfast Quinoa with Figs and Walnuts

Prep time: 10 minutes | Cook time: 12 minutes | Serves 4

- 1½ cups quinoa, rinsed and drained
- 2½ cups water
- 1 cup almond milk
- 2 tablespoons honey
- 1 teaspoon vanilla extract
- ½ teaspoon ground
- cinnamon
- ¼ teaspoon salt
- ½ cup low-fat plain Greek yogurt
- 8 fresh figs, quartered
- 1 cup chopped toasted walnuts

1. Add the quinoa, water, almond milk, honey, vanilla extract, cinnamon, and salt to the Instant Pot®. Stir everything together until well mixed. Secure the lid, set the steam release to Sealing, press the Rice button, and adjust the cooking time to 12 minutes. Once the timer goes off, allow the pressure to release naturally for about 20 minutes to ensure a tender texture. 2. After the pressure has released, press the Cancel button and open the lid. Use a fork to fluff the quinoa to achieve a light and fluffy consistency. Serve the quinoa warm, topped with a dollop of yogurt, fresh figs, and a sprinkle of chopped walnuts for added texture and flavor. Enjoy this comforting breakfast or snack!

Per Serving:
calories: 413 | fat: 25g | protein: 10g | carbs: 52g | fiber: 7g | sodium: 275mg

Savory Cottage Cheese Breakfast Bowl

- 2 cups low-fat cottage cheese
- 2 tablespoons chopped mixed fresh herbs, such as basil, dill, flat-leaf parsley, and oregano
- ½ teaspoon ground black pepper
- 1 large tomato, chopped
- 1 small cucumber, peeled and chopped
- ¼ cup pitted kalamata olives, halved
- 1 tablespoon extra-virgin olive oil

1. In a medium bowl, mix the cottage cheese with the fresh herbs and ground black pepper until well combined. 2. Add in the chopped tomato, cucumber, and olives, gently folding them into the cottage cheese mixture to keep the vegetables intact. 3. Drizzle the mixture with olive oil just before serving for a finishing touch. Serve immediately and enjoy a light, refreshing dish.

Per Serving:
calories: 181 | fat: 10g | protein: 15g | carbs: 8g | fiber: 1g | sodium: 788mg

Strawberry Vanilla Collagen Smoothie

- 3 ounces (85 g) fresh or frozen strawberries
- ¾ cup unsweetened almond milk
- ¼ cup coconut cream or goat's cream
- 1 large egg
- 1 tablespoon chia seeds or flax meal
- 2 tablespoons grass-fed collagen powder
- ¼ teaspoon vanilla powder or 1 teaspoon unsweetened vanilla extract
- Zest from ½ lemon
- 1 tablespoon macadamia oil
- Optional: ice cubes, to taste

1. Place all of the ingredients in a blender and pulse until smooth and frothy. Serve immediately.

Per Serving:
calories: 515 | fat: 42g | protein: 10g | carbs: 30g | fiber: 4g | sodium: 202mg

Baked Harissa Shakshuka with Fresh Basil

- 1½ tablespoons extra-virgin olive oil
- 2 tablespoons harissa
- 1 tablespoon tomato paste
- ½ onion, diced
- 1 bell pepper, seeded and diced
- 3 garlic cloves, minced
- 1 (28-ounce / 794-g) can no-salt-added diced tomatoes
- ½ teaspoon kosher salt
- 4 large eggs
- 2 to 3 tablespoons fresh basil, chopped or cut into ribbons

1. Preheat the oven to 375°F (190°C). 2. Heat the olive oil in a 12-inch cast-iron pan or ovenproof skillet over medium heat. Add the harissa, tomato paste, onion, and bell pepper; sauté for 3 to 4 minutes. Add the garlic and cook until fragrant, about 30 seconds. Add the diced tomatoes and salt and simmer for about 10 minutes. 3. Make 4 wells in the sauce and gently break 1 egg into each. Transfer to the oven and bake until the whites are cooked and the yolks are set, 10 to 12 minutes. 4. Allow to cool for 3 to 5 minutes, garnish with the basil, and carefully spoon onto plates.

Per Serving:
calories: 190 | fat: 10g | protein: 9g | carbs: 15g | fiber: 4g | sodium: 255mg

Pumpkin Spice Greek Yogurt Parfait

- 1 (15-ounce / 425-g) can pure pumpkin purée
- 4 teaspoons honey, additional to taste
- 1 teaspoon pumpkin pie spice
- ¼ teaspoon ground cinnamon
- 2 cups plain, unsweetened, full-fat Greek yogurt
- 1 cup honey granola

1. In a large bowl, mix the pumpkin purée, honey, pumpkin pie spice, and cinnamon. Cover and refrigerate for at least 2 hours. 2. To make the parfaits, in each cup, pour ¼ cup pumpkin mix, ¼ cup yogurt and ¼ cup granola. Repeat Greek yogurt and pumpkin layers and top with honey granola.

Per Serving:
calories: 264 | fat: 9g | protein: 15g | carbs: 35g | fiber: 6g | sodium: 90mg

Spinach, Sun-Dried Tomato, and Feta Egg Wraps

- 1 tablespoon olive oil
- ¼ cup minced onion
- 3 to 4 tablespoons minced sun-dried tomatoes in olive oil and herbs
- 3 large eggs, beaten
- 1½ cups packed baby spinach
- 1 ounce (28 g) crumbled feta cheese
- Salt
- 2 (8-inch) whole-wheat tortillas

1. Heat the olive oil in a large skillet over medium-high heat. Add the chopped onion and diced tomatoes, sautéing for about 3 minutes until the vegetables soften and release their juices. 2. Reduce the heat to medium and pour in the beaten eggs. Stir constantly to scramble them, ensuring the eggs cook evenly without sticking. 3. Once the eggs are mostly set, add the fresh spinach and stir to combine, allowing it to wilt. Sprinkle crumbled feta cheese over the scrambled eggs, and add salt to taste. 4. Warm the tortillas in the microwave for about 20 seconds each, or until soft and pliable. 5. Spoon half of the egg mixture onto each tortilla. Fold the tortillas in half or roll them up tightly to create a wrap. Serve warm for a satisfying and flavorful breakfast or brunch option.

Per Serving:
calories: 435 | fat: 28g | protein: 17g | carbs: 31g | fiber: 6g | sodium: 552mg

Chapter 3

Beans and Grains

Mediterranean Tomato Rice with Fresh Herbs

Prep time: 10 minutes | Cook time: 25 minutes | Serves 3

- 2 tablespoons extra virgin olive oil
- 1 medium onion (any variety), chopped
- 1 garlic clove, finely chopped
- 1 cup uncooked medium-grain rice
- 1 tablespoon tomato paste
- 1 pound (454 g) canned

- crushed tomatoes, or 1 pound (454 g) fresh tomatoes (puréed in a food processor)
- ¾ teaspoon fine sea salt
- 1 teaspoon granulated sugar
- 2 cups hot water
- 2 tablespoons chopped fresh mint or basil

1. Heat the olive oil in a wide, deep pan over medium heat. When the oil begins to shimmer, add the onion and sauté for 3–4 minutes or until soft, then add the garlic and sauté for an additional 30 seconds. 2. Add the rice and stir until the rice is coated with the oil, then add the tomato paste and stir rapidly. Add the tomatoes, sea salt, and sugar, and then stir again. 3. Add the hot water, stir, then reduce the heat to low and simmer, covered, for 20 minutes or until the rice is soft. (If the rice appears to need more cooking time, add a small amount of hot water to the pan and continue cooking.) Remove the pan from the heat. 4. Add the chopped mint or basil, and let the rice sit for 10 minutes before serving. Store covered in the refrigerator for up to 4 days.

Per Serving:
calories: 359 | fat: 11g | protein: 7g | carbs: 60g | fiber: 6g | sodium: 607mg

Instant Pot Polenta with Arugula, Figs, and Blue Cheese

Prep time: 15 minutes | Cook time: 40 minutes | Serves 4

- 1 cup coarse-ground cornmeal
- ½ cup oil-packed sun-dried tomatoes, chopped
- 1 teaspoon minced fresh thyme or ¼ teaspoon dried
- ½ teaspoon table salt
- ¼ teaspoon pepper
- 3 tablespoons extra-virgin olive oil, divided

- 2 ounces (57 g) baby arugula
- 4 figs, cut into ½-inch-thick wedges
- 1 tablespoon balsamic vinegar
- 2 ounces (57 g) blue cheese, crumbled (½ cup)
- 2 tablespoons pine nuts, toasted

1. Arrange trivet included with Instant Pot in base of insert and add 1 cup water. Fold sheet of aluminum foil into 16 by 6-inch sling, then rest 1½-quart round soufflé dish in center of sling. Whisk 4 cups water, cornmeal, tomatoes, thyme, salt, and pepper together in bowl, then transfer mixture to soufflé dish. Using sling, lower soufflé dish into pot and onto trivet; allow narrow edges of sling to rest along sides of insert. 2. Lock lid in place and close pressure release valve. Select high pressure cook function and cook for 40 minutes. Turn off Instant Pot and quick-release pressure. Carefully remove lid, allowing steam to escape away from you. 3. Using sling, transfer soufflé dish to wire rack. Whisk 1 tablespoon oil into polenta, smoothing out any lumps. Let sit until thickened slightly, about 10 minutes. Season with salt and pepper to taste. 4. Toss arugula and figs with vinegar and remaining 2 tablespoons oil in bowl, and season with salt and pepper to taste. Divide polenta among individual serving plates and top with arugula mixture, blue cheese, and pine nuts. Serve.

Per Serving:
calories: 360 | fat: 21g | protein: 7g | carbs: 38g | fiber: 8g | sodium: 510mg

Lentils with Artichoke, Tomato, and Feta

Prep time: 10 minutes | Cook time: 12 minutes | Serves 6

- 2 cups dried red lentils, rinsed and drained
- ½ teaspoon salt
- 4 cups water
- 1 (12-ounce / 340-g) jar marinated artichokes, drained and chopped
- 2 medium vine-ripe tomatoes, chopped
- ½ medium red onion, peeled and diced

- ½ large English cucumber, diced
- ½ cup crumbled feta cheese
- ¼ cup chopped fresh flat-leaf parsley
- 3 tablespoons extra-virgin olive oil
- 2 tablespoons balsamic vinegar
- ½ teaspoon ground black pepper

1. Add the lentils, salt, and water to the Instant Pot®. Secure the lid, set the steam release to Sealing, press the Manual button, and set the cooking time to 12 minutes. Once the timer beeps, perform a quick-release until the float valve drops. Carefully open the lid and drain any excess liquid from the lentils. Allow the lentils to cool to room temperature, which will take about 30 minutes. 2. In a large mixing bowl, combine the cooled lentils with the artichoke hearts, diced tomatoes, chopped onion, cucumber, crumbled feta cheese, and fresh parsley. Drizzle with olive oil and red wine vinegar, and season with black pepper. Toss everything together until well mixed. Transfer the salad to a serving bowl. You can serve it immediately at room temperature or refrigerate for at least 2 hours to allow the flavors to develop. Enjoy this fresh and hearty salad as a side dish or light meal.

Per Serving:
calories: 332 | fat: 13g | protein: 17g | carbs: 40g | fiber: 6g | sodium: 552mg

Instant Pot Farro Mushroom Risotto

Prep time: 10 minutes | Cook time: 20 minutes | Serves 6

- 2 tablespoons olive oil
- 1 medium yellow onion, peeled and diced
- 16 ounces (454 g) sliced button mushrooms
- ½ teaspoon salt
- ½ teaspoon ground black pepper
- ½ teaspoon dried thyme
- ½ teaspoon dried oregano
- 1 clove garlic, peeled and minced
- 1 cup farro, rinsed and drained
- 1½ cups vegetable broth
- ¼ cup grated Parmesan cheese
- 2 tablespoons minced fresh flat-leaf parsley

1. Press the Sauté button on the Instant Pot® and heat oil. Add onion and mushrooms and sauté 8 minutes. Add salt, pepper, thyme, and oregano and cook 30 seconds. Add garlic and cook for 30 seconds. Press the Cancel button. 2. Stir in farro and broth. Close lid, set steam release to Sealing, press the Manual button, and set time to 10 minutes. When timer beeps, let pressure release naturally for 10 minutes, then quick-release the remaining pressure until the float valve drops. 3. Top with cheese and parsley before serving.

Per Serving:
calories: 215 | fat: 8g | protein: 11g | carbs: 24g | fiber: 3g | sodium: 419mg

Farro Salad with Tomatoes and Olives

Prep time: 10 minutes | Cook time: 20 minutes | Serves 6

- 10 ounces (283 g) farro, rinsed and drained
- 4 cups water
- 4 Roma tomatoes, seeded and chopped
- 4 scallions, green parts only, thinly sliced
- ½ cup sliced black olives
- ¼ cup minced fresh flat-leaf parsley
- ¼ cup extra-virgin olive oil
- 2 tablespoons balsamic vinegar
- ¼ teaspoon ground black pepper

1. Add the farro and water to the Instant Pot®. Close the lid securely and set the steam release to Sealing. Press the Multigrain button and adjust the time to 20 minutes. Once the timer beeps, allow the pressure to release naturally, which will take about 30 minutes, ensuring the farro is tender. 2. Carefully open the lid and fluff the farro with a fork to release any steam and separate the grains. Transfer the farro to a mixing bowl and let it cool for about 30 minutes. Once cooled, add the diced tomatoes, sliced scallions, black olives, and chopped parsley, mixing everything thoroughly. 3. In a small bowl, whisk together the olive oil, balsamic vinegar, and freshly ground black pepper until well combined. Drizzle the dressing over the farro mixture and toss to coat evenly. Cover and refrigerate the salad for at least 4 hours to let the flavors meld together. Serve chilled or at room temperature for a refreshing, hearty dish.

Per Serving:
calories: 288 | fat: 14g | protein: 7g | carbs: 31g | fiber: 3g | sodium: 159mg

Instant Pot Lemon Garlic Brown Rice Pilaf

Prep time: 10 minutes | Cook time: 34 minutes | Serves 8

- 2 tablespoons olive oil
- 1 medium yellow onion, peeled and chopped
- 4 cloves garlic, peeled and minced
- 1 tablespoon grated lemon zest
- ½ teaspoon ground black
- pepper
- 1 teaspoon dried thyme
- 1 teaspoon dried oregano
- ¼ teaspoon salt
- 2 tablespoons white wine
- 2 tablespoons lemon juice
- 2 cups brown rice
- 2 cups vegetable broth

1. Press the Sauté button on the Instant Pot® and heat oil. Add onion and cook until soft, about 6 minutes. Add garlic and cook until fragrant, about 30 seconds. Add lemon zest, pepper, thyme, oregano, and salt. Cook until fragrant, about 1 minute. 2. Add wine and lemon juice and cook, stirring well, until liquid has almost evaporated, about 1 minute. Add rice and cook, stirring constantly, until coated and starting to toast, about 3 minutes. Press the Cancel button. 3. Stir in broth. Close lid, set steam release to Sealing, press the Manual button, and set time to 22 minutes. 4. When the timer beeps, let pressure release naturally for 10 minutes, then quick-release the remaining pressure until the float valve drops. Open lid and fluff rice with a fork. Serve warm.

Per Serving:
calories: 202 | fat: 5g | protein: 4g | carbs: 37g | fiber: 1g | sodium: 274mg

Asparagus-Spinach Farro

Prep time: 5 minutes | Cook time: 16 minutes | Serves 4

- 2 tablespoons olive oil
- 1 cup quick-cooking farro
- ½ shallot, finely chopped
- 4 garlic cloves, minced
- Sea salt
- Freshly ground black pepper
- 2½ cups water, vegetable broth, or chicken broth
- 8 ounces (227 g) asparagus, woody ends trimmed, cut into 2-inch pieces
- 3 ounces (85 g) fresh baby spinach
- ½ cup grated Parmesan cheese

1. Heat the olive oil in a large skillet over medium-high heat. Add the farro, minced shallot, and garlic, seasoning with salt and black pepper. Cook for about 4 minutes, stirring occasionally, until the shallot softens and the farro begins to toast. Pour in the water and bring the mixture to a boil. Once boiling, reduce the heat to low, cover, and let it simmer for about 10 minutes or as directed on the package of farro until the farro is tender but still chewy. 2. Add the asparagus pieces to the skillet and cook for about 5 minutes until they are tender but still crisp. Stir in the fresh spinach, cooking for an additional 30 seconds until it wilts and blends into the mixture. 3. Finish by sprinkling the top with grated Parmesan cheese. Serve the dish warm for a hearty and nutritious meal, full of texture and flavor.

Per Serving:
calories: 277 | fat: 11g | protein: 10g | carbs: 38g | fiber: 7g | sodium: 284mg

Slow Cooker Mediterranean Chicken Fried Rice

Prep time: 15 minutes | Cook time: 3 to 5 hours | Serves 4

- Nonstick cooking spray
- 1 cup raw long-grain brown rice, rinsed
- 2½ cups low-sodium chicken broth
- 2 tablespoons extra-virgin olive oil
- 2 tablespoons balsamic vinegar
- 2 zucchini, diced
- 4 ounces (113 g) mushrooms, diced
- 1 small onion, diced
- 2 garlic cloves, minced
- 1 carrot, diced
- 1 bell pepper, any color, seeded and diced
- ¼ cup peas (raw, frozen, or canned)
- 1 teaspoon sea salt
- 1 pound (454 g) boneless, skinless chicken breast, cut into ½-inch pieces
- 2 large eggs

1. Generously coat a slow-cooker insert with cooking spray. Put the rice, chicken broth, olive oil, vinegar, zucchini, mushrooms, onion, garlic, carrot, bell pepper, peas, and salt in a slow cooker. Stir to mix well. 2. Nestle the chicken into the rice mixture. 3. Cover the cooker and cook for 3 to 5 hours on Low heat. 4. In a small bowl, whisk the eggs. Pour the eggs over the chicken and rice. Replace the cover on the cooker and cook for 15 to 30 minutes on Low heat, or until the eggs are scrambled and cooked through. 5. Fluff the rice with a fork before serving.

Per Serving:
calories: 431 | fat: 14g | protein: 35g | carbs: 48g | fiber: 5g | sodium: 876mg

Simple Tri-Color Lentil Salad

Prep time: 15 minutes | Cook time: 12 minutes | Serves 6

- 2 cups tri-color dried lentils, rinsed and drained
- ½ teaspoon salt
- 4 cups water
- 1 medium red onion, peeled and diced
- 1 stalk celery, diced
- 1 cup sliced cherry tomatoes
- ½ medium yellow bell pepper, seeded and diced
- ¼ cup chopped fresh cilantro
- ¼ cup extra-virgin olive oil
- ¼ cup red wine vinegar
- 1 tablespoon chopped fresh oregano
- 1 teaspoon fresh thyme leaves
- ¼ teaspoon ground black pepper
- ½ cup crumbled feta cheese
- ½ cup halved Kalamata olives

1. Add the lentils, salt, and water to the Instant Pot®. Secure the lid and set the steam release to Sealing. Press the Manual button and set the cooking time to 12 minutes. When the timer goes off, quick-release the pressure until the float valve drops. Carefully open the lid and drain any excess liquid from the lentils. Let the lentils cool to room temperature, which will take about 30 minutes. 2. In a large mixing bowl, combine the cooled lentils with the chopped onion, celery, tomatoes, bell pepper, and cilantro. Add the olive oil, vinegar, oregano, thyme, and black pepper, then toss everything together until well mixed. Transfer the lentil mixture to a serving bowl and garnish with crumbled feta cheese and olives. Serve the salad at room temperature or refrigerate it for at least 2 hours to allow the flavors to meld before serving. Enjoy this vibrant, refreshing dish as a side or light main.

Per Serving:
calories: 469 | fat: 19g | protein: 14g | carbs: 62g | fiber: 4g | sodium: 730mg

Instant Pot Cilantro Lime Brown Rice

Prep time: 10 minutes | Cook time: 32 minutes | Serves 8

- 2 tablespoons extra-virgin olive oil
- ½ medium yellow onion, peeled and chopped
- 2 cloves garlic, peeled and minced
- ½ cup chopped fresh cilantro, divided
- 2 cups brown rice
- 2¼ cups water
- 2 tablespoons lime juice
- 1 tablespoon grated lime zest
- ¼ teaspoon salt
- ½ teaspoon ground black pepper

1. Press the Sauté button on the Instant Pot® and heat oil. Add onion and cook until soft, about 6 minutes. Add garlic and ¼ cup cilantro and cook until fragrant, about 30 seconds. Add rice and cook, stirring constantly, until well coated and starting to toast, about 3 minutes. Press the Cancel button. 2. Stir in water. Close lid, set steam release to Sealing, press the Manual button, and set time to 22 minutes. When the timer beeps, let pressure release naturally for 10 minutes, then quick-release the remaining pressure. Open lid and fluff rice with a fork. Fold in remaining ¼ cup cilantro, lime juice, lime zest, salt, and pepper. Serve warm.

Per Serving:
calories: 95 | fat: 4g | protein: 1g | carbs: 14g | fiber: 1g | sodium: 94mg

Lentils with Cilantro and Lime

Prep time: 15 minutes | Cook time: 20 minutes | Serves 6

- 2 tablespoons olive oil
- 1 medium yellow onion, peeled and chopped
- 1 medium carrot, peeled and chopped
- ¼ cup chopped fresh cilantro
- ½ teaspoon ground cumin
- ½ teaspoon salt
- 2 cups dried green lentils, rinsed and drained
- 4 cups low-sodium chicken broth
- 2 tablespoons lime juice

1. Press the Sauté button on the Instant Pot® and heat the oil. Once hot, add the chopped onion and carrot, cooking for about 3 minutes until they are just tender. Stir in the chopped cilantro, ground cumin, and salt, and cook for about 30 seconds until the spices become fragrant. Press the Cancel button to stop the sauté function. 2. Add the lentils and vegetable broth to the pot, stirring to combine. Secure the lid, set the steam release valve to Sealing, press the Manual button, and adjust the cooking time to 15 minutes. 3. When the timer beeps, let the pressure release naturally for about 25 minutes to ensure the lentils are perfectly tender. Carefully open the lid and stir in the fresh lime juice for a bright and zesty finish. Serve the lentil dish warm, and enjoy its comforting and aromatic flavors.

Per Serving:
calories: 316 | fat: 5g | protein: 20g | carbs: 44g | fiber: 21g | sodium: 349mg

Chickpea and Green Bean Salad with Herbs and Mushrooms

Prep time: 20 minutes | Cook time: 40 minutes | Serves 8

- 2 cups dried chickpeas, soaked overnight and drained
- ½ teaspoon salt
- 9 cups water, divided
- ½ pound (227 g) fresh green beans, trimmed and cut into 1" pieces
- 4 ounces (113 g) sliced button mushrooms
- ½ red bell pepper, seeded, thinly sliced, and cut into 1" pieces
- ½ medium red onion, peeled and diced
- ¼ cup chopped fresh flat-
- leaf parsley
- 2 tablespoons chopped fresh chives
- 2 tablespoons chopped fresh tarragon
- ¼ cup extra-virgin olive oil
- 2 tablespoons red wine vinegar
- 1 teaspoon Dijon mustard
- 1 teaspoon honey
- ½ teaspoon ground black pepper
- ¼ teaspoon salt
- ¼ cup grated Parmesan cheese

1. Add chickpeas, salt, and 8 cups water to the Instant Pot®. Close lid, set steam release to Sealing, press the Manual button, and set time to 40 minutes. 2. When the timer beeps, let pressure release naturally for 10 minutes, then quick-release the remaining pressure. Press the Cancel button. Open lid and drain chickpeas. Transfer to a large bowl and cool to room temperature. 3. Add remaining 1 cup water to the Instant Pot®. Add rack to pot, top with steamer basket, and add green beans. Close lid, set steam release to Sealing, press the Manual button, and set time to 0 minutes. When the timer beeps, open lid, remove steamer basket, and rinse green beans with cool water. Add to bowl with chickpeas. 4. Add to the bowl mushrooms, bell pepper, red onion, parsley, chives, and tarragon. Toss to mix. In a small bowl, combine olive oil, vinegar, mustard, honey, black pepper, and salt. Whisk to combine, then pour over chickpea and green bean mixture, and toss to coat. Top with cheese and serve immediately.

Per Serving:
calories: 291 | fat: 12g | protein: 13g | carbs: 33g | fiber: 10g | sodium: 312mg

Chili-Spiced Beans

Prep time: 10 minutes | Cook time: 30 minutes | Serves 8

- 1 pound (454 g) dried pinto beans, soaked overnight and drained
- 1 medium onion, peeled and chopped
- ¼ cup chopped fresh cilantro
- 1 (15-ounce / 425-g) can tomato sauce
- ¼ cup chili powder
- 2 tablespoons smoked paprika
- 1 teaspoon ground cumin
- 1 teaspoon ground coriander
- ½ teaspoon ground black pepper
- 2 cups vegetable broth
- 1 cup water

1. Add all the ingredients to the Instant Pot® and stir to combine them thoroughly. Make sure everything is well mixed for even cooking. 2. Secure the lid on the Instant Pot®, set the steam release to Sealing, press the Chili button, and cook for the default time of 30 minutes. Once the timer beeps, perform a quick-release by turning the steam release valve until the float valve drops completely. Carefully open the lid and stir the mixture well. If the beans are too thin, press the Cancel button, then press the Sauté button, and let the beans simmer uncovered until they reach your desired consistency. Serve the beans warm for a hearty and comforting dish.

Per Serving:
calories: 86 | fat: 0g | protein: 5g | carbs: 17g | fiber: 4g | sodium: 323mg

Pasta E Fagioli with Rosemary and Parmesan

Prep time: 15 minutes | Cook time: 50 minutes | Serves 2

- 1 cup uncooked borlotti (cranberry) beans or pinto beans
- 3 tablespoons extra virgin olive oil, divided
- 1 small carrot, finely chopped
- ½ medium onion (white or red), finely chopped
- 1 celery stalk, finely chopped
- 1 bay leaf
- 1 tablespoon tomato paste
- 2 cups cold water
- 1 rosemary sprig plus ½ teaspoon chopped fresh
- rosemary needles
- ¼ teaspoon fine sea salt
- ¼ teaspoon freshly ground black pepper plus more to taste
- 1½ ounces (43 g) uncooked egg fettuccine or other egg noodles
- 1 garlic clove, peeled and finely sliced
- ¼ teaspoon red pepper flakes
- 2 teaspoons grated Parmesan cheese
- Pinch of coarse sea salt, for serving

1. Place the beans in a large bowl and cover with cold water by 3 inches (7.5cm) to allow for expansion. Soak for 12 hours or overnight, then drain and rinse. 2. Add 2 tablespoons of the olive oil to a medium pot over medium heat. When the oil begins to shimmer, add the carrot, onions, celery, and bay leaf. Sauté for 3 minutes, then add the tomato paste and continue sautéing and stirring for 2 more minutes. 3. Add the beans, cold water, and rosemary sprig. Cover, bring to a boil, then reduce the heat to low and simmer for 30–40 minutes or until the beans are soft, but not falling apart. Remove the rosemary sprig and bay leaf. Use a slotted spoon to remove about 1 cup of the beans. Set aside. 4. Using an immersion blender, blend the remaining beans in the pot, then add the whole beans back to the pot along with the sea salt and ¼ teaspoon of the black pepper. Increase the heat to medium. When the mixture begins to bubble, add the pasta and cook until done, about 3 minutes. 5. While the pasta is cooking, heat 1 teaspoon of the olive oil in a small pan over medium heat. Add the garlic, red pepper flakes, and chopped rosemary needles. Sauté for 2 minutes, then transfer the mixture to the beans and stir. 6. When the pasta is done cooking, remove from the heat and set aside to cool for 5 minutes before dividing between 2 plates. Drizzle 1 teaspoon of the olive oil and sprinkle 1 teaspoon of the grated Parmesan over each serving. Season with freshly ground pepper to taste and a pinch of coarse sea salt. This dish is best served promptly, but can be stored in the refrigerator for up to 2 days.

Per Serving:
calories: 409 | fat: 22g | protein: 12g | carbs: 42g | fiber: 11g | sodium: 763mg

Buckwheat and Halloumi Bowl with Mint Dressing

Prep time: 20 minutes | Cook time: 12 minutes | Serves 4

- 1 cup raw buckwheat groats, rinsed and drained
- 1¼ cups water
- ¼ teaspoon salt
- 2 tablespoons light olive oil, divided
- 8 ounces (227 g) Halloumi, cut into ¼" slices
- 4 cups chopped kale or spinach
- ½ medium red onion, peeled and diced
- ½ large English cucumber, chopped
- 1 cup halved cherry tomatoes
- ½ cup pitted Kalamata olives
- ¼ cup lemon juice
- ¼ cup extra-virgin olive oil
- ¼ cup fresh mint leaves
- 1 teaspoon honey
- 1 teaspoon Dijon mustard
- ¼ teaspoon ground black pepper

1. Add the buckwheat, water, salt, and 1 tablespoon of light olive oil to the Instant Pot®. Stir the mixture well to ensure everything is evenly combined. Secure the lid, set the steam release to Sealing, press the Manual button, and set the cooking time to 6 minutes. 2. When the timer beeps, let the pressure release naturally for about 20 minutes. Carefully open the lid and transfer the cooked buckwheat to a medium bowl. Clean and dry the Instant Pot® insert, then press the Cancel button to stop the cooking process. 3. Press the Sauté button on the Instant Pot® and heat the remaining 1 tablespoon of light olive oil. Add the Halloumi slices to the pot and cook until browned, about 3 minutes per side, ensuring they are nicely golden and crisp. 4. To assemble the bowls, start by placing a layer of mixed greens in each of the four bowls. Top each bowl with a portion of the cooked buckwheat, followed by the browned Halloumi slices, sliced onion, cucumber, cherry tomatoes, and olives. 5. In a blender, combine the lemon juice, extra-virgin olive oil, fresh mint, honey, Dijon mustard, and black pepper. Blend for about 30 seconds until the dressing is completely smooth and well mixed. Drizzle the dressing over each bowl and serve immediately for a fresh and flavorful meal.

Per Serving:
calories: 453 | fat: 25g | protein: 12g | carbs: 46g | fiber: 8g | sodium: 246mg

Fava and Garbanzo Bean Fūl

Prep time: 10 minutes | Cook time: 10 minutes | Serves 6

- 1 (16-ounce/ 454-g) can garbanzo beans, rinsed and drained
- 1 (15-ounce/ 425-g) can fava beans, rinsed and drained
- 3 cups water
- ½ cup lemon juice
- 3 cloves garlic, peeled and minced
- 1 teaspoon salt
- 3 tablespoons extra-virgin olive oil

1. In a 3-quart pot over medium heat, combine the garbanzo beans, fava beans, and water. Cook for about 10 minutes until the beans are heated through and tender. 2. After cooking, reserve 1 cup of the liquid from the pot, then drain the beans and transfer them to a large mixing bowl. 3. In a separate bowl, mix together the reserved bean liquid, lemon juice, minced garlic, and salt. Pour this mixture over the drained beans. Using a potato masher, mash about half of the beans in the bowl, leaving some whole for texture. 4. After mashing, stir the mixture thoroughly to ensure the beans are evenly distributed and well combined. 5. Drizzle the olive oil over the top for a rich finishing touch. 6. Serve this dish warm or cold with pita bread for a delicious and hearty meal or snack.

Per Serving:
calories: 199 | fat: 9g | protein: 10g | carbs: 25g | fiber: 9g | sodium: 395mg

Hearty Three-Bean Vegan Chili

Prep time: 20 minutes | Cook time: 30 minutes | Serves 12

- 1 cup dried pinto beans, soaked overnight and drained
- 1 cup dried red beans, soaked overnight and drained
- 1 cup dried black beans, soaked overnight and drained
- 2 medium white onions, peeled and chopped
- 2 medium red bell peppers, seeded and chopped
- 2 stalks celery, chopped
- 1 (28-ounce / 794-g) can diced tomatoes
- 1 (15-ounce / 425-g) can tomato sauce
- ¼ cup chili powder
- 2 tablespoons smoked paprika
- 1 teaspoon ground cumin
- 1 teaspoon ground coriander
- ½ teaspoon salt
- ½ teaspoon ground black pepper
- 3 cups vegetable broth
- 1 cup water

1. Place all ingredients in the Instant Pot® and stir to combine. Close lid, set steam release to Sealing, press the Chili button, and cook for the default time of 30 minutes. 2. When the timer beeps, quick-release the pressure until the float valve drops, then open lid and stir well. If chili is too thin, press the Cancel button and then press the Sauté button and let chili simmer, uncovered, until desired thickness is reached. Serve warm.

Per Serving:
calories: 195 | fat: 1g | protein: 10g | carbs: 35g | fiber: 10g | sodium: 521mg

Slow Cooker White Beans with Kale

Prep time: 15 minutes | Cook time: 7½ hours | Serves 2

- 1 onion, chopped
- 1 leek, white part only, sliced
- 2 celery stalks, sliced
- 2 garlic cloves, minced
- 1 cup dried white lima beans or cannellini beans, sorted and rinsed
- 2 cups vegetable broth
- ½ teaspoon salt
- ½ teaspoon dried thyme leaves
- ⅛ teaspoon freshly ground black pepper
- 3 cups torn kale

1. In the slow cooker, combine all the ingredients except the kale. 2. Cover and cook on low for 7 hours, or until the beans are tender. 3. Add the kale and stir. 4. Cover and cook on high for 30 minutes, or until the kale is tender but still firm, and serve.

Per Serving:
calories: 176 | fat: 1g | protein: 9g | carbs: 36g | fiber: 9g | sodium: 616mg

Moroccan Lamb with White Beans and Spices

- 1½ tablespoons table salt, for brining
- 1 pound (454 g) dried great Northern beans, picked over and rinsed
- 1 (12-ounce/ 340-g) lamb shoulder chop (blade or round bone), ¾ to 1 inch thick, trimmed and halved
- ½ teaspoon table salt
- 2 tablespoons extra-virgin olive oil, plus extra for serving
- 1 onion, chopped
- 1 red bell pepper, stemmed, seeded, and chopped
- 2 tablespoons tomato paste
- 3 garlic cloves, minced
- 2 teaspoons paprika
- 2 teaspoons ground cumin
- 1½ teaspoons ground ginger
- ¼ teaspoon cayenne pepper
- ½ cup dry white wine
- 2 cups chicken broth
- 2 tablespoons minced fresh parsley

1. Dissolve 1½ tablespoons salt in 2 quarts cold water in large container. Add beans and soak at room temperature for at least 8 hours or up to 24 hours. Drain and rinse well. 2. Pat lamb dry with paper towels and sprinkle with ½ teaspoon salt. Using highest sauté function, heat oil in Instant Pot for 5 minutes (or until just smoking). Brown lamb, about 5 minutes per side; transfer to plate. 3. Add onion and bell pepper to fat left in pot and cook, using highest sauté function, until softened, about 5 minutes. Stir in tomato paste, garlic, paprika, cumin, ginger, and cayenne and cook until fragrant, about 30 seconds. Stir in wine, scraping up any browned bits, then stir in broth and beans. 4. Nestle lamb into beans and add any accumulated juices. Lock lid in place and close pressure release valve. Select high pressure cook function and cook for 1 minute. Turn off Instant Pot and let pressure release naturally for 15 minutes. Quick-release any remaining pressure, then carefully remove lid, allowing steam to escape away from you. 5. Transfer lamb to cutting board, let cool slightly, then shred into bite-size pieces using 2 forks; discard excess fat and bones. Stir lamb and parsley into beans, and season with salt and pepper to taste. Drizzle individual portions with extra oil before serving.

Per Serving:
calories: 350 | fat: 12g | protein: 20g | carbs: 40g | fiber: 15g | sodium: 410mg

Instant Pot Creamy Yellow Lentil Soup

- 2 tablespoons olive oil
- 1 medium yellow onion, peeled and chopped
- 1 medium carrot, peeled and chopped
- 2 cloves garlic, peeled and minced
- 1 teaspoon ground cumin
- ½ teaspoon ground black pepper
- ¼ teaspoon salt
- 2 cups dried yellow lentils, rinsed and drained
- 6 cups water

1. Press the Sauté button on the Instant Pot® and heat oil. Add onion and carrot and cook until just tender, about 3 minutes. Add garlic, cumin, pepper, and salt and cook until fragrant, about 30 seconds. Press the Cancel button. 2. Add lentils and water, close lid, set steam release to Sealing, press the Manual button, and set time to 15 minutes. When the timer beeps, let pressure release naturally, about 15 minutes. Open lid and purée with an immersion blender or in batches in a blender. Serve warm.

Per Serving:
calories: 248 | fat: 5g | protein: 15g | carbs: 35g | fiber: 8g | sodium: 118mg

Herbed Lima Beans

- 1 pound (454 g) frozen baby lima beans, thawed
- 2 cloves garlic, peeled and minced
- 2 thyme sprigs
- 1 bay leaf
- 2 tablespoons extra-virgin olive oil
- 3 cups water
- 1 tablespoon chopped fresh dill
- 1 tablespoon chopped fresh tarragon
- 1 tablespoon chopped fresh mint

1. Add the lima beans, minced garlic, fresh thyme, bay leaf, olive oil, and water to the Instant Pot®. Close the lid securely, set the steam release to Sealing, press the Manual button, and set the cooking time to 6 minutes. Once the timer beeps, perform a quick-release until the float valve drops. Open the lid, remove and discard the thyme sprigs and bay leaf, and give the mixture a good stir. 2. Stir in the fresh dill, tarragon, and mint. Allow the mixture to stand for about 10 minutes on the Keep Warm setting so the flavors can blend nicely before serving. Enjoy the beans as a side dish or as part of a hearty meal.

Per Serving:
calories: 134 | fat: 5g | protein: 5g | carbs: 17g | fiber: 4g | sodium: 206mg

Chicken Artichoke Rice Bake

- Nonstick cooking spray
- 1 cup raw long-grain brown rice, rinsed
- 2½ cups low-sodium chicken broth
- 1 (14-ounce/ 397-g) can artichoke hearts, drained and rinsed
- ½ small onion, diced
- 2 garlic cloves, minced
- 10 ounces (283 g) fresh spinach, chopped
- 1 teaspoon dried thyme
- ½ teaspoon sea salt
- ½ teaspoon freshly ground black pepper
- 1 pound (454 g) boneless, skinless chicken breast

1. Generously spray the inside of the slow cooker with cooking spray to prevent sticking. Add the rice, chicken broth, artichoke hearts, chopped onion, minced garlic, spinach, dried thyme, salt, and black pepper to the slow cooker. Gently stir everything together until well mixed. 2. Place the chicken breasts directly on top of the rice mixture, ensuring they are centered and not submerged. 3. Cover the slow cooker and cook on Low heat for 3 to 5 hours, until the rice is tender and the chicken is cooked through. 4. Once done, remove the chicken from the slow cooker and shred it using two forks. Stir the shredded chicken back into the rice mixture to incorporate it evenly. Serve warm for a comforting and hearty meal.

Per Serving:
calories: 323 | fat: 4g | protein: 32g | carbs: 44g | fiber: 6g | sodium: 741mg

Black Chickpeas

Prep time: 11 minutes | Cook time: 9 to 11 hours | Serves 6

- 1 tablespoon rapeseed oil
- 2 teaspoons cumin seeds
- 2 cups dried whole black chickpeas, washed
- 4 cups hot water
- 1 onion, roughly chopped
- 2-inch piece fresh ginger, peeled and roughly chopped
- 4 garlic cloves
- 3 fresh green chiles
- 1 tomato, roughly chopped
- 1 teaspoon turmeric
- 1 teaspoon Kashmiri chili powder
- 1 teaspoon sea salt
- Handful fresh coriander leaves, chopped
- Juice of 1 lemon

1. Heat the oil in a frying pan over medium heat, or directly in the slow cooker if it has a sear setting. Add the cumin seeds, allowing them to sizzle until fragrant, then transfer them into the slow cooker. 2. Set the slow cooker to high heat, then add the chickpeas along with the water, stirring to combine. 3. In a blender, purée the onion, ginger, garlic, green chiles, and tomato until smooth to form a paste. Pour this mixture into the slow cooker and add the turmeric, chili powder, and salt. Stir everything to mix well. 4. Cover the slow cooker and let it cook for 9 hours on high, or 11 hours on low, until the chickpeas are tender and the flavors have melded. 5. Once the chickpeas are done cooking, check and adjust the seasoning if needed. Stir in the fresh coriander leaves and lemon juice for added freshness and acidity. Serve hot, and enjoy the rich, spiced chickpea curry as a comforting meal.

Per Serving:
calories: 129 | fat: 4g | protein: 5g | carbs: 19g | fiber: 5g | sodium: 525mg

Za'atar Chickpeas and Chicken

Prep time: 10 minutes | Cook time: 4 to 6 hours | Serves 4

- 2 pounds (907 g) bone-in chicken thighs or legs
- 1 (15-ounce/ 425-g) can reduced-sodium chickpeas, drained and rinsed
- ½ cup low-sodium chicken broth
- Juice of 1 lemon
- 1 tablespoon extra-virgin olive oil
- 2 teaspoons white vinegar
- 2 tablespoons za'atar
- 1 garlic clove, minced
- ½ teaspoon sea salt
- ¼ teaspoon freshly ground black pepper

1. Place the chicken and chickpeas in the slow cooker, stirring to combine them evenly. 2. In a small bowl, whisk together the chicken broth, lemon juice, olive oil, vinegar, za'atar seasoning, minced garlic, salt, and black pepper until the mixture is well blended. Pour the mixture over the chicken and chickpeas in the slow cooker, ensuring everything is coated. 3. Cover the slow cooker and set it to cook on Low heat for 4 to 6 hours, until the chicken is tender and infused with the flavorful spices. Serve warm, garnished with fresh herbs if desired, for a simple and delicious meal.

Per Serving:
calories: 647 | fat: 41g | protein: 46g | carbs: 23g | fiber: 7g | sodium: 590mg

Skillet Bulgur with Kale and Tomatoes

Prep time: 15 minutes | Cook time: 8 minutes | Serves 2

- 2 tablespoons olive oil
- 2 cloves garlic, minced
- 1 bunch kale, trimmed and cut into bite-sized pieces
- Juice of 1 lemon
- 2 cups cooked bulgur wheat
- 1 pint cherry tomatoes, halved
- Sea salt and freshly ground pepper, to taste

1. Heat the olive oil in a large skillet over medium heat. Once hot, add the minced garlic and sauté for about 1 minute until it becomes fragrant but not browned. 2. Add the kale leaves, stirring to coat them evenly with the oil and garlic. Cook for about 5 minutes, stirring occasionally, until the kale is completely wilted and tender. 3. Stir in the lemon juice, followed by the bulgur and diced tomatoes. Mix everything thoroughly and season with sea salt and freshly ground black pepper to taste. Cook for another minute until the flavors meld together. Serve warm as a healthy side dish or light meal.

Per Serving:
calories: 311 | fat: 14g | protein: 8g | carbs: 43g | fiber: 10g | sodium: 21mg

French Green Lentils with Swiss Chard and Almonds

Prep time: 15 minutes | Cook time: 17 minutes | Serves 6

- 2 tablespoons extra-virgin olive oil, plus extra for drizzling
- 12 ounces (340 g) Swiss chard, stems chopped fine, leaves sliced into ½-inch-wide strips
- 1 onion, chopped fine
- ½ teaspoon table salt
- 2 garlic cloves, minced
- 1 teaspoon minced fresh thyme or ¼ teaspoon dried
- 2½ cups water
- 1 cup French green lentils, picked over and rinsed
- 3 tablespoons whole-grain mustard
- ½ teaspoon grated lemon zest plus 1 teaspoon juice
- 3 tablespoons sliced almonds, toasted
- 2 tablespoons chopped fresh parsley

1. Using highest sauté function, heat oil in Instant Pot until shimmering. Add chard stems, onion, and salt and cook until vegetables are softened, about 5 minutes. Stir in garlic and thyme and cook until fragrant, about 30 seconds. Stir in water and lentils. 2. Lock lid in place and close pressure release valve. Select high pressure cook function and cook for 11 minutes. Turn off Instant Pot and let pressure release naturally for 15 minutes. Quick-release any remaining pressure, then carefully remove lid, allowing steam to escape away from you. 3. Stir chard leaves into lentils, 1 handful at a time, and let cook in residual heat until wilted, about 5 minutes. Stir in mustard and lemon zest and juice. Season with salt and pepper to taste. Transfer to serving dish, drizzle with extra oil, and sprinkle with almonds and parsley. Serve.

Per Serving:
calories: 190 | fat: 8g | protein: 9g | carbs: 23g | fiber: 6g | sodium: 470mg

Vegetarian Dinner Loaf

- 1 cup dried pinto beans, soaked overnight and drained
- 8 cups water, divided
- 1 tablespoon vegetable oil
- 1 teaspoon salt
- 1 cup diced onion
- 1 cup chopped walnuts
- ½ cup rolled oats
- 1 large egg, beaten
- ¾ cup ketchup
- 1 teaspoon garlic powder
- 1 teaspoon dried basil
- 1 teaspoon dried parsley
- ½ teaspoon salt
- ½ teaspoon ground black pepper

1. Add the beans and 4 cups of water to the Instant Pot®. Secure the lid, set the steam release to Sealing, press the Manual button, and set the cooking time to 1 minute. Once the timer beeps, quickly release the pressure until the float valve drops. Press the Cancel button to stop the cooking process. 2. Open the lid, then drain and rinse the beans thoroughly. Return them to the Instant Pot® and add the remaining 4 cups of water. Allow the beans to soak for 1 hour in the water. 3. Preheat your oven to 350ºF (175ºC) to prepare for baking. 4. After soaking, add the olive oil and salt to the beans in the pot. Close the lid, set the steam release to Sealing, press the Manual button, and set the cooking time to 11 minutes. Once the timer beeps, allow the pressure to release naturally for about 25 minutes, then open the lid. Drain the beans and transfer them to a large mixing bowl. 5. Add the chopped onion, walnuts, oats, beaten egg, ketchup, garlic powder, dried basil, parsley, salt, and pepper to the bowl with the cooked beans. Stir the mixture until well combined. Spread the mixture evenly into a greased loaf pan and bake in the preheated oven for 30 to 35 minutes until set and lightly browned on top. Let the loaf cool in the pan for 20 minutes before slicing and serving. Enjoy this hearty and flavorful bean loaf as a comforting plant-based meal.

Per Serving:

calories: 278 | fat: 17g | protein: 9g | carbs: 27g | fiber: 6g | sodium: 477mg

Quinoa with Kale, Carrots, and Walnuts

- 1 cup quinoa, rinsed and drained
- 2 cups water
- ¼ cup olive oil
- 2 tablespoons apple cider vinegar
- 1 clove garlic, peeled and minced
- ½ teaspoon ground black pepper
- ½ teaspoon salt
- 2 cups chopped kale
- 1 cup shredded carrot
- 1 cup toasted walnut pieces
- ½ cup crumbled feta cheese

1. Add the quinoa and water to the Instant Pot® and stir well to combine. Secure the lid and set the steam release to Sealing. Press the Manual button and adjust the time to 20 minutes. Once the timer beeps, allow the pressure to release naturally for about 20 minutes before opening the lid. Fluff the quinoa with a fork to separate the grains, then transfer it to a medium bowl and let it cool to room temperature for about 40 minutes. 2. Once the quinoa has cooled, add the olive oil, vinegar, minced garlic, black pepper, salt, chopped kale, grated carrot, walnuts, and crumbled feta. Toss everything together until all ingredients are well mixed and coated. Cover and refrigerate the salad for at least 4 hours to allow the flavors to meld together before serving. Enjoy this nutritious and flavorful dish as a side or light meal.

Per Serving:

calories: 625 | fat: 39g | protein: 19g | carbs: 47g | fiber: 10g | sodium: 738mg

South Indian Sambar with Mixed Vegetables

Sambar Masala:
- 1 teaspoon rapeseed oil
- 3 tablespoons coriander seeds
- 2 tablespoons split gram
- 1 teaspoon black peppercorns

Sambar:
- 1½ cups split yellow pigeon peas, washed
- 2 fresh green chiles, sliced lengthwise
- 2 garlic cloves, chopped
- 6 pearl onions
- 4 to 5 tablespoons sambar masala
- 2 teaspoons salt
- 1 to 2 carrots, peeled and chopped
- 1 red potato, peeled and diced
- 1 white radish (mooli), peeled and chopped into 2¾-inch sticks
- 1 tomato, roughly chopped

- ½ teaspoon fenugreek seeds
- ½ teaspoon mustard seeds
- ¼ teaspoon cumin seeds
- 12 whole dried red chiles

- 4 cups water
- 2 to 3 moringa seed pods, or ⅓ pound (151 g) green beans or asparagus, chopped into 2¾-inch lengths
- 2 tablespoons tamarind paste
- ½ teaspoon asafetida
- 2 teaspoons coconut oil
- 1 teaspoon mustard seeds
- 20 curry leaves
- 2 dried red chilies
- Handful fresh coriander leaves, chopped (optional)

Make the Sambar Masala: 1. Add the oil to a medium nonstick skillet. Add all of the remaining ingredients and roast for a few minutes until fragrant. The spices will brown a little, but don't let them burn. 2. Remove from the heat and pour onto a plate to cool. Once cooled, place into your spice grinder or mortar and pestle and grind to a powder. Set aside. Make the Sambar: 3. Heat the slow cooker to high and add the pigeon peas, green chiles, garlic, pearl onions, sambar masala, salt, carrots, potatoes, radish, tomato, and water. 4. Cover and cook for 4 hours on high, or for 6 hours on low. 5. Add the moringa (or green beans or asparagus), tamarind paste, and asafetida. Cover and cook for another 30 minutes. 6. When you're ready to serve, heat the coconut oil in a frying pan and pop the mustard seeds with the curry leaves and dried chiles. Pour over the sambar. Top with coriander leaves (if using) and serve.

Per Serving:
calories: 312 | fat: 7g | protein: 12g | carbs: 59g | fiber: 16g | sodium: 852mg

Black Bean Salad with Corn and Tomato Relish

- ½ pound (227 g) dried black beans, soaked overnight and drained
- 1 medium white onion, peeled and sliced in half
- 2 cloves garlic, peeled and lightly crushed
- 8 cups water
- 1 cup corn kernels
- 1 large tomato, seeded and chopped
- ½ medium red onion, peeled and chopped

- ¼ cup minced fresh cilantro
- ½ teaspoon ground cumin
- ¼ teaspoon smoked paprika
- ¼ teaspoon ground black pepper
- ¼ teaspoon salt
- 3 tablespoons extra-virgin olive oil
- 3 tablespoons lime juice

1. Add beans, white onion, garlic, and water to the Instant Pot®. Close lid, set steam release to Sealing, press the Bean button, and cook for the default time of 30 minutes. When the timer beeps, let pressure release naturally, about 20 minutes. 2. Open lid and remove and discard onion and garlic. Drain beans well and transfer to a medium bowl. Cool to room temperature, about 30 minutes. 3. In a separate small bowl, combine corn, tomato, red onion, cilantro, cumin, paprika, pepper, and salt. Toss to combine. Add to black beans and gently fold to mix. Whisk together olive oil and lime juice in a small bowl and pour over black bean mixture. Gently toss to coat. Serve at room temperature or refrigerate for at least 2 hours.

Per Serving:
calories: 216 | fat: 7g | protein: 8g | carbs: 28g | fiber: 6g | sodium: 192mg

Chapter 4

Vegetables and Sides

Chapter 4 Vegetables and Sides

Chili Lime Cauliflower with Cilantro

Prep time: 10 minutes | Cook time: 7 minutes | Serves 4

- 2 cups chopped cauliflower florets
- 2 tablespoons coconut oil, melted
- 2 teaspoons chili powder
- ½ teaspoon garlic powder
- 1 medium lime
- 2 tablespoons chopped cilantro

1. In a large bowl, toss cauliflower with coconut oil. Sprinkle with chili powder and garlic powder. Place seasoned cauliflower into the air fryer basket. 2. Adjust the temperature to 350ºF (177ºC) and set the timer for 7 minutes. 3. Cauliflower will be tender and begin to turn golden at the edges. Place into a serving bowl. 4. Cut the lime into quarters and squeeze juice over cauliflower. Garnish with cilantro.

Per Serving:

calories: 80 | fat: 7g | protein: 1g | carbs: 5g | fiber: 2g | sodium: 55mg

Stuffed Artichokes

Prep time: 20 minutes | Cook time: 5 to 7 hours | Serves 4 to 6

- 4 to 6 fresh large artichokes
- ½ cup bread crumbs
- ½ cup grated Parmesan cheese or Romano cheese
- 4 garlic cloves, minced
- ½ teaspoon sea salt
- ½ teaspoon freshly ground
- black pepper
- ¼ cup water
- 2 tablespoons extra-virgin olive oil
- 2 tablespoons chopped fresh parsley for garnish (optional)

1. To prepare the artichokes, cut off the stem base and trim about 1 inch from the top of each artichoke. Remove and discard the lowest leaves near the stem end. Trim any sharp tips from the leaves to prevent any pointy edges. Set the artichokes aside. 2. In a small mixing bowl, combine the bread crumbs, grated Parmesan cheese, minced garlic, salt, and black pepper. Mix until well blended. 3. Gently spread the artichoke leaves apart and stuff the bread-crumb mixture between the leaves, pressing the mixture down to the base of the artichokes. 4. Pour water into the bottom of a slow cooker to help create steam. 5. Arrange the prepared artichokes in a single layer in the slow cooker. Drizzle olive oil over each artichoke to add richness and enhance flavor. 6. Cover the slow cooker and set it to cook on Low heat for 5 to 7 hours, or until the artichokes are tender when pierced with a knife. 7. Garnish with fresh parsley before serving if desired, for an added touch of color and freshness. Enjoy the tender, flavorful artichokes as an appetizer or side dish.

Per Serving:

calories: 224 | fat: 12g | protein: 12g | carbs: 23g | fiber: 8g | sodium: 883mg

Slow Cooker Root Vegetable Hash with Plums

Prep time: 20 minutes | Cook time: 8 hours | Makes 9 (¾-cup) servings

- 4 carrots, peeled and cut into 1-inch cubes
- 3 large russet potatoes, peeled and cut into 1-inch cubes
- 1 onion, diced
- 3 garlic cloves, minced
- ½ teaspoon salt
- ⅛ teaspoon freshly ground black pepper
- ½ teaspoon dried thyme leaves
- 1 sprig rosemary
- ½ cup vegetable broth
- 3 plums, cut into 1-inch pieces

1. In the slow cooker, combine the carrots, potatoes, onion, and garlic. Sprinkle with the salt, pepper, and thyme, and stir. 2. Imbed the rosemary sprig in the vegetables. 3. Pour the broth over everything. 4. Cover and cook on low for 7½ hours, or until the vegetables are tender. 5. Stir in the plums, cover, and cook on low for 30 minutes, until tender. 6. Remove and discard the rosemary sprig, and serve.

Per Serving:

calories: 137 | fat: 0g | protein: 3g | carbs: 32g | fiber: 4g | sodium: 204mg

Braised Eggplant and Tomatoes

Prep time: 10 minutes | Cook time: 40 minutes | Serves 4

- 1 large eggplant, peeled and diced
- Pinch sea salt
- 1 (15-ounce / 425-g) can chopped tomatoes and juices
- 1 cup chicken broth
- 2 garlic cloves, smashed
- 1 tablespoon Italian seasoning
- 1 bay leaf
- Sea salt and freshly ground pepper, to taste

1. Slice the eggplant and sprinkle salt on both sides to help draw out any bitter juices. Let the salted eggplant sit for 20 minutes, then rinse well under cold water and pat dry with a paper towel. 2. Dice the eggplant into bite-sized pieces. 3. In a large saucepot, combine the diced eggplant, tomatoes, chicken broth, garlic cloves, seasoning blend, and bay leaf. Stir everything together to mix well. 4. Bring the mixture to a boil over medium-high heat, then reduce the heat to a simmer. 5. Cover the pot and let it simmer for 30 to 40 minutes, or until the eggplant is tender and has absorbed the flavors. Once cooked, remove the garlic cloves and bay leaf. Taste and adjust the seasoning as needed before serving. Enjoy the warm, savory dish on its own or with crusty bread.

Per Serving:

calories: 70 | fat: 1g | protein: 4g | carbs: 14g | fiber: 6g | sodium: 186mg

Savory Butternut Squash and Apples

Prep time: 20 minutes | Cook time: 4 hours |
Serves 10

- 1 (3-pound / 1.4-kg) butternut squash, peeled, seeded, and cubed
- 4 cooking apples (granny smith or honeycrisp work well), peeled, cored, and chopped
- ¾ cup dried currants
- ½ sweet yellow onion such as vidalia, sliced thin
- 1 tablespoon ground cinnamon
- 1½ teaspoons ground nutmeg

1. Add the squash, apples, currants, and chopped onion to the slow cooker, mixing to combine evenly. Sprinkle the mixture with ground cinnamon and nutmeg for a warm, aromatic flavor. 2. Set the slow cooker to high and cook for about 4 hours, or until the squash is tender and easily pierced with a fork. Stir occasionally during cooking to ensure the ingredients are well mixed and the flavors blend together. Serve warm for a comforting, spiced dish that's perfect as a side or dessert.

Per Serving:
calories: 114 | fat: 0g | protein: 2g | carbs: 28g | fiber: 6g | sodium: 8mg

Roasted Vegetables with Lemon Tahini Dressing

Prep time: 15 minutes | Cook time: 25 minutes | Serves 4

For the Dressing:
- ½ cup tahini
- ½ cup water, as needed
- 3 tablespoons freshly

For the Vegetables:
- 8 ounces (227 g) baby potatoes, halved
- 8 ounces (227 g) baby carrots
- 1 head cauliflower, cored and cut into large chunks
- 2 red bell peppers, quartered
- 1 zucchini, cut into 1-inch

squeezed lemon juice
- Sea salt

pieces
- ¼ cup olive oil
- 1½ teaspoons garlic powder
- ¼ teaspoon dried oregano
- ¼ teaspoon dried thyme
- Sea salt
- Freshly ground black pepper
- Red pepper flakes (optional)

Make the Dressing: 1. In a small bowl, stir together the tahini, water, and lemon juice until well blended. 2. Taste, season with salt, and set aside. Make the Vegetables: 3. Preheat the oven to 425°F(220°C). Line a baking sheet with parchment paper. 4. Place the potatoes in a microwave-safe bowl with 3 tablespoons water, cover with a paper plate, and microwave on high for 4 minutes. Drain any excess water. 5. Transfer the potatoes to a large bowl and add the carrots, cauliflower, bell peppers, zucchini, olive oil, garlic powder, oregano, and thyme. Season with salt and black pepper. 6. Spread the vegetables in a single layer on the prepared baking sheet and roast until fork-tender and a little charred, about 25 minutes. 7. Transfer the vegetables to a large bowl and add the dressing and red pepper flakes, if desired. Toss to coat. 8. Serve the roasted vegetables alongside your favorite chicken or fish dish.

Per Serving:
calories: 412 | fat: 30g | protein: 9g | carbs: 31g | fiber: 9g | sodium: 148mg

Sweet and Crispy Roasted Pearl Onions

Prep time: 5 minutes | Cook time: 18 minutes | Serves 3

- 1 (14½ ounces / 411 g) package frozen pearl onions (do not thaw)
- 2 tablespoons extra-virgin olive oil
- 2 tablespoons balsamic
- vinegar
- 2 teaspoons finely chopped fresh rosemary
- ½ teaspoon kosher salt
- ¼ teaspoon black pepper

1. In a medium bowl, mix the sliced onions with the olive oil, vinegar, chopped rosemary, salt, and black pepper until the onions are evenly coated. 2. Transfer the seasoned onions to the air fryer basket, spreading them out in an even layer. Set the air fryer to 400°F (204°C) and cook for 18 minutes, stirring once or twice during the cooking process to ensure even cooking, until the onions are tender and have a light char. Serve warm as a flavorful side or topping.

Per Serving:
calories: 145 | fat: 9g | protein: 2g | carbs: 15g | fiber: 2g | sodium: 396mg

Sweet Potato Gorgonzola Veggie Burgers

Prep time: 10 minutes |Cook time: 15 minutes| Serves: 4

- 1 large sweet potato (about 8 ounces / 227 g)
- 2 tablespoons extra-virgin olive oil, divided
- 1 cup chopped onion (about ½ medium onion)
- 1 cup old-fashioned rolled oats
- 1 large egg
- 1 tablespoon balsamic vinegar
- 1 tablespoon dried oregano
- 1 garlic clove
- ¼ teaspoon kosher or sea salt
- ½ cup crumbled Gorgonzola or blue cheese (about 2 ounces / 57 g)
- Salad greens or 4 whole-wheat rolls, for serving (optional)

1. Using a fork, pierce the sweet potato all over and microwave on high for 4 to 5 minutes, until tender in the center. Cool slightly, then slice in half. 2. While the sweet potato is cooking, in a large skillet over medium-high heat, heat 1 tablespoon of oil. Add the onion and cook for 5 minutes, stirring occasionally. 3. Using a spoon, carefully scoop the sweet potato flesh out of the skin and put the flesh in a food processor. Add the onion, oats, egg, vinegar, oregano, garlic, and salt. Process until smooth. Add the cheese and pulse four times to barely combine. With your hands, form the mixture into four (½-cup-size) burgers. Place the burgers on a plate, and press to flatten each to about ¾-inch thick. 4. Wipe out the skillet with a paper towel, then heat the remaining 1 tablespoon of oil over medium-high heat until very hot, about 2 minutes. Add the burgers to the hot oil, then turn the heat down to medium. Cook the burgers for 5 minutes, flip with a spatula, then cook an additional 5 minutes. Enjoy as is or serve on salad greens or whole-wheat rolls.

Per Serving:
calories: 337 | fat: 16g | protein: 13g | carbs: 38g | fiber: 6g | sodium: 378mg

Cauliflower and Carrot Skillet Hash

Prep time: 10 minutes | Cook time: 10 minutes | Serves 4

- 3 tablespoons extra-virgin olive oil
- 1 large onion, chopped
- 1 tablespoon garlic, minced
- 2 cups carrots, diced
- 4 cups cauliflower pieces, washed
- 1 teaspoon salt
- ½ teaspoon ground cumin

1. In a large skillet over medium heat, cook the olive oil, onion, garlic, and carrots for 3 minutes. 2. Cut the cauliflower into 1 inch or bite-size pieces. Add the cauliflower, salt, and cumin to the skillet and toss to combine with the carrots and onions. 3. Cover and cook for 3 minutes. 4. Toss the vegetables and continue to cook uncovered for an additional 3 to 4 minutes. 5. Serve warm.

Per Serving:
calories: 159 | fat: 11g | protein: 3g | carbs: 15g | fiber: 5g | sodium: 657mg

Fresh Stuffed Cucumbers with Avocado and Tomato

Prep time: 10 minutes | Cook time: 0 minutes | Serves 2

- 1 English cucumber
- 1 tomato, diced
- 1 avocado, diced
- Dash of lime juice
- Sea salt and freshly ground pepper, to taste
- Small bunch cilantro, chopped

1. Cut the cucumber in half lengthwise and scoop out the flesh and seeds into a small bowl. 2. Without mashing too much, gently combine the cucumber flesh and seeds with the tomato, avocado, and lime juice. 3. Season with sea salt and freshly ground pepper to taste. 4. Put mixture back into cucumber halves and cut each piece in half. Garnish with the cilantro and serve.

Per Serving:
calories: 189 | fat: 15g | protein: 3g | carbs: 15g | fiber: 8g | sodium: 13mg

Radish Chips

Prep time: 10 minutes | Cook time: 5 minutes | Serves 4

- 2 cups water
- 1 pound (454 g) radishes
- ¼ teaspoon onion powder
- ¼ teaspoon paprika
- ½ teaspoon garlic powder
- 2 tablespoons coconut oil, melted

1. Fill a medium saucepan with water and bring it to a boil over medium-high heat on the stovetop. 2. While the water is heating, remove both the top and bottom ends from each radish. Use a mandoline to slice each radish thinly and uniformly, or use a food processor fitted with the slicing blade for more convenience. 3. Once the water is boiling, add the radish slices to the pot. Let them cook for about 5 minutes or until they turn translucent. Drain the radish slices and place them onto a clean kitchen towel, patting them dry to remove excess moisture. 4. In a large bowl, toss the radish slices with the remaining ingredients—olive oil, salt, pepper, and any desired seasoning—until they are evenly coated. Transfer the radish chips to the air fryer basket, spreading them out as evenly as possible. 5. Set the air fryer to 320°F (160°C) and air fry the radish chips for about 5 minutes, shaking the basket two or three times during cooking to ensure the chips cook evenly. 6. Once they are crispy and golden, remove the radish chips from the air fryer. Serve them warm for a light, healthy, and crunchy snack.

Per Serving:
calories: 81 | fat: 7g | protein: 1g | carbs: 5g | fiber: 2g | sodium: 27mg

Air-Fried Zucchini Boats with Tomatoes and Feta

Prep time: 5 minutes | Cook time: 10 minutes | Serves 4

- 1 large zucchini, ends removed, halved lengthwise
- 6 grape tomatoes, quartered
- ¼ teaspoon salt
- ¼ cup feta cheese
- 1 tablespoon balsamic vinegar
- 1 tablespoon olive oil

1. Use a spoon to scoop out 2 tablespoons from center of each zucchini half, making just enough space to fill with tomatoes and feta. 2. Place tomatoes evenly in centers of zucchini halves and sprinkle with salt. Place into ungreased air fryer basket. Adjust the temperature to 350°F (177°C) and roast for 10 minutes. When done, zucchini will be tender. 3. Transfer boats to a serving tray and sprinkle with feta, then drizzle with vinegar and olive oil. Serve warm.

Per Serving:
calories: 92 | fat: 6g | protein: 3g | carbs: 8g | fiber: 2g | sodium: 242mg

Five-Spice Roasted Sweet Potatoes

Prep time: 10 minutes | Cook time: 12 minutes | Serves 4

- ½ teaspoon ground cinnamon
- ¼ teaspoon ground cumin
- ¼ teaspoon paprika
- 1 teaspoon chile powder
- ⅛ teaspoon turmeric
- ½ teaspoon salt (optional)
- Freshly ground black pepper, to taste
- 2 large sweet potatoes, peeled and cut into ¾-inch cubes (about 3 cups)
- 1 tablespoon olive oil

1. In a large mixing bowl, combine the ground cinnamon, cumin, paprika, chile powder, turmeric, salt, and black pepper to taste. Stir the spices until they are well mixed. 2. Add the diced potatoes to the bowl and toss to coat them thoroughly with the spice blend. 3. Drizzle the potatoes with olive oil, stirring to ensure they are evenly coated with both the oil and the spices. 4. Transfer the seasoned potatoes to a baking pan or an ovenproof dish that fits comfortably inside your air fryer basket. 5. Place the pan in the air fryer and cook the potatoes at 390°F (199°C) for 6 minutes. Stop and stir the potatoes well to ensure even cooking. 6. Continue cooking for an additional 6 minutes until the potatoes are tender on the inside and crispy on the outside. Serve immediately for a deliciously spiced side dish or snack.

Per Serving:
calories: 14 | fat: 3g | protein: 1g | carbs: 14g | fiber: 2g | sodium: 327mg

Roasted Fennel with Za'atar

Prep time: 10 minutes | Cook time: 30 minutes | Serves 4

- 4 fennel bulbs, quartered
- 1 tablespoon olive oil
- 1 tablespoon za'atar
- seasoning
- ¼ teaspoon salt

1. Preheat your oven to 425°F (220°C). This high temperature will help the fennel roast to a nice caramelized finish. 2. In a large mixing bowl, toss the sliced fennel bulbs with olive oil, za'atar seasoning, and a pinch of salt. Make sure the fennel is evenly coated with the oil and seasoning. 3. Spread the seasoned fennel on a large baking sheet in a single layer to ensure even roasting. Place the baking sheet in the preheated oven and roast for 25 to 30 minutes, tossing the fennel once after 15 minutes to promote even cooking. Roast until the fennel is soft and caramelized, with golden-brown edges. Serve warm as a delicious side dish or add to salads for extra flavor.

Per Serving:
calories: 109 | fat: 3g | protein: 3g | carbs: 18g | fiber: 7g | sodium: 422mg

Air Fryer Almond Flour Dinner Rolls

Prep time: 10 minutes | Cook time: 12 minutes | Serves 6

- 1 cup shredded Mozzarella cheese
- 1 ounce (28 g) full-fat cream cheese
- 1 cup blanched finely
- ground almond flour
- ¼ cup ground flaxseed
- ½ teaspoon baking powder
- 1 large egg

1. Place Mozzarella, cream cheese, and almond flour in a large microwave-safe bowl. Microwave for 1 minute. Mix until smooth. 2. Add flaxseed, baking powder, and egg until fully combined and smooth. Microwave an additional 15 seconds if it becomes too firm. 3. Separate the dough into six pieces and roll into balls. Place the balls into the air fryer basket. 4. Adjust the temperature to 320ºF (160ºC) and air fry for 12 minutes. 5. Allow rolls to cool completely before serving.

Per Serving:
calories: 223 | fat: 17g | protein: 13g | carbs: 7g | fiber: 4g | sodium: 175mg

Lebanese Baba Ghanoush

Prep time: 15 minutes | Cook time: 20 minutes | Serves 4

- 1 medium eggplant
- 2 tablespoons vegetable oil
- 2 tablespoons tahini (sesame paste)
- 2 tablespoons fresh lemon juice
- ½ teaspoon kosher salt
- 1 tablespoon extra-virgin olive oil
- ½ teaspoon smoked paprika
- 2 tablespoons chopped fresh parsley

1. Rub the entire surface of the eggplant with vegetable oil until it is evenly coated. Place the eggplant into the air fryer basket, setting the air fryer to 400°F (204°C) for 20 minutes, or until the skin of the eggplant is blistered and charred. This will give the eggplant a smoky flavor. 2. Once the eggplant is done, carefully transfer it to a resealable plastic bag. Seal the bag and set it aside for 15 minutes, allowing the eggplant to continue cooking in the residual heat and steam, making it easier to peel. 3. After resting, transfer the eggplant to a large mixing bowl. Peel off and discard the charred skin, leaving only the softened flesh. Roughly mash the eggplant with a fork or masher, then add the tahini, lemon juice, and salt. Stir the mixture until all ingredients are well combined and smooth. 4. Transfer the mashed eggplant to a serving bowl. Drizzle with olive oil for added richness, and sprinkle with paprika and fresh parsley for garnish. Serve this smoky and creamy dish as a dip with pita bread or vegetables.

Per Serving:
calories: 171 | fat: 15g | protein: 3g | carbs: 10g | fiber: 5g | sodium: 303mg

Baked Stuffed Eggplant with Caramelized Onions and Feta

Prep time: 10 minutes | Cook time:1 hour 30 minutes | Serves 4

- 4 medium, long eggplant, washed and stemmed
- 6 tablespoons extra virgin olive oil, divided, plus 1 teaspoon for brushing
- 1⅛ teaspoon fine sea salt, divided
- 3 medium red onions, finely chopped
- 5 garlic cloves, finely
- chopped
- 1 teaspoon granulated sugar
- 15 ounces (425 g) chopped tomatoes (fresh or canned)
- 1 cinnamon stick
- ½ cup chopped fresh parsley
- ¼ teaspoon freshly ground black pepper
- 4 tablespoons crumbled feta
- 4 cherry tomatoes, sliced

1. Preheat the oven to 400ºF (205ºC). Make 3 end-to-end slits, each about 1 inch deep, along the length of each eggplant, making sure not to cut completely through. (The slits should be about ¾ inch apart.) 2. Place the eggplant in a large baking pan, slit side up. Brush with 1 teaspoon of the olive oil, and season with ⅛ teaspoon of the sea salt. Transfer to the oven and roast for 45 minutes. 3. While the eggplant are roasting, begin preparing the filling by heating 3 tablespoons of the olive oil in a deep pan placed over medium heat. When the oil starts to shimmer, add the onions and garlic and sauté for 3 minutes. 4. Sprinkle the sugar and ¼ teaspoon of the sea salt over the onions. Stir, then reduce the heat to medium-low and cook for 15 minutes or until the onions are caramelized. (Reduce the heat if the onions begin to burn.) 5. Add the tomatoes, cinnamon stick, parsley, black pepper, and remaining ¾ teaspoon of sea salt. Stir, increase the heat to medium, and cook for 3–4 minutes. 6. When the eggplant are done roasting, remove them from the oven, carefully pull the slits open, and stuff each eggplant with the filling. 7. Place the stuffed eggplant snugly in a baking dish. Drizzle the remaining 3 tablespoons of olive oil over the eggplant, ensuring the outsides of the eggplant are coated with the oil. Sprinkle 1 tablespoon of feta over each eggplant and then top with 3–4 slices of cherry tomatoes. 8. Place the stuffed eggplant back in the oven and bake for 15 minutes, then lower the heat to 350ºF (180ºC) and bake for 30 more minutes. Remove from the oven and set aside to cool for at least 15 minutes before serving. Store covered in the refrigerator for up to 3 days.

Per Serving:
calories: 408 | fat: 24g | protein: 9g | carbs: 48g | fiber: 20g | sodium: 771mg

Sesame Carrots and Sugar Snap Peas

Prep time: 10 minutes | Cook time: 16 minutes | Serves 4

- 1 pound (454 g) carrots, peeled sliced on the bias (½-inch slices)
- 1 teaspoon olive oil
- Salt and freshly ground black pepper, to taste
- ⅓ cup honey
- 1 tablespoon sesame oil
- 1 tablespoon soy sauce
- ½ teaspoon minced fresh ginger
- 4 ounces (113 g) sugar snap peas (about 1 cup)
- 1½ teaspoons sesame seeds

1. Preheat the air fryer to 360°F (182°C) to get it ready for cooking. 2. In a mixing bowl, toss the carrot sticks with olive oil, then season with salt and black pepper. Place the carrots in the air fryer basket and cook for 10 minutes, shaking the basket once or twice during cooking to ensure even roasting. 3. In a large bowl, whisk together the honey, sesame oil, soy sauce, and minced ginger until well combined. Add the sugar snap peas and the air-fried carrots to the honey mixture, tossing to coat the vegetables evenly. Return everything to the air fryer basket for the next cooking step. 4. Increase the temperature to 400°F (204°C) and air fry for an additional 6 minutes, shaking the basket halfway through to ensure even cooking. This will help the sugar snap peas and carrots develop a light glaze and more intense flavor. 5. Transfer the air-fried carrots and sugar snap peas to a serving bowl. Pour any remaining sauce from the air fryer over the vegetables and sprinkle with sesame seeds for added texture and flavor. Serve immediately for a delicious, sweet, and savory side dish.

Per Serving:
calories: 202 | fat: 6g | protein: 2g | carbs: 37g | fiber: 4g | sodium: 141mg

Sicilian-Style Roasted Cauliflower with Capers, Currants, and Crispy Breadcrumbs

Prep time: 10 minutes | Cook time: 55 minutes | Serves 4

- 1 large head of cauliflower (2 pounds / 907 g), cut into 2-inch florets
- 6 tablespoons olive oil, divided
- 1 teaspoon salt
- ½ teaspoon freshly ground black pepper
- 3 garlic cloves, thinly sliced
- 2 tablespoons salt-packed capers, soaked, rinsed, and
- patted dry
- ¾ cup fresh whole-wheat breadcrumbs
- ½ cup chicken broth
- 1 teaspoon anchovy paste
- ⅓ cup golden raisins
- 1 tablespoon white wine vinegar
- 2 tablespoons chopped flat-leaf parsley

1. Preheat your oven to 425°F (220°C). This high heat will help the cauliflower develop a nice, crispy exterior. 2. In a medium bowl, toss the cauliflower florets with 3 tablespoons of olive oil, salt, and black pepper, ensuring the florets are evenly coated. Spread the seasoned cauliflower in a single layer on a large, rimmed baking sheet. Roast the cauliflower in the preheated oven for about 45 minutes, stirring occasionally, until it turns golden brown with crispy edges. 3. While the cauliflower is roasting, heat the remaining 3 tablespoons of olive oil in a small saucepan

over medium-low heat. Add the minced garlic and cook, stirring frequently, for about 5 minutes until the garlic starts to turn golden. Stir in the capers and cook for an additional 3 minutes. Then, add the breadcrumbs and stir until they are evenly coated in the oil, cooking until the breadcrumbs are golden brown and crisp. Use a slotted spoon to transfer the breadcrumbs to a bowl or plate to cool. 4. In the same saucepan, combine the broth and anchovy paste, bringing the mixture to a boil over medium-high heat. Add the raisins and vinegar, stirring occasionally, and cook for about 5 minutes until most of the liquid is absorbed. This will help create a flavorful, tangy sauce to complement the roasted cauliflower. 5. When the cauliflower is finished roasting, transfer it to a large serving bowl. Pour the raisin mixture over the cauliflower and toss everything together to combine the flavors. Top the cauliflower with the crispy garlic breadcrumbs for added texture, and garnish with fresh parsley for a burst of color. Serve immediately while warm for the best flavor and texture.

Per Serving:
calories: 364 | fat: 22g | protein: 8g | carbs: 37g | fiber: 6g | sodium: 657mg

Slow Cooker Spicy Creamer Potatoes

Prep time: 10 minutes | Cook time: 8 hours | Makes 7 (1-cup) servings

- 2 pounds (907 g) creamer potatoes
- 1 onion, chopped
- 3 garlic cloves, minced
- 1 chipotle chile in adobo sauce, minced
- 2 tablespoons freshly
- squeezed lemon juice
- 2 tablespoons water
- 1 tablespoon chili powder
- ½ teaspoon ground cumin
- ½ teaspoon salt
- ⅛ teaspoon freshly ground black pepper

1. In the slow cooker, combine all the ingredients and stir. 2. Cover and cook on low for 7 to 8 hours, or until the potatoes are tender, and serve.

Per Serving:
calories: 113 | fat: 0g | protein: 3g | carbs: 25g | fiber: 4g | sodium: 208mg

Tomato Stewed Okra with Cilantro

Prep time: 5 minutes | Cook time: 25 minutes | Serves 4

- ¼ cup extra-virgin olive oil
- 1 large onion, chopped
- 4 cloves garlic, finely chopped
- 1 teaspoon salt
- 1 pound (454 g) fresh or frozen okra, cleaned
- 1 (15-ounce / 425-g) can plain tomato sauce
- 2 cups water
- ½ cup fresh cilantro, finely chopped
- ½ teaspoon freshly ground black pepper

1. In a large pot over medium heat, stir and cook the olive oil, onion, garlic, and salt for 1 minute. 2. Stir in the okra and cook for 3 minutes. 3. Add the tomato sauce, water, cilantro, and black pepper; stir, cover, and let cook for 15 minutes, stirring occasionally. 4. Serve warm.

Per Serving:
calories: 202 | fat: 14g | protein: 4g | carbs: 19g | fiber: 6g | sodium: 607mg

Caponata (Sicilian Eggplant)

Prep time: 1 hour 5 minutes | Cook time: 40 minutes | Serves 2

- 3 medium eggplant, cut into ½-inch cubes (about 1½ pounds / 680 g)
- ½ teaspoon fine sea salt
- ¼ cup extra virgin olive oil
- 1 medium onion (red or white), chopped
- 1 tablespoon dried oregano
- ½ cup green olives, pitted and halved
- 2 tablespoons capers, rinsed
- 3 medium tomatoes (about

- 15 ounces / 425 g), chopped
- 3 tablespoons red wine vinegar
- 2 tablespoons granulated sugar
- Salt to taste
- Freshly ground black pepper to taste
- 2 tablespoons chopped fresh basil
- 1 tablespoon toasted pine nuts (optional)

1. Place the diced eggplant in a large colander and sprinkle with ½ teaspoon of sea salt. Let the eggplant rest for about an hour to draw out any bitterness. After an hour, rinse the eggplant under cold water and pat dry with paper towels. 2. Heat the olive oil in a large pan over medium heat. Once the oil begins to shimmer, add the eggplant and sauté for about 5 minutes, or until it begins to turn golden brown. Add the chopped onions and continue to sauté until the onions are soft and translucent, about 5 more minutes. 3. Stir in the dried oregano, olives, capers, and canned tomatoes along with their juices. Mix well, reduce the heat to medium-low, and let the mixture simmer gently for about 20 to 25 minutes, allowing all the flavors to meld together. 4. While the mixture is simmering, combine the vinegar and sugar in a small bowl, stirring until the sugar is fully dissolved. Pour the vinegar-sugar mixture into the pan, stirring well, and cook for another 2 to 3 minutes until the sharp vinegar smell dissipates. Remove the pan from the heat once everything is well incorporated. 5. Season the dish to taste with additional salt and freshly ground black pepper. Just before serving, garnish each portion with a sprinkle of chopped fresh basil and toasted pine nuts for added flavor and texture. Serve this dish warm or at room temperature, and store any leftovers in the refrigerator for up to 3 days for an easy, flavorful meal.

Per Serving:
calories: 473 | fat: 32g | protein: 6g | carbs: 47g | fiber: 15g | sodium: 702mg

Zucchini Ribbons with Lemon Ricotta and Fresh Herbs

Prep time: 20 minutes | Cook time: 0 minutes | Serves 4

- 2 medium zucchini or yellow squash
- ½ cup ricotta cheese
- 2 tablespoons fresh mint, chopped, plus additional mint leaves for garnish
- 2 tablespoons fresh parsley, chopped

- Zest of ½ lemon
- 2 teaspoons lemon juice
- ½ teaspoon kosher salt
- ¼ teaspoon freshly ground black pepper
- 1 tablespoon extra-virgin olive oil

1. Using a vegetable peeler, make ribbons by peeling the summer squash lengthwise. The squash ribbons will resemble the wide pasta, pappardelle. 2. In a medium bowl, combine the ricotta cheese, mint, parsley, lemon zest, lemon juice, salt, and black pepper. 3. Place mounds of the squash ribbons evenly on 4 plates then dollop the ricotta mixture on top. Drizzle with the olive oil and garnish with the mint leaves.

Per Serving:
calories: 90 | fat: 6g | protein: 5g | carbs: 5g | fiber: 1g | sodium: 180mg

Crispy Green Beans

Prep time: 5 minutes | Cook time: 8 minutes | Serves 4

- 2 teaspoons olive oil
- ½ pound (227 g) fresh green beans, ends trimmed

- ¼ teaspoon salt
- ¼ teaspoon ground black pepper

1. In a large mixing bowl, drizzle the green beans with olive oil and sprinkle with salt and black pepper. Toss the green beans to ensure they are evenly coated with the oil and seasoning. 2. Transfer the seasoned green beans to the air fryer basket, spreading them out in an even layer. Set the air fryer temperature to 350°F (177°C) and cook for 8 minutes, shaking the basket twice during the cooking process to promote even browning. The green beans will be golden and crispy at the edges when done. Serve them warm as a simple yet tasty side dish.

Per Serving:
calories: 33 | fat: 3g | protein: 1g | carbs: 3g | fiber: 1g | sodium: 147mg

Fried Zucchini Salad

Prep time: 10 minutes | Cook time: 5 to 7 minutes | Serves 4

- 2 medium zucchini, thinly sliced
- 5 tablespoons olive oil, divided
- ¼ cup chopped fresh parsley
- 2 tablespoons chopped fresh

- mint
- Zest and juice of ½ lemon
- 1 clove garlic, minced
- ¼ cup crumbled feta cheese
- Freshly ground black pepper, to taste

1. Preheat the air fryer to 400°F (204°C) to get it ready for cooking the zucchini. 2. In a large bowl, toss the zucchini slices with 1 tablespoon of olive oil, making sure each slice is evenly coated. 3. Working in batches if necessary, arrange the zucchini slices in an even layer in the air fryer basket. Cook for 5 to 7 minutes, pausing halfway through to shake the basket for even cooking. The zucchini should be soft and lightly browned on each side when done. 4. While the zucchini is cooking, prepare the dressing. In a small bowl, mix the remaining 4 tablespoons of olive oil with the chopped parsley, mint, lemon zest, lemon juice, and minced garlic until well combined. 5. Arrange the cooked zucchini slices on a serving plate and drizzle with the prepared herb dressing. Sprinkle crumbled feta cheese and a bit of black pepper over the top. Serve warm or at room temperature for a light and refreshing dish.

Per Serving:
calories: 194 | fat: 19g | protein: 3g | carbs: 4g | fiber: 1g | sodium: 96mg

Roasted Broccoli with Tahini Yogurt Sauce

For the Broccoli:
- 1½ to 2 pounds (680 to 907 g) broccoli, stalk trimmed and cut into slices, head cut into florets
- 1 lemon, sliced into ¼-inch-thick rounds

For the Tahini Yogurt Sauce:
- ½ cup plain Greek yogurt
- 2 tablespoons tahini
- 1 tablespoon lemon juice

- 3 tablespoons extra-virgin olive oil
- ½ teaspoon kosher salt
- ¼ teaspoon freshly ground black pepper

- ¼ teaspoon kosher salt
- 1 teaspoon sesame seeds, for garnish (optional)

Make the Broccoli: 1. Preheat your oven to 425°F (220°C). Line a baking sheet with parchment paper or foil to prevent sticking and make cleanup easier. 2. In a large bowl, gently toss the broccoli florets with the lemon slices, olive oil, salt, and black pepper until everything is evenly coated. Spread the broccoli mixture in a single layer on the prepared baking sheet for even roasting. Roast for 15 minutes, then stir the broccoli, and continue roasting for an additional 15 minutes, or until the broccoli is tender and golden brown.
Make the Tahini Yogurt Sauce: 3. In a medium bowl, combine the yogurt, tahini, lemon juice, and salt, mixing until smooth and well combined.
Assemble:
4. Spread the tahini yogurt sauce evenly on a serving platter or large plate. Arrange the roasted broccoli and lemon slices over the sauce. Garnish with sesame seeds, if desired, for added texture and flavor. Serve warm for a delicious side dish or appetizer.

Per Serving:
calories: 245 | fat: 16g | protein: 12g | carbs: 20g | fiber: 7g | sodium: 305mg

Freekeh Pilaf with Walnuts and Spiced Yogurt

- 2½ cups freekeh
- 3 tablespoons extra-virgin olive oil, divided
- 2 medium onions, diced
- ¼ teaspoon ground cinnamon
- ¼ teaspoon ground allspice
- 5 cups chicken stock

- ½ cup chopped walnuts
- Salt
- Freshly ground black pepper
- ½ cup plain, unsweetened, full-fat Greek yogurt
- 1½ teaspoons freshly squeezed lemon juice
- ½ teaspoon garlic powder

1. In a small bowl, soak the freekeh covered in cold water for 5 minutes. Drain and rinse the freekeh, then rinse one more time. 2. In a large sauté pan or skillet, heat 2 tablespoons oil, then add the onions and cook until fragrant. Add the freekeh, cinnamon, and allspice. Stir periodically for 1 minute. 3. Add the stock and walnuts and season with salt and pepper. Bring to a simmer. 4. Cover and reduce the heat to low. Cook for 15 minutes. Once freekeh is tender, remove from the heat and allow to rest for 5 minutes. 5. In a small bowl, combine the yogurt, lemon juice, and garlic powder. You may need to add salt to bring out the flavors. Add the yogurt mixture to the freekeh and serve immediately.

Per Serving:
calories: 653 | fat: 25g | protein: 23g | carbs: 91g | fiber: 12g | sodium: 575mg

Air-Fried Garlic Roasted Eggplant

- 1 large eggplant
- 2 tablespoons olive oil

- ¼ teaspoon salt
- ½ teaspoon garlic powder

1. Remove top and bottom from eggplant. Slice eggplant into ¼-inch-thick round slices. 2. Brush slices with olive oil. Sprinkle with salt and garlic powder. Place eggplant slices into the air fryer basket. 3. Adjust the temperature to 390ºF (199ºC) and set the timer for 15 minutes. 4. Serve immediately.

Per Serving:
calories: 98 | fat: 7g | protein: 2g | carbs: 8g | fiber: 3g | sodium: 200mg

Garlic-Parmesan Crispy Baby Potatoes

- Oil, for spraying
- 1 pound (454 g) baby potatoes
- ½ cup grated Parmesan cheese, divided
- 3 tablespoons olive oil
- 2 teaspoons granulated garlic
- ½ teaspoon onion powder
- ½ teaspoon salt
- ¼ teaspoon freshly ground black pepper
- ¼ teaspoon paprika
- 2 tablespoons chopped fresh parsley, for garnish

1. Place parchment in the air fryer basket and spray lightly with oil. 2. Rinse the potatoes well, pat them dry with paper towels, and put them in a large mixing bowl. 3. In a small bowl, combine ¼ cup Parmesan cheese, olive oil, garlic, onion powder, salt, black pepper, and paprika. Pour the mixture over the potatoes and toss until evenly coated. 4. Arrange the potatoes in a single layer in the air fryer basket, keeping them from touching. Work in batches if needed, depending on the size of your air fryer. 5. Air fry at 400°F (204°C) for 15 minutes, stirring after 7 to 8 minutes, or until the potatoes are tender when pierced with a fork. Cook an extra 1 to 2 minutes if necessary. 6. Garnish with parsley and sprinkle the remaining Parmesan cheese before serving.

Per Serving:
calories: 234 | fat: 14g | protein: 6g | carbs: 22g | fiber: 3g | sodium: 525mg

Zucchini Noodles Pomodoro

- 1 tablespoon vegetable oil
- 1 large onion, peeled and diced
- 3 cloves garlic, peeled and minced
- 1 (28-ounce / 794-g) can diced tomatoes, including juice
- ½ cup water
- 1 tablespoon Italian seasoning
- ½ teaspoon salt
- ½ teaspoon ground black pepper
- 2 medium zucchini, trimmed and spiralized

1. Press the Sauté button on the Instant Pot® and heat oil. Add onion and cook until translucent, about 5 minutes. Add garlic and cook for an additional 30 seconds. Add tomatoes, water, Italian seasoning, salt, and pepper. Add zucchini and toss to combine. Press the Cancel button. 2. Close lid, set steam release to Sealing, press the Manual button, and set time to 1 minute. When the timer beeps, let pressure release naturally for 5 minutes. Quick-release any remaining pressure until the float valve drops and open lid. Press the Cancel button. 3. Transfer zucchini to four bowls. Press the Sauté button, then press the Adjust button to change the temperature to Less, and simmer sauce in the Instant Pot® uncovered for 5 minutes. Ladle over zucchini and serve immediately.

Per Serving:
calories: 72 | fat: 4g | protein: 2g | carbs: 9g | fiber: 2g | sodium: 476mg

Chapter **5**

Vegetarian Mains

Chapter 5 Vegetarian Mains

Eggs Poached in Moroccan Tomato Sauce

Prep time: 10 minutes | Cook time: 35 minutes | Serves 4

- 1 tablespoon olive oil
- 1 medium yellow onion, diced
- 2 red bell peppers, seeded and diced
- 1¾ teaspoons sweet paprika
- 1 teaspoon ras al hanout
- ½ teaspoon cayenne pepper
- 1 teaspoon salt
- ¼ cup tomato paste
- 1 (28-ounce / 794-g) can diced tomatoes, drained
- 8 eggs
- ¼ cup chopped cilantro

1. Heat olive oil in a skillet over medium-high heat. Add the onion and bell peppers, stirring frequently for about 5 minutes until they soften. Add paprika, ras al hanout, cayenne, salt, and tomato paste, cooking and stirring occasionally for another 5 minutes. 2. Mix in the diced tomatoes, then reduce the heat to medium-low. Let the mixture simmer for about 15 minutes until the tomatoes break down and the sauce thickens. 3. Create 8 wells in the sauce and crack an egg into each one. Cover the skillet and cook for about 10 minutes, or until the egg whites are set while the yolks remain runny. 4. Scoop the eggs and sauce into serving bowls, garnish with fresh cilantro, and serve hot.

Per Serving:
calories: 238 | fat: 13g | protein: 15g | carbs: 18g | fiber: 5g | sodium: 735mg

Cheese Stuffed Zucchini

Prep time: 20 minutes | Cook time: 8 minutes | Serves 4

- 1 large zucchini, cut into four pieces
- 2 tablespoons olive oil
- 1 cup Ricotta cheese, room temperature
- 2 tablespoons scallions, chopped
- 1 heaping tablespoon fresh parsley, roughly chopped
- 1 heaping tablespoon coriander, minced
- 2 ounces (57 g) Cheddar cheese, preferably freshly grated
- 1 teaspoon celery seeds
- ½ teaspoon salt
- ½ teaspoon garlic pepper

1. Place the zucchini in the air fryer basket and cook at 350ºF (177ºC) for about 10 minutes. Check the doneness and cook for an extra 2-3 minutes if necessary. 2. While the zucchini cooks, prepare the stuffing by combining the remaining ingredients. 3. Once the zucchini is tender, remove them and fill each piece with the prepared stuffing. Return the stuffed zucchini to the air fryer and cook for an additional 5 minutes.

Per Serving:
calories: 242 | fat: 20g | protein: 12g | carbs: 5g | fiber: 1g | sodium: 443mg

Three-Cheese Zucchini Boats

Prep time: 15 minutes | Cook time: 20 minutes | Serves 2

- 2 medium zucchini
- 1 tablespoon avocado oil
- ¼ cup low-carb, no-sugar-added pasta sauce
- ¼ cup full-fat ricotta cheese
- ¼ cup shredded Mozzarella cheese
- ¼ teaspoon dried oregano
- ¼ teaspoon garlic powder
- ½ teaspoon dried parsley
- 2 tablespoons grated vegetarian Parmesan cheese

1. Trim about 1 inch off both ends of each zucchini. Slice the zucchini lengthwise, then scoop out some of the flesh with a spoon to create space for the filling. Brush the zucchini with oil and add 2 tablespoons of pasta sauce into each half. 2. In a medium mixing bowl, combine ricotta, Mozzarella, oregano, garlic powder, and parsley. Fill each zucchini half with the cheese mixture. Arrange the stuffed zucchini in the air fryer basket. 3. Set the air fryer to 350ºF (177ºC) and cook for 20 minutes. 4. Use tongs or a spatula to carefully lift the zucchini out of the basket. Sprinkle with Parmesan cheese on top and serve immediately.

Per Serving:
calories: 208 | fat: 14g | protein: 12g | carbs: 11g | fiber: 3g | sodium: 247mg

Mediterranean Roasted Chickpeas with Tomatoes and Feta

Prep time: 15 minutes | Cook time: 15 minutes | Serves 4

- 1 tablespoon extra-virgin olive oil
- ½ medium onion, chopped
- 3 garlic cloves, chopped
- 2 teaspoons smoked paprika
- ¼ teaspoon ground cumin
- 4 cups halved cherry tomatoes
- 2 (15-ounce / 425-g) cans chickpeas, drained and rinsed
- ½ cup plain, unsweetened, full-fat Greek yogurt, for serving
- 1 cup crumbled feta, for serving

1. Preheat the oven to 425ºF (220ºC). 2. In an oven-safe sauté pan or skillet, heat the oil over medium heat and sauté the onion and garlic. Cook for about 5 minutes, until softened and fragrant. Stir in the paprika and cumin and cook for 2 minutes. Stir in the tomatoes and chickpeas. 3. Bring to a simmer for 5 to 10 minutes before placing in the oven. 4. Roast in oven for 25 to 30 minutes, until bubbling and thickened. To serve, top with Greek yogurt and feta.

Per Serving:
calories: 412 | fat: 15g | protein: 20g | carbs: 51g | fiber: 13g | sodium: 444mg

Balsamic Marinated Tofu with Basil and Oregano

Prep time: 10 minutes | Cook time: 30 minutes | Serves 4

- ¼ cup extra-virgin olive oil
- ¼ cup balsamic vinegar
- 2 tablespoons low-sodium soy sauce or gluten-free tamari
- 3 garlic cloves, grated
- 2 teaspoons pure maple syrup
- Zest of 1 lemon
- 1 teaspoon dried basil
- 1 teaspoon dried oregano
- ½ teaspoon dried thyme
- ½ teaspoon dried sage
- ¼ teaspoon kosher salt
- ¼ teaspoon freshly ground black pepper
- ¼ teaspoon red pepper flakes (optional)
- 1 (16-ounce / 454-g) block extra firm tofu, drained and patted dry, cut into ½-inch or 1-inch cubes

1. Combine the olive oil, vinegar, soy sauce, garlic, maple syrup, lemon zest, basil, oregano, thyme, sage, salt, black pepper, and red pepper flakes (optional) in a bowl or large zip-top bag. Add the tofu, mixing gently to coat it well. Seal and refrigerate for at least 30 minutes or leave overnight for stronger flavor. 2. Preheat the oven to 425°F (220°C) and line a baking sheet with parchment paper or foil. Arrange the marinated tofu pieces in a single layer on the baking sheet. Bake for 20 to 30 minutes, flipping the tofu halfway through cooking, until it becomes slightly crispy outside while remaining tender inside.

Per Serving:
calories: 225 | fat: 16g | protein: 13g | carbs: 9g | fiber: 2g | sodium: 265mg

Creamy Chickpea Sauce with Whole-Wheat Fusilli

Prep time: 15 minutes | Cook time: 20 minutes | Serves 4

- ¼ cup extra-virgin olive oil
- ½ large shallot, chopped
- 5 garlic cloves, thinly sliced
- 1 (15-ounce / 425-g) can chickpeas, drained and rinsed, reserving ½ cup canning liquid
- Pinch red pepper flakes
- 1 cup whole-grain fusilli pasta
- ¼ teaspoon salt
- ⅛ teaspoon freshly ground black pepper
- ¼ cup shaved fresh Parmesan cheese
- ¼ cup chopped fresh basil
- 2 teaspoons dried parsley
- 1 teaspoon dried oregano
- Red pepper flakes

1. Heat oil in a medium pan over medium heat. Add shallot and garlic, sautéing for 3 to 5 minutes until garlic turns golden. Stir in ¾ of the chickpeas along with 2 tablespoons of liquid from the can, and bring it all to a simmer. 2. Remove from heat and transfer the mixture into a blender. Blend until smooth, then stir in the remaining chickpeas. If the sauce is too thick, add more reserved chickpea liquid to adjust the consistency. 3. In a separate large pot, bring salted water to a boil and cook the pasta until al dente, about 8 minutes. Reserve ½ cup of the pasta water, then drain the pasta and return it to the pot. 4. Pour the chickpea sauce over the pasta and mix in up to ¼ cup of reserved pasta water. Add more if needed until you reach the desired consistency. 5. Place the pasta pot over medium heat, stirring occasionally until the sauce thickens. Season with salt and pepper to taste. 6. Serve the pasta garnished with Parmesan cheese, fresh basil, parsley, oregano, and red pepper flakes.

Per Serving:
1 cup pasta: calories: 310 | fat: 17g | protein: 10g | carbs: 33g | fiber: 7g | sodium: 243mg

Grilled Eggplant Mozzarella Stacks

Prep time: 20 minutes | Cook time: 10 minutes | Serves 2

- 1 medium eggplant, cut crosswise into 8 slices
- ¼ teaspoon salt
- 1 teaspoon Italian herb seasoning mix
- 2 tablespoons olive oil
- 1 large tomato, cut into 4 slices
- 4 (1-ounce / 28-g) slices of buffalo mozzarella
- Fresh basil, for garnish

1. Place the eggplant slices in a colander set in the sink or over a bowl. Sprinkle both sides with the salt. Let the eggplant sit for 15 minutes. 2. While the eggplant is resting, heat the grill to medium-high heat (about 350°F / 180°C). 3. Pat the eggplant dry with paper towels and place it in a mixing bowl. Sprinkle it with the Italian herb seasoning mix and olive oil. Toss well to coat. 4. Grill the eggplant for 5 minutes, or until it has grill marks and is lightly charred. Flip each eggplant slice over, and grill on the second side for another 5 minutes. 5. Flip the eggplant slices back over and top four of the slices with a slice of tomato and a slice of mozzarella. Top each stack with one of the remaining four slices of eggplant. 6. Turn the grill down to low and cover it to let the cheese melt. Check after 30 seconds and remove when the cheese is soft and mostly melted. 7. Sprinkle with fresh basil slices.

Per Serving:
calories: 354 | fat: 29g | protein: 13g | carbs: 19g | fiber: 9g | sodium: 340mg

Air-Fried Mushroom Zucchini Veggie Burgers

Prep time: 10 minutes | Cook time: 12 minutes | Serves 4

- 8 ounces (227 g) cremini mushrooms
- 2 large egg yolks
- ½ medium zucchini, trimmed and chopped
- ¼ cup peeled and chopped
- yellow onion
- 1 clove garlic, peeled and finely minced
- ½ teaspoon salt
- ¼ teaspoon ground black pepper

1. Place all ingredients into a food processor and pulse twenty times until finely chopped and combined. 2. Separate mixture into four equal sections and press each into a burger shape. Place burgers into ungreased air fryer basket. Adjust the temperature to 375°F (191°C) and air fry for 12 minutes, turning burgers halfway through cooking. Burgers will be browned and firm when done. 3. Place burgers on a large plate and let cool 5 minutes before serving.

Per Serving:
calories: 50 | fat: 3g | protein: 3g | carbs: 4g | fiber: 1g | sodium: 299mg

Baked Tofu with Artichokes and Sun-Dried Tomatoes

- 1 (16-ounce / 454-g) package extra-firm tofu, drained and patted dry, cut into 1-inch cubes
- 2 tablespoons extra-virgin olive oil, divided
- 2 tablespoons lemon juice, divided
- 1 tablespoon low-sodium soy sauce or gluten-free tamari
- 1 onion, diced
- ½ teaspoon kosher salt
- 2 garlic cloves, minced
- 1 (14-ounce / 397-g) can artichoke hearts, drained
- 8 sun-dried tomato halves packed in oil, drained and chopped
- ¼ teaspoon freshly ground black pepper
- 1 tablespoon white wine vinegar
- Zest of 1 lemon
- ¼ cup fresh parsley, chopped

1. Preheat the oven to 400ºF (205ºC). Line a baking sheet with foil or parchment paper. 2. In a bowl, combine the tofu, 1 tablespoon of the olive oil, 1 tablespoon of the lemon juice, and the soy sauce. Allow to sit and marinate for 15 to 30 minutes. Arrange the tofu in a single layer on the prepared baking sheet and bake for 20 minutes, turning once, until light golden brown. 3. Heat the remaining 1 tablespoon olive oil in a large skillet or sauté pan over medium heat. Add the onion and salt; sauté until translucent, 5 to 6 minutes. Add the garlic and sauté for 30 seconds. Add the artichoke hearts, sun-dried tomatoes, and black pepper and sauté for 5 minutes. Add the white wine vinegar and the remaining 1 tablespoon lemon juice and deglaze the pan, scraping up any brown bits. Remove the pan from the heat and stir in the lemon zest and parsley. Gently mix in the baked tofu.

Per Serving:
calories: 230 | fat: 14g | protein: 14g | carbs: 13g | fiber: 5g | sodium: 500mg

One-Pan Mushroom Pasta with Mascarpone

- 2 tablespoons olive oil
- 1 large shallot, minced
- 8 ounces (227 g) baby bella (cremini) mushrooms, sliced
- ¼ cup dry sherry
- 1 teaspoon dried thyme
- 2 cups low-sodium
- vegetable stock
- 6 ounces (170 g) dry pappardelle pasta
- 2 tablespoons mascarpone cheese
- Salt
- Freshly ground black pepper

1. In a large sauté pan, heat olive oil over medium-high heat. Add shallots and mushrooms, cooking for about 10 minutes until the mushrooms release most of their liquid. 2. Pour in the sherry, add thyme, and stir in the vegetable stock. Bring the mixture to a boil. 3. Add the pasta, breaking it into pieces as needed so it fits in the pan and is submerged in the liquid. Bring it back to a boil, then cover and reduce heat to medium-low. Cook the pasta for about 10 minutes or until al dente, stirring occasionally to prevent sticking. If the sauce begins to dry out, add a little water or extra vegetable stock. 4. Once the pasta is tender, stir in the mascarpone cheese and season with salt and pepper to taste. 5. Remove from heat and let the sauce thicken slightly before serving.

Per Serving:
calories: 517 | fat: 18g | protein: 16g | carbs: 69g | fiber: 3g | sodium: 141mg

Air-Fried Caprese Eggplant Stacks

- 1 medium eggplant, cut into ¼-inch slices
- 2 large tomatoes, cut into ¼-inch slices
- 4 ounces (113 g) fresh
- Mozzarella, cut into ½-ounce / 14-g slices
- 2 tablespoons olive oil
- ¼ cup fresh basil, sliced

1. In a baking dish, place four slices of eggplant on the bottom. Place a slice of tomato on top of each eggplant round, then Mozzarella, then eggplant. Repeat as necessary. 2. Drizzle with olive oil. Cover dish with foil and place dish into the air fryer basket. 3. Adjust the temperature to 350ºF (177ºC) and bake for 12 minutes. 4. When done, eggplant will be tender. Garnish with fresh basil to serve.

Per Serving:
calories: 97 | fat: 7g | protein: 2g | carbs: 8g | fiber: 4g | sodium: 11mg

Warm Mediterranean Farro Bowl with Chickpeas and Artichokes

- ⅓ cup extra-virgin olive oil
- ½ cup chopped red bell pepper
- ⅓ cup chopped red onions
- 2 garlic cloves, minced
- 1 cup zucchini, cut in ½-inch slices
- ½ cup canned chickpeas, drained and rinsed
- ½ cup coarsely chopped artichokes
- 3 cups cooked farro
- Salt
- Freshly ground black pepper
- ¼ cup sliced olives, for serving (optional)
- ½ cup crumbled feta cheese, for serving (optional)
- 2 tablespoons fresh basil, chiffonade, for serving (optional)
- 3 tablespoons balsamic reduction, for serving (optional)

1. In a large sauté pan or skillet, heat the oil over medium heat and sauté the pepper, onions, and garlic for about 5 minutes, until tender. 2. Add the zucchini, chickpeas, and artichokes, then stir and continue to sauté vegetables, approximately 5 more minutes, until just soft. 3. Stir in the cooked farro, tossing to combine and cooking enough to heat through. Season with salt and pepper and remove from the heat. 4. Transfer the contents of the pan into the serving vessels or bowls. 5. Top with olives, feta, and basil (if using). Drizzle with balsamic reduction (if using) to finish.

Per Serving:
calories: 367 | fat: 20g | protein: 9g | carbs: 51g | fiber: 9g | sodium: 87mg

Tangy Asparagus and Broccoli

- ½ pound (227 g) asparagus, cut into 1½-inch pieces
- ½ pound (227 g) broccoli, cut into 1½-inch pieces
- 2 tablespoons olive oil
- Salt and white pepper, to taste
- ½ cup vegetable broth
- 2 tablespoons apple cider vinegar

1. Arrange the vegetables in a single layer inside the air fryer basket that has been lightly greased. Drizzle olive oil evenly over the vegetables. 2. Season with salt and white pepper. 3. Set the air fryer to 380ºF (193ºC) and cook for 15 minutes, shaking the basket halfway through to ensure even cooking. 4. Meanwhile, pour ½ cup of vegetable broth into a saucepan and bring it to a rapid boil. Add the vinegar and let it cook for 5 to 7 minutes, or until the sauce reduces by half. 5. Drizzle the reduced sauce over the warm vegetables and serve immediately. Enjoy!

Per Serving:
calories: 93 | fat: 7g | protein: 3g | carbs: 6g | fiber: 3g | sodium: 89mg

Quinoa with Almonds and Cranberries

- 2 cups cooked quinoa
- ⅓ teaspoon cranberries or currants
- ¼ cup sliced almonds
- 2 garlic cloves, minced
- 1¼ teaspoons salt
- ½ teaspoon ground cumin
- ½ teaspoon turmeric
- ¼ teaspoon ground cinnamon
- ¼ teaspoon freshly ground black pepper

1. In a large mixing bowl, combine the quinoa, cranberries, almonds, garlic, salt, cumin, turmeric, cinnamon, and black pepper. Toss everything together until evenly mixed. Serve on its own as a flavorful side dish or pair it with roasted cauliflower for a complete meal.

Per Serving:
calories: 194 | fat: 6g | protein: 7g | carbs: 31g | fiber: 4g | sodium: 727mg

Air-Fried Eggplant Parmesan

- 1 medium eggplant, ends trimmed, sliced into ½-inch rounds
- ¼ teaspoon salt
- 2 tablespoons coconut oil
- ½ cup grated Parmesan cheese
- 1 ounce (28 g) 100% cheese crisps, finely crushed
- ½ cup low-carb marinara sauce
- ½ cup shredded Mozzarella cheese

1. Sprinkle eggplant rounds with salt on both sides and wrap in a kitchen towel for 30 minutes. Press to remove excess water, then drizzle rounds with coconut oil on both sides. 2. In a medium bowl, mix Parmesan and cheese crisps. Press each eggplant slice into mixture to coat both sides. 3. Place rounds into ungreased air fryer basket. Adjust the temperature to 350ºF (177ºC) and air fry for 15 minutes, turning rounds halfway through cooking. They will be crispy around the edges when done. 4. Spoon marinara over rounds and sprinkle with Mozzarella. Continue cooking an additional 2 minutes at 350ºF (177ºC) until cheese is melted. Serve warm.

Per Serving:
calories: 208 | fat: 13g | protein: 12g | carbs: 13g | fiber: 5g | sodium: 531mg

Fava Bean Purée with Sautéed Chicory

- ½ pound (227 g) dried fava beans, soaked in water overnight and drained
- 1 pound (454 g) chicory leaves
- ¼ cup olive oil
- 1 small onion, chopped
- 1 clove garlic, minced
- Salt

1. In a saucepan, cover the fava beans by at least an inch of water and bring to a boil over medium-high heat. Reduce the heat to low, cover, and simmer until very tender, about 2 hours. Check the pot from time to time to make sure there is enough water and add more as needed. 2. Drain off any excess water and then mash the beans with a potato masher. 3. While the beans are cooking, bring a large pot of salted water to a boil. Add the chicory and cook for about 3 minutes, until tender. Drain. 4. In a medium skillet, heat the olive oil over medium-high heat. Add the onion and a pinch of salt and cook, stirring frequently, until softened and beginning to brown, about 5 minutes. Add the garlic and cook, stirring, for another minute. Transfer half of the onion mixture, along with the oil, to the bowl with the mashed beans and stir to mix. Taste and add salt as needed. 5. Serve the purée topped with some of the remaining onions and oil, with the chicory leaves on the side.

Per Serving:
calories: 336 | fat: 14g | protein: 17g | carbs: 40g | fiber: 19g | sodium: 59mg

Air-Fried Crustless Spinach and Cheddar Pie

- 6 large eggs
- ¼ cup heavy whipping cream
- 1 cup frozen chopped
- spinach, drained
- 1 cup shredded sharp Cheddar cheese
- ¼ cup diced yellow onion

1. In a medium bowl, whisk eggs and add cream. Add remaining ingredients to bowl. 2. Pour into a round baking dish. Place into the air fryer basket. 3. Adjust the temperature to 320ºF (160ºC) and bake for 20 minutes. 4. Eggs will be firm and slightly browned when cooked. Serve immediately.

Per Serving:
calories: 263 | fat: 20g | protein: 18g | carbs: 4g | fiber: 1g | sodium: 321mg

Cauliflower Steaks with Olive Citrus Sauce

- 1 or 2 large heads cauliflower (at least 2 pounds / 907 g, enough for 4 portions)
- ⅓ cup extra-virgin olive oil
- ¼ teaspoon kosher salt
- ⅛ teaspoon ground black pepper
- Juice of 1 orange
- Zest of 1 orange
- ¼ cup black olives, pitted and chopped
- 1 tablespoon Dijon or grainy mustard
- 1 tablespoon red wine vinegar
- ½ teaspoon ground coriander

1. Preheat your oven to 400ºF (205ºC) and line a baking sheet with parchment paper or foil for easy cleanup. 2. Trim the stem of the cauliflower to allow it to sit flat, then slice it vertically into four thick "steaks." Arrange these cauliflower slabs on the baking sheet, drizzle with olive oil, and season generously with salt and black pepper. Bake for around 30 minutes, flipping halfway through, until the cauliflower turns tender and golden brown. 3. Meanwhile, in a medium bowl, whisk together orange juice, orange zest, olives, mustard, vinegar, and coriander until well combined. 4. Serve the roasted cauliflower either warm or at room temperature, topped with the prepared orange-olive sauce for added flavor.

Per Serving:

calories: 265 | fat: 21g | protein: 5g | carbs: 19g | fiber: 4g | sodium: 310mg

Baked Ratatouille with Herbed Breadcrumbs and Goat Cheese

- 6 tablespoons olive oil, divided
- 2 medium onions, diced
- 2 cloves garlic, minced
- 2 medium eggplants, halved lengthwise and cut into ¾-inch thick half rounds
- 3 medium zucchini, halved lengthwise and cut into ¾-inch thick half rounds
- 2 red bell peppers, seeded and cut into 1½-inch pieces
- 1 green bell pepper, seeded and cut into 1½-inch pieces
- 1 (14-ounce / 397-g) can diced tomatoes, drained
- 1 teaspoon salt
- ½ teaspoon freshly ground black pepper
- 8 ounces (227 g) fresh breadcrumbs
- 1 tablespoon chopped fresh parsley
- 1 tablespoon chopped fresh basil
- 1 tablespoon chopped fresh chives
- 6 ounces (170 g) soft, fresh goat cheese

1. Preheat the oven to 375°F (190°C). 2. Heat 5 tablespoons of the olive oil in a large skillet over medium heat. Add the onions and garlic and cook, stirring frequently, until the onions are soft and beginning to turn golden, about 8 minutes. Add the eggplant, zucchini, and bell peppers and cook, turning the vegetables occasionally, for another 10 minutes. Stir in the tomatoes, salt, and pepper and let simmer for 15 minutes. 3. While the vegetables are simmering, stir together the breadcrumbs, the remaining tablespoon of olive oil, the parsley, basil, and chives. 4. Transfer the vegetable mixture to a large baking dish, spreading it out into an even layer. Crumble the goat cheese over the top, then sprinkle the breadcrumb mixture evenly over the top. Bake in the preheated oven for about 30 minutes, until the topping is golden brown and crisp. Serve hot.

Per Serving:

calories: 644 | fat: 37g | protein: 21g | carbs: 63g | fiber: 16g | sodium: 861mg

Moroccan Red Lentil and Pumpkin Stew

- 2 tablespoons olive oil
- 1 teaspoon ground cumin
- 1 teaspoon ground turmeric
- 1 tablespoon curry powder
- 1 large onion, diced
- 1 teaspoon salt
- 2 tablespoons minced fresh ginger
- 4 cloves garlic, minced
- 1 pound (454 g) pumpkin, peeled, seeded, and cut into 1-inch dice
- 1 red bell pepper, seeded and diced
- 1½ cups red lentils, rinsed
- 6 cups vegetable broth
- ¼ cup chopped cilantro, for garnish

1. Warm olive oil in a stockpot over medium heat. Add cumin, turmeric, and curry powder, stirring for about 1 minute until the spices release their aroma. Add the onion and salt, and cook for about 5 minutes, stirring often until the onion softens. Stir in the ginger and garlic, cooking for another 2 minutes while stirring frequently. Mix in the pumpkin, bell pepper, lentils, and broth, then bring everything to a boil. 2. Lower the heat and let the mixture simmer uncovered for about 20 minutes, or until the lentils are fully tender. Serve hot with a garnish of fresh cilantro.

Per Serving:

calories: 405 | fat: 9g | protein: 20g | carbs: 66g | fiber: 11g | sodium: 594mg

Chapter **6**

Fish and Seafood

Chapter 6 Fish and Seafood

Cod with Lemon Parsley Pistou

Prep time: 15 minutes | Cook time: 10 minutes | Serves 4

- 1 cup packed roughly chopped fresh flat-leaf Italian parsley
- 1 to 2 small garlic cloves, minced
- Zest and juice of 1 lemon
- 1 teaspoon salt
- ½ teaspoon freshly ground black pepper
- 1 cup extra-virgin olive oil, divided
- 1 pound (454 g) cod fillets, cut into 4 equal-sized pieces

1. In a food processor, combine the parsley, garlic, lemon zest and juice, salt, and pepper. Pulse to chop well. 2. While the food processor is running, slowly stream in ¾ cup olive oil until well combined. Set aside. 3. In a large skillet, heat the remaining ¼ cup olive oil over medium-high heat. Add the cod fillets, cover, and cook 4 to 5 minutes on each side, or until cooked through. Thicker fillets may require a bit more cooking time. Remove from the heat and keep warm. 4. Add the pistou to the skillet and heat over medium-low heat. Return the cooked fish to the skillet, flipping to coat in the sauce. Serve warm, covered with pistou.

Per Serving:
calories: 580 | fat: 55g | protein: 21g | carbs: 2g | fiber: 1g | sodium: 591mg

Salmon with Wild Rice and Citrus Mint Salad

Prep time: 20 minutes | Cook time: 18 minutes | Serves 4

- 1 cup wild rice, picked over and rinsed
- 3 tablespoons extra-virgin olive oil, divided
- 1½ teaspoon table salt, for cooking rice
- 2 oranges, plus ⅛ teaspoon grated orange zest
- 4 (6-ounce / 170-g) skinless salmon fillets, 1½ inches thick
- 1 teaspoon ground dried Aleppo pepper
- ½ teaspoon table salt
- 1 small shallot, minced
- 1 tablespoon red wine vinegar
- 2 teaspoons Dijon mustard
- 1 teaspoon honey
- 2 carrots, peeled and shredded
- ¼ cup chopped fresh mint

1. Combine 6 cups water, rice, 1 tablespoon oil, and 1½ teaspoons salt in Instant Pot. Lock lid in place and close pressure release valve. Select high pressure cook function and cook for 15 minutes. Turn off Instant Pot and let pressure release naturally for 15 minutes. Quick-release any remaining pressure, then carefully remove lid, allowing steam to escape away from you. Drain rice and set aside to cool slightly. Wipe pot clean with paper towels. 2. Add ½ cup water to now-empty Instant Pot. Fold sheet of aluminum foil into 16 by 6-inch sling. Slice 1 orange ¼ inch thick and shingle widthwise in 3 rows across center of sling. Sprinkle flesh side of salmon with Aleppo pepper and ½ teaspoon salt, then arrange skinned side down on top of orange slices. Using sling, lower salmon into Instant Pot; allow narrow edges of sling to rest along sides of insert. Lock lid in place and close pressure release valve. Select high pressure cook function and cook for 3 minutes. 3. Meanwhile, cut away peel and pith from remaining 1 orange. Quarter orange, then slice crosswise into ¼-inch pieces. Whisk remaining 2 tablespoons oil, shallot, vinegar, mustard, honey, and orange zest together in large bowl. Add rice, orange pieces, carrots, and mint, and gently toss to combine. Season with salt and pepper to taste. 4. Turn off Instant Pot and quick-release pressure. Carefully remove lid, allowing steam to escape away from you. Using sling, transfer salmon to large plate. Gently lift and tilt fillets with spatula to remove orange slices. Serve salmon with salad.

Per Serving:
calories: 690 | fat: 34g | protein: 43g | carbs: 51g | fiber: 5g | sodium: 770mg

Seafood Paella

Prep time: 20 minutes | Cook time: 13 minutes | Serves 4

- ½ teaspoon saffron threads
- 2 cups vegetable broth
- 2 tablespoons olive oil
- 1 medium yellow onion, peeled and diced
- 1 cup diced carrot
- 1 medium green bell pepper, seeded and diced
- 1 cup fresh or frozen green peas
- 2 cloves garlic, peeled and minced
- 1 cup basmati rice
- ¼ cup chopped fresh flat-leaf parsley
- ½ pound (227 g) medium shrimp, peeled and deveined
- ½ pound (227 g) mussels, scrubbed and beards removed
- ½ pound (227 g) clams, rinsed
- ¼ teaspoon ground black pepper

1. In a medium microwave-safe bowl, combine saffron and broth, stirring well. Microwave on High for 30 seconds to warm the broth slightly, then set aside. 2. Press the Sauté button on the Instant Pot® and heat the oil. Add onion, carrot, bell pepper, and peas, and cook for about 5 minutes until they start to soften. Add garlic and rice, stirring until the rice is well coated. Pour in the saffron broth and add parsley, then press the Cancel button. 3. Secure the Instant Pot® lid, set the steam release handle to Sealing, press the Manual button, and set the timer for 7 minutes. Once the timer goes off, quickly release the pressure until the float valve drops, then open the lid and press the Cancel button. 4. Stir the rice mixture and layer the shrimp, mussels, and clams on top. Close the lid again, set steam release to Sealing, press the Manual button, and set the timer for 1 minute. When the timer beeps, let the pressure release naturally for 10 minutes, then quick-release any remaining pressure until the float valve drops. Open the lid and discard any mussels that haven't opened. Season with black pepper before serving.

Per Serving:
calories: 434 | fat: 11g | protein: 33g | carbs: 52g | fiber: 5g | sodium: 633mg

Steamed River Trout with Fresh Herb Sauce

Prep time: 10 minutes | Cook time: 3 minutes | Serves 4

- 4 (½-pound / 227-g) fresh river trout, rinsed and patted dry
- 1 teaspoon salt, divided
- 1 teaspoon white wine vinegar
- ½ cup water
- ½ cup minced fresh flat-leaf parsley
- 2 tablespoons chopped fresh oregano
- 1 teaspoon fresh thyme leaves
- 1 small shallot, peeled and minced
- 2 tablespoons olive oil
- ½ teaspoon lemon juice

1. Sprinkle trout with ¾ teaspoon salt inside and out. Combine vinegar and water, pour into the Instant Pot®, and place rack inside. Place trout on rack. 2. Close lid, set steam release to Sealing, press the Manual button, and set time to 3 minutes. When the timer beeps, let pressure release naturally for 3 minutes. Quick-release any remaining pressure until the float valve drops and then open lid. 3. Transfer fish to a serving plate. Peel and discard skin from fish. Remove and discard the heads if desired. 4. In a small bowl, mix together parsley, oregano, thyme, shallot, olive oil, lemon juice, and remaining ¼ teaspoon salt. Pour evenly over fish. Serve immediately.

Per Serving:

calories: 344 | fat: 18g | protein: 45g | carbs: 1g | fiber: 0g | sodium: 581mg

Olive Oil Poached Tuna with Fresh Herbs

Prep time: 5 minutes | Cook time: 45 minutes | Serves 4

- 1 cup extra-virgin olive oil, plus more if needed
- 4 (3- to 4-inch) sprigs fresh rosemary
- 8 (3- to 4-inch) sprigs fresh thyme
- 2 large garlic cloves, thinly
- sliced
- 2 (2-inch) strips lemon zest
- 1 teaspoon salt
- ½ teaspoon freshly ground black pepper
- 1 pound (454 g) fresh tuna steaks (about 1 inch thick)

1. Select a thick pot just large enough to fit the tuna in a single layer on the bottom. The larger the pot, the more olive oil you will need to use. Combine the olive oil, rosemary, thyme, garlic, lemon zest, salt, and pepper over medium-low heat and cook until warm and fragrant, 20 to 25 minutes, lowering the heat if it begins to smoke. 2. Remove from the heat and allow to cool for 25 to 30 minutes, until warm but not hot. 3. Add the tuna to the bottom of the pan, adding additional oil if needed so that tuna is fully submerged, and return to medium-low heat. Cook for 5 to 10 minutes, or until the oil heats back up and is warm and fragrant but not smoking. Lower the heat if it gets too hot. 4. Remove the pot from the heat and let the tuna cook in warm oil 4 to 5 minutes, to your desired level of doneness. For a tuna that is rare in the center, cook for 2 to 3 minutes. 5. Remove from the oil and serve warm, drizzling 2 to 3 tablespoons seasoned oil over the tuna. 6. To store for later use, remove the tuna from the oil and place in a container with a lid. Allow tuna and oil to cool separately. When both have cooled, remove the herb stems with a slotted spoon and pour the cooking oil over the tuna.

Cover and store in the refrigerator for up to 1 week. Bring to room temperature to allow the oil to liquify before serving.

Per Serving:

calories: 606 | fat: 55g | protein: 28g | carbs: 1g | fiber: 0g | sodium: 631mg

Cod and Cauliflower Chowder

Prep time: 15 minutes | Cook time: 40 minutes | Serves 4

- 2 tablespoons extra-virgin olive oil
- 1 leek, white and light green parts only, cut in half lengthwise and sliced thinly
- 4 garlic cloves, sliced
- 1 medium head cauliflower, coarsely chopped
- 1 teaspoon kosher salt
- ¼ teaspoon freshly ground
- black pepper
- 2 pints cherry tomatoes
- 2 cups no-salt-added vegetable stock
- ¼ cup green olives, pitted and chopped
- 1 to 1½ pounds (454 to 680 g) cod
- ¼ cup fresh parsley, minced

1. In a Dutch oven or large pot, heat olive oil over medium heat. Add the leek and sauté for about 5 minutes until lightly golden. Stir in the garlic and cook for another 30 seconds. Add the cauliflower along with salt and black pepper, and sauté for 2 to 3 more minutes. 2. Pour in the tomatoes and vegetable stock, then increase the heat to high to bring the mixture to a boil. Once boiling, reduce the heat to low and let it simmer for 10 minutes. 3. Stir in the olives, then gently add the fish. Cover the pot and let it simmer for 20 minutes, or until the fish becomes opaque and flakes apart easily. Carefully fold in the fresh parsley before serving.

Per Serving:

calories: 270 | fat: 9g | protein: 30g | carbs: 19g | fiber: 5g | sodium: 545mg

Air-Fried Salmon Spring Rolls with Fresh Herbs

Prep time: 20 minutes | Cook time: 8 to 10 minutes | Serves 4

- ½ pound (227 g) salmon fillet
- 1 teaspoon toasted sesame oil
- 1 onion, sliced
- 8 rice paper wrappers
- 1 yellow bell pepper, thinly sliced
- 1 carrot, shredded
- ⅓ cup chopped fresh flat-leaf parsley
- ¼ cup chopped fresh basil

1. Put the salmon in the air fryer basket and drizzle with the sesame oil. Add the onion. Air fry at 370°F (188°C) for 8 to 10 minutes, or until the salmon just flakes when tested with a fork and the onion is tender. 2. Meanwhile, fill a small shallow bowl with warm water. One at a time, dip the rice paper wrappers into the water and place on a work surface. 3. Top each wrapper with one-eighth each of the salmon and onion mixture, yellow bell pepper, carrot, parsley, and basil. Roll up the wrapper, folding in the sides, to enclose the ingredients. 4. If you like, bake in the air fryer at 380°F (193°C) for 7 to 9 minutes, until the rolls are crunchy. Cut the rolls in half to serve.

Per Serving:

calories: 197 | fat: 4g | protein: 14g | carbs: 26g | fiber: 2g | sodium: 145mg

Salmon with Broccoli Rabe, White Beans, and Garlic Chips

Prep time: 20 minutes | Cook time: 10 minutes | Serves 4

- 2 tablespoons extra-virgin olive oil, plus extra for drizzling
- 4 garlic cloves, sliced thin
- ½ cup chicken or vegetable broth
- ¼ teaspoon red pepper flakes
- 1 lemon, sliced ¼ inch thick, plus lemon wedges for serving
- 4 (6-ounce / 170-g) skinless salmon fillets, 1½ inches thick
- ½ teaspoon table salt
- ¼ teaspoon pepper
- 1 pound (454 g) broccoli rabe, trimmed and cut into 1-inch pieces
- 1 (15-ounce / 425-g) can cannellini beans, rinsed

1. Using highest sauté function, cook oil and garlic in Instant Pot until garlic is fragrant and light golden brown, about 3 minutes. Using slotted spoon, transfer garlic to paper towel–lined plate and season with salt to taste; set aside for serving. Turn off Instant Pot, then stir in broth and pepper flakes. 2. Fold sheet of aluminum foil into 16 by 6-inch sling. Arrange lemon slices widthwise in 2 rows across center of sling. Sprinkle flesh side of salmon with salt and pepper, then arrange skinned side down on top of lemon slices. Using sling, lower salmon into Instant Pot; allow narrow edges of sling to rest along sides of insert. Lock lid in place and close pressure release valve. Select high pressure cook function and cook for 3 minutes. 3. Turn off Instant Pot and quick-release pressure. Carefully remove lid, allowing steam to escape away from you. Using sling, transfer salmon to large plate. Tent with foil and let rest while preparing broccoli rabe mixture. 4. Stir broccoli rabe and beans into cooking liquid, partially cover, and cook, using highest sauté function, until broccoli rabe is tender, about 5 minutes. Season with salt and pepper to taste. Gently lift and tilt salmon fillets with spatula to remove lemon slices. Serve salmon with broccoli rabe mixture and lemon wedges, sprinkling individual portions with garlic chips and drizzling with extra oil.

Per Serving:
calories: 510 | fat: 30g | protein: 43g | carbs: 15g | fiber: 6g | sodium: 650mg

Sautéed Garlic Prawns with Tomatoes and Fresh Basil

Prep time: 10 minutes | Cook time: 10 minutes | Serves 4

- 2 tablespoons olive oil
- 1¼ pounds (567 g) shrimp, peeled and deveined
- 3 cloves garlic, minced
- ⅛ teaspoon crushed red pepper flakes
- ¾ cup dry white wine
- 1½ cups grape tomatoes
- ¼ cup finely chopped fresh basil, plus more for garnish
- ¾ teaspoon salt
- ½ teaspoon freshly ground black pepper

1. Heat the olive oil in a medium skillet over medium-high heat. Add the shrimp and cook about 1 minute on each side, until just cooked through. Transfer the shrimp to a plate, leaving the oil in the pan. 2. Add the garlic and red pepper flakes to the oil in the pan and cook, stirring, for 30 seconds. Stir in the wine and cook until it is reduced by about half. Add the tomatoes and cook, stirring, for 3 to 4 minutes more, until the tomatoes begin to break down. Stir in the basil, salt, pepper, and the reserved shrimp. Cook 1 to 2 minutes more, until heated through. Serve hot, garnished with the remaining basil.

Per Serving:
calories: 282 | fat: 10g | protein: 33g | carbs: 7g | fiber: 1g | sodium: 299mg

Lemon Pesto Salmon

Prep time: 5 minutes | Cook time: 10 minutes | Serves 2

- 10 ounces (283 g) salmon fillet (1 large piece or 2 smaller ones)
- Salt
- Freshly ground black pepper
- 2 tablespoons prepared pesto sauce
- 1 large fresh lemon, sliced

1. Preheat the grill to medium-high heat and lightly oil the grill grates. Alternatively, you can set your oven to 350ºF (180ºC) for roasting. 2. Season the salmon with salt and freshly ground black pepper, then spread a generous layer of pesto sauce on top. 3. Arrange fresh lemon slices on the hot grill or on a baking sheet if roasting, creating a bed slightly larger than the salmon fillet. Lay the salmon on top of the lemon slices and add extra lemon slices on top of the fillet if desired. 4. Grill the salmon for 6 to 10 minutes until it becomes opaque and easily flakes with a fork. If you're roasting the salmon, cook it for around 20 minutes. There's no need to flip the salmon during cooking.

Per Serving:
calories: 315 | fat: 21g | protein: 29g | carbs: 1g | fiber: 0g | sodium: 176mg

Air-Fried Hake Gratin with Creamy Swiss Topping

Prep time: 30 minutes | Cook time: 17 minutes | Serves 4

- 1 tablespoon avocado oil
- 1 pound (454 g) hake fillets
- 1 teaspoon garlic powder
- Sea salt and ground white pepper, to taste
- 2 tablespoons shallots, chopped
- 1 bell pepper, seeded and
- chopped
- ½ cup Cottage cheese
- ½ cup sour cream
- 1 egg, well whisked
- 1 teaspoon yellow mustard
- 1 tablespoon lime juice
- ½ cup Swiss cheese, shredded

1. Brush the bottom and sides of a casserole dish with avocado oil. Add the hake fillets to the casserole dish and sprinkle with garlic powder, salt, and pepper. 2. Add the chopped shallots and bell peppers. 3. In a mixing bowl, thoroughly combine the Cottage cheese, sour cream, egg, mustard, and lime juice. Pour the mixture over fish and spread evenly. 4. Cook in the preheated air fryer at 370ºF (188ºC) for 10 minutes. 5. Top with the Swiss cheese and cook an additional 7 minutes. Let it rest for 10 minutes before slicing and serving. Bon appétit!

Per Serving:
calories: 256 | fat: 12g | protein: 28g | carbs: 8g | fiber: 1g | sodium: 523mg

Moroccan Braised Halibut with Cinnamon and Capers

Prep time: 5 minutes | Cook time: 20 minutes | Serves 4

- ¼ cup olive oil
- ¾ teaspoon ground cumin
- 1 (15-ounce / 425-g) can diced tomatoes, drained
- 1½ tablespoons drained capers
- ½ teaspoon cinnamon
- ½ teaspoon salt, divided
- ½ teaspoon freshly ground black pepper, divided
- 4 halibut fillets, about 6 ounces (170 g) each and 1-inch-thick

1. In a large skillet, heat the olive oil over medium heat. Add the cumin and stir for 1 minute until fragrant. Add the tomatoes, capers, cinnamon, ¼ teaspoon salt, and ¼ teaspoon black pepper, cooking for around 10 minutes or until the mixture thickens. 2. Pat the fish dry with paper towels and season evenly with the remaining ¼ teaspoon salt and ¼ teaspoon black pepper. Place the seasoned fish into the skillet with the sauce, cover, and let it simmer for 8 to 10 minutes until the fish is fully cooked. Serve immediately while hot.

Per Serving:
calories: 309 | fat: 14g | protein: 40g | carbs: 5g | fiber: 2g | sodium: 525mg

Air-Fried Blackened Red Snapper with Lemon

Prep time: 13 minutes | Cook time: 8 to 10 minutes | Serves 4

- 1½ teaspoons black pepper
- ¼ teaspoon thyme
- ¼ teaspoon garlic powder
- ⅛ teaspoon cayenne pepper
- 1 teaspoon olive oil
- 4 (4 ounces / 113 g) red snapper fillet portions, skin on
- 4 thin slices lemon
- Cooking spray

1. Mix the spices and oil together to make a paste. Rub into both sides of the fish. 2. Spray the air fryer basket with nonstick cooking spray and lay snapper steaks in basket, skin-side down. 3. Place a lemon slice on each piece of fish. 4. Roast at 390ºF (199ºC) for 8 to 10 minutes. The fish will not flake when done, but it should be white through the center.

Per Serving:
calories: 128 | fat: 3g | protein: 23g | carbs: 1g | fiber: 1g | sodium: 73mg

Pistachio-Crusted Whitefish

Prep time: 10 minutes | Cook time: 20 minutes | Serves 2

- ¼ cup shelled pistachios
- 1 tablespoon fresh parsley
- 1 tablespoon grated Parmesan cheese
- 1 tablespoon panko bread crumbs
- 2 tablespoons olive oil
- ¼ teaspoon salt
- 10 ounces (283 g) skinless whitefish (1 large piece or 2 smaller ones)

1. Preheat your oven to 350°F (180ºC) and place the oven rack in the middle position. Line a sheet pan with foil or parchment paper for easy cleanup. 2. In a mini food processor, blend all of the ingredients except for the fish until the nuts are finely ground. If you don't have a food processor, mince the nuts with a chef's knife and mix the ingredients together by hand in a small bowl. 3. Place the fish fillets on the prepared sheet pan. Evenly spread the nut mixture over the top of the fish, pressing it down gently to adhere. 4. Bake the fish for 20 to 30 minutes, depending on the thickness, until it is opaque and flakes easily when tested with a fork.

Per Serving:
calories: 267 | fat: 18g | protein: 28g | carbs: 1g | fiber: 0g | sodium: 85mg

Almond-Crusted Salmon with Honey Thyme Glaze

Prep time: 10 minutes | Cook time: 12 minutes | Serves 4

- ¼ cup olive oil
- 1 tablespoon honey
- ¼ cup breadcrumbs
- ½ cup finely chopped 4 salmon steaks
- almonds, lightly toasted
- ½ teaspoon dried thyme
- Sea salt and freshly ground pepper, to taste

1. Preheat the oven to 350ºF (180ºC). 2. Combine the olive oil with the honey. (Soften the honey in the microwave for 15 seconds, if necessary, for easier blending.) 3. In a shallow dish, combine the breadcrumbs, almonds, thyme, sea salt, and freshly ground pepper. 4. Coat the salmon steaks with the olive oil mixture, then the almond mixture. 5. Place on a baking sheet brushed with olive oil and bake 8–12 minutes, or until the almonds are lightly browned and the salmon is firm.

Per Serving:
calories: 634 | fat: 34g | protein: 69g | carbs: 12g | fiber: 2g | sodium: 289mg

Cod with Tomatoes and Garlic

Prep time: 10 minutes | Cook time: 20 minutes | Serves 4

- 1 pound (454 g) cod or your favorite white-fleshed fish
- Sea salt
- Freshly ground black pepper
- 2 tablespoons olive oil
- 2 garlic cloves, minced
- 1 (15-ounce / 425-g) can diced tomatoes, with their juices
- ¼ cup white wine
- ¼ cup chopped fresh Italian parsley

1. Use paper towels to pat the fish dry, then season both sides with salt and black pepper. 2. Heat olive oil in a large skillet over medium heat. Place the cod in the skillet and cook for 3 to 5 minutes per side, or until the fish is fully cooked and flakes easily. Transfer the fish to a plate, loosely cover with aluminum foil, and set it aside. 3. Add garlic to the same skillet and sauté for about 3 minutes until fragrant. Pour in the tomatoes and wine, and increase the heat to medium-high. Let the mixture cook for approximately 4 minutes until it starts to thicken, then season with salt and black pepper to taste. 4. Return the fish to the skillet and spoon the tomato mixture over it. Serve immediately, garnished with fresh parsley.

Per Serving:
calories: 170 | fat: 7g | protein: 18g | carbs: 5g | fiber: 2g | sodium: 507mg

Caramelized Fennel and Sardines with Penne

Prep time: 15 minutes | Cook time: 30 minutes | Serves 4

- 8 ounces (227 g) whole-wheat penne
- 2 tablespoons extra-virgin olive oil
- 1 bulb fennel, cored and thinly sliced, plus ¼ cup fronds
- 2 celery stalks, thinly sliced, plus ½ cup leaves
- 4 garlic cloves, sliced
- ¾ teaspoon kosher salt
- ¼ teaspoon freshly ground black pepper
- Zest of 1 lemon
- Juice of 1 lemon
- 2 (4.4-ounce / 125-g) cans boneless/skinless sardines packed in olive oil, undrained

1. Cook the penne according to the package instructions. Drain the pasta, saving 1 cup of the cooking water for later use. 2. In a large skillet or sauté pan, heat olive oil over medium heat. Add fennel and celery, cooking for 10 to 12 minutes while stirring often until they become tender and golden. Stir in the garlic and cook for another minute. 3. Add the cooked penne, reserved pasta water, salt, and black pepper to the skillet. Increase the heat to medium-high and cook for 1 to 2 minutes, stirring to combine. 4. Take the skillet off the heat and mix in lemon zest, lemon juice, fennel fronds, and celery leaves. Break the sardines into bite-size pieces and gently fold them in, including the oil they were packed in, until everything is well combined.

Per Serving:
calories: 400 | fat: 15g | protein: 22g | carbs: 46g | fiber: 6g | sodium: 530mg

Olive Oil Poached Fish with Citrus Arugula Salad

Prep time: 10 minutes | Cook time: 25 minutes | Serves 4

Fish

- 4 skinless white fish fillets (1¼ to 1½ pounds / 567 to 680 g total), such as halibut, sole, or cod, ¾'–1' thick
- ¼ teaspoon kosher salt
- ¼ teaspoon ground black pepper
- 5–7 cups olive oil
- 1 lemon, thinly sliced

Salad

- ¼ cup white wine vinegar
- 1 Earl Grey tea bag
- 2 blood oranges or tangerines
- 1 ruby red grapefruit or pomelo
- 6 kumquats, thinly sliced, or 2 clementines, peeled and sectioned
- 4 cups baby arugula
- ½ cup pomegranate seeds
- ¼ cup extra-virgin olive oil
- 2 teaspoons minced shallot
- ½ teaspoon kosher salt
- ¼ teaspoon ground black pepper
- ¼ cup mint leaves, coarsely chopped

1. Make the fish: Season the fish with the salt and pepper and set aside for 30 minutes. 2. Preheat the oven to 225°F. 3. In a large high-sided ovenproof skillet or roasting pan over medium heat, warm 1' to 1½' of the oil and the lemon slices until the temperature reaches 120°F (use a candy thermometer). Add the fish fillets to the oil, without overlapping, making sure they're completely submerged. 4. Transfer the skillet or pan to the oven, uncovered. Bake for 25 minutes. Transfer the fish to a rack to drain for 5 minutes. 5. Make the salad: In a small saucepan, heat the vinegar until almost boiling. Add the tea bag and set aside to steep for 10 minutes. 6. Meanwhile, with a paring knife, cut off enough of the top and bottom of 1 of the oranges or tangerines to reveal the flesh. Cut along the inside of the peel, between the pith and the flesh, taking off as much pith as possible. Over a large bowl, hold the orange in 1 hand. With the paring knife, cut along the membranes between each section, allowing the fruit to fall into the bowl. Once all the fruit segments have been released, squeeze the remaining membranes over a small bowl. Repeat with the second orange and the grapefruit or pomelo. 7. In the large bowl with the segmented fruit, add the kumquats or clementines, arugula, and pomegranate seeds. Gently toss to distribute. 8. Remove the tea bag from the vinegar and squeeze out as much liquid as possible. Discard the bag and add the vinegar to the small bowl with the citrus juice. Slowly whisk in the oil, shallot, salt, and pepper. Drizzle 3 to 4 tablespoons over the salad and gently toss. (Store the remaining vinaigrette in the refrigerator for up to 1 week.) 9. Sprinkle the salad with the mint and serve with the fish.

Per Serving:
calories: 280 | fat: 7g | protein: 29g | carbs: 25g | fiber: 6g | sodium: 249mg

One-Pot Shrimp Fried Rice

Prep time: 10 minutes | Cook time: 25 minutes | Serves 4

Shrimp:

- 1 teaspoon cornstarch
- ½ teaspoon kosher salt
- ¼ teaspoon black pepper
- 1 pound (454 g) jumbo raw shrimp (21 to 25 count), peeled and deveined

Rice:

- 2 cups cold cooked rice
- 1 cup frozen peas and carrots, thawed
- ¼ cup chopped green onions (white and green parts)
- 3 tablespoons toasted sesame oil
- 1 tablespoon soy sauce
- ½ teaspoon kosher salt
- 1 teaspoon black pepper

Eggs:

- 2 large eggs, beaten
- ¼ teaspoon kosher salt
- ¼ teaspoon black pepper

1. Prepare the shrimp by whisking cornstarch, salt, and pepper in a small bowl until well mixed. Place shrimp in a large bowl and sprinkle the seasoned cornstarch over them. Toss to ensure each shrimp is evenly coated, then set aside. 2. For the rice, combine rice, peas and carrots, green onions, sesame oil, soy sauce, salt, and pepper in a baking pan. Stir until everything is evenly distributed. 3. Place the baking pan in the air fryer basket. Set the air fryer to 350ºF (177ºC) and cook for 15 minutes, stirring the rice halfway through to ensure even cooking. 4. Once the rice is partially cooked, arrange the shrimp on top of it. Set the air fryer to 350ºF (177ºC) for an additional 5 minutes. 5. While the shrimp cooks, beat the eggs with salt and pepper in a medium bowl. 6. After the shrimp has cooked for 5 minutes, open the air fryer and pour the beaten eggs evenly over the shrimp and rice mixture. Set the air fryer again to 350ºF (177ºC) for another 5 minutes. 7. Remove the baking pan from the air fryer, then stir to break up the rice and mix in the shrimp and cooked eggs until everything is well combined.

Per Serving:
calories: 364 | fat: 15g | protein: 30g | carbs: 28g | fiber: 3g | sodium: 794mg

Mediterranean Fish Stew

Prep time: 15 minutes | Cook time: 13 minutes | Serves 4

- 4 tablespoons olive oil
- 1 medium yellow onion, peeled and diced
- 2 cloves garlic, peeled and minced
- ½ teaspoon dried oregano leaves
- ½ teaspoon ground fennel
- ¼ teaspoon dried thyme leaves
- 1 (14½-ounce / 411-g) can

diced tomatoes
- 1 cup seafood stock
- ½ cup white wine
- 1 pound (454 g) white fish fillets, such as halibut or sea bass, cut into 2" pieces
- ¼ teaspoon salt
- ¼ teaspoon ground black pepper
- ½ teaspoon hot sauce

1. Press the Sauté button on the Instant Pot® and add the oil to heat. Once hot, add the onion and cook for about 4 minutes until softened. Stir in the garlic, oregano, fennel, and thyme, cooking for another 30 seconds until fragrant. Add the tomatoes, seafood stock, and wine, stirring well to combine. Press the Cancel button. 2. Secure the lid, set the steam release handle to Sealing, press the Manual button, and set the cook time to 3 minutes. 3. When the timer goes off, quick-release the pressure until the float valve drops, then open the lid. Press the Cancel button, then press the Sauté button again and add the fish. Cook for about 5 minutes, or until the fish is opaque and cooked through. Season with salt and pepper to taste, and add hot sauce just before serving.

Per Serving:
calories: 282 | fat: 15g | protein: 26g | carbs: 8g | fiber: 2g | sodium: 456mg

Parchment-Baked Halibut with Fennel and Carrot Medley

Prep time: 10 minutes | Cook time: 25 minutes | Serves 4

- 1 bulb fennel, cored, thinly sliced, and fronds reserved
- 1 bunch young carrots, quartered and tops removed
- 1 small shallot, sliced
- 4 skinless halibut fillets (6 ounces / 170 geach)

- ½ teaspoon kosher salt
- ¼ teaspoon ground black pepper
- 4 slices orange
- 8 sprigs thyme
- 4 leaves fresh sage, sliced
- ½ cup white wine

1. Preheat the oven to 425°F(220°C). Tear 4 squares of parchment paper, about 15' × 15'. 2. In the middle of a piece of parchment, set ¼ of the fennel, carrots, and shallot, topped by 1 piece of fish. Sprinkle with ⅛ teaspoon of the salt and a pinch of the pepper. Lay 1 slice of the orange, 2 sprigs of the thyme, ¼ of the sage, and a bit of fennel frond on top. Drizzle 2 tablespoons of the wine around the fish. 3. Bring up the opposite sides of the parchment and fold them together, like you're folding the top of a paper bag, to seal all the edges. Set the packet on a baking sheet, and repeat with the remaining ingredients. 4. Bake until the packets are slightly browned and puffed, about 13 minutes. Allow to rest for 2 to 3 minutes. Set individual packets on plates and with kitchen shears or a small knife, carefully cut open at the table. (Caution: The escaping steam will be hot.)

Per Serving:
calories: 253 | fat: 3g | protein: 34g | carbs: 18g | fiber: 5g | sodium: 455mg

Creamy Pesto Shrimp with Zucchini Noodles

Prep time: 10 minutes | Cook time: 10 minutes | Serves 4

- 1 pound (454 g) peeled and deveined fresh shrimp
- Salt
- Freshly ground black pepper
- 2 tablespoons extra-virgin olive oil
- ½ small onion, slivered
- 8 ounces (227 g) store-bought jarred pesto

- ¾ cup crumbled goat or feta cheese, plus more for serving
- 6 cups zucchini noodles (from about 2 large zucchini), for serving
- ¼ cup chopped flat-leaf Italian parsley, for garnish

1. In a bowl, season the shrimp with salt and pepper and set aside. 2. In a large skillet, heat the olive oil over medium-high heat. Sauté the onion until just golden, 5 to 6 minutes. 3. Reduce the heat to low and add the pesto and cheese, whisking to combine and melt the cheese. Bring to a low simmer and add the shrimp. Reduce the heat back to low and cover. Cook until the shrimp is cooked through and pink, another 3 to 4 minutes. 4. Serve warm over zucchini noodles, garnishing with chopped parsley and additional crumbled cheese, if desired.

Per Serving:
calories: 608 | fat: 49g | protein: 37g | carbs: 9g | fiber: 3g | sodium: 564mg

Citrus Shrimp Ceviche Salad with Avocado

Prep time: 15 minutes | Cook time: 0 minutes | Serves 4

- 1 pound (454 g) fresh shrimp, peeled and deveined
- 1 small red or yellow bell pepper, cut into ½-inch chunks
- ½ English cucumber, peeled and cut into ½-inch chunks
- ½ small red onion, cut into thin slivers
- ¼ cup chopped fresh cilantro or flat-leaf Italian parsley
- ⅓ cup freshly squeezed lime

juice
- 2 tablespoons freshly squeezed lemon juice
- 2 tablespoons freshly squeezed clementine juice or orange juice
- ½ cup extra-virgin olive oil
- 1 teaspoon salt
- ½ teaspoon freshly ground black pepper
- 2 ripe avocados, peeled, pitted, and cut into ½-inch chunks

1. Cut the shrimp in half lengthwise. In a large glass bowl, combine the shrimp, bell pepper, cucumber, onion, and cilantro. 2. In a small bowl, whisk together the lime, lemon, and clementine juices, olive oil, salt, and pepper. Pour the mixture over the shrimp and veggies and toss to coat. Cover and refrigerate for at least 2 hours, or up to 8 hours. Give the mixture a toss every 30 minutes for the first 2 hours to make sure all the shrimp "cook" in the juices. 3. Add the cut avocado just before serving and toss to combine.

Per Serving:
calories: 520 | fat: 42g | protein: 26g | carbs: 14g | fiber: 8g | sodium: 593mg

Southern Italian Seafood Stew in Tomato Broth

Prep time: 15 minutes | Cook time: 1 hour 20 minutes | Serves 6

- ½ cup olive oil
- 1 fennel bulb, cored and finely chopped
- 2 stalks celery, finely chopped
- 1 medium onion, finely chopped
- 1 tablespoon dried oregano
- ½ teaspoon crushed red pepper flakes
- 1½ pounds (680 g) cleaned squid, bodies cut into ½-inch rings, tentacles halved
- 2 cups dry white wine
- 1 (28-ounce / 794-g) can tomato purée
- 1 bay leaf
- 1 teaspoon salt
- ½ teaspoon freshly ground black pepper
- 1 cup bottled clam juice
- 1 pound (454 g) whole head-on prawns
- 1½ pounds (680 g) mussels, scrubbed
- 1 lemon, cut into wedges, for serving

1. Heat olive oil in a large Dutch oven over medium-high heat. Add fennel, celery, onion, oregano, and red pepper flakes, then lower the heat to medium. Cook, stirring occasionally, for 15 minutes or until the vegetables soften. Add the squid and reduce the heat to low, allowing it to simmer for 15 minutes. 2. Pour in the wine and raise the heat to medium-high, bringing it to a boil. Stir occasionally until the wine evaporates. Lower the heat and add tomato purée, bay leaf, salt, and pepper. Let it cook gently for about 40 minutes, stirring occasionally, until the sauce thickens well. 3. Add 2 cups of water and clam juice, then increase the heat to medium-high and bring to a boil. 4. Add the shrimp and mussels, cover, and cook for roughly 5 minutes, or until the mussels have opened and the shrimp turn pink. 5. Spoon the seafood and broth into bowls, garnish with lemon wedges, and serve hot.

Per Serving:
calories: 490 | fat: 23g | protein: 48g | carbs: 22g | fiber: 5g | sodium: 899mg

Halibut in Parchment with Zucchini, Shallots, and Herbs

Prep time: 15 minutes | Cook time: 15 minutes | Serves 4

- ½ cup zucchini, diced small
- 1 shallot, minced
- 4 (5-ounce / 142-g) halibut fillets (about 1 inch thick)
- 4 teaspoons extra-virgin olive oil
- ¼ teaspoon kosher salt
- ⅛ teaspoon freshly ground black pepper
- 1 lemon, sliced into ⅛-inch-thick rounds
- 8 sprigs of thyme

1. Preheat your oven to 450°F (235°C). In a medium bowl, mix together the zucchini and shallots until well combined. 2. Cut four 15-by-24-inch pieces of parchment paper. Fold each sheet in half horizontally. Draw a large half-heart shape on one side, with the fold running along the center, then cut out the heart shape and open the parchment flat. 3. Place a fish fillet near the center of each parchment heart. Drizzle each fillet with 1 teaspoon of olive oil, then season with salt and black pepper. Top each fillet with a few lemon slices and 2 sprigs of fresh thyme. Divide the zucchini and shallot mixture evenly, placing one-quarter of the mixture over each

fillet. Fold the parchment over the fish. 4. Starting at the top of each parchment heart, fold the edges over tightly, continuing all the way around to create a sealed packet. Twist the end securely to keep it closed. 5. Arrange the parchment packets on a baking sheet and bake for about 15 minutes. Transfer each packet to a plate, carefully cut them open, and serve immediately while hot.

Per Serving:
calories: 190 | fat: 7g | protein: 27g | carbs: 5g | fiber: 1g | sodium: 170mg

Seasoned Steamed Crab

Prep time: 10 minutes | Cook time: 3 minutes | Serves 2

- 1 tablespoon extra-virgin olive oil
- ½ teaspoon Old Bay seafood seasoning
- ½ teaspoon smoked paprika
- ¼ teaspoon cayenne pepper
- 2 cloves garlic, peeled and minced
- 2 (2-pound / 907-g) Dungeness crabs
- 1 cup water

1. In a medium bowl, mix together oil, seafood seasoning, smoked paprika, cayenne pepper, and garlic until well combined. Coat the crabs thoroughly in this seasoning mixture, ensuring they're evenly covered, and place them in the steamer basket. 2. Pour water into the Instant Pot®, then insert the steamer basket with the seasoned crabs. Secure the lid, set the steam release handle to Sealing, press the Manual button, and set the timer for 3 minutes. 3. Once the timer goes off, quick-release the pressure until the float valve drops. Press Cancel, open the lid, and carefully transfer the crabs to a serving platter. Serve them hot and enjoy.

Per Serving:
calories: 185 | fat: 8g | protein: 25g | carbs: 1g | fiber: 0g | sodium: 434mg

Asian Swordfish

Prep time: 10 minutes | Cook time: 6 to 11 minutes | Serves 4

- 4 (4-ounce / 113-g) swordfish steaks
- ½ teaspoon toasted sesame oil
- 1 jalapeño pepper, finely minced
- 2 garlic cloves, grated
- 1 tablespoon grated fresh
- ginger
- ½ teaspoon Chinese five-spice powder
- ⅛ teaspoon freshly ground black pepper
- 2 tablespoons freshly squeezed lemon juice

1. Place the swordfish steaks on a work surface and drizzle with sesame oil, ensuring they are evenly coated. 2. In a small bowl, combine the jalapeño, garlic, ginger, five-spice powder, black pepper, and lemon juice. Rub this mixture all over the swordfish steaks and let them marinate for about 10 minutes. 3. Preheat your air fryer to 380°F (193°C). Arrange the marinated swordfish in the air fryer basket and roast for 6 to 11 minutes, or until the fish reaches an internal temperature of at least 140°F (60°C). Serve immediately while hot.

Per Serving:
calories: 175 | fat: 8g | protein: 22g | carbs: 2g | fiber: 0g | sodium: 93mg

Cod with Warm Tabbouleh Salad

Prep time: 10 minutes | Cook time: 6 minutes | Serves 4

- 1 cup medium-grind bulgur, rinsed
- 1 teaspoon table salt, divided
- 1 lemon, sliced ¼ inch thick, plus 2 tablespoons juice
- 4 (6-ounce / 170-g) skinless cod fillets, 1½ inches thick
- 3 tablespoons extra-virgin olive oil, divided, plus extra for drizzling
- ¼ teaspoon pepper
- 1 small shallot, minced
- 10 ounces (283 g) cherry tomatoes, halved
- 1 cup chopped fresh parsley
- ½ cup chopped fresh mint

1. Place the trivet into the base of the Instant Pot insert and add ½ cup water. Fold a sheet of aluminum foil into a 16 by 6-inch sling, then place a 1½-quart round soufflé dish in the center of the sling. In the soufflé dish, combine 1 cup water, bulgur, and ½ teaspoon salt. Lower the dish into the Instant Pot using the sling, with the narrow edges resting along the sides of the pot. 2. Secure the lid and close the pressure release valve. Select the high pressure cook function and set the timer for 3 minutes. When cooking is complete, turn off the Instant Pot and quick-release the pressure. Carefully remove the lid, keeping your face away from the escaping steam. Use the sling to transfer the soufflé dish to a wire rack and allow it to cool. Remove the trivet from the Instant Pot, but keep the sling and water in the insert. 3. Lay the lemon slices in two rows across the center of the sling. Brush the cod fillets with 1 tablespoon of oil and season with the remaining ½ teaspoon salt and black pepper. Arrange the cod fillets, skinned side down, in an even layer on top of the lemon slices. Lower the cod into the Instant Pot using the sling, allowing the narrow edges to rest along the sides. Lock the lid and close the pressure release valve. Select the high pressure cook function and set the timer for 3 minutes. 4. While the cod cooks, whisk the remaining 2 tablespoons of oil, lemon juice, and shallot in a large bowl. Add the cooked bulgur, tomatoes, parsley, and mint, gently tossing to combine. Season with salt and pepper to taste. 5. Turn off the Instant Pot and quick-release the pressure. Carefully remove the lid, allowing steam to vent away from you. Use the sling to transfer the cod to a large plate. Use a spatula to gently lift and remove the lemon slices from under the fillets. Serve the cod alongside the bulgur salad, drizzling each portion with a little extra olive oil.

Per Serving:

calories: 380 | fat: 12g | protein: 36g | carbs: 32g | fiber: 6g | sodium: 690mg

Wild Cod Oreganata

Prep time: 10 minutes | Cook time: 20 minutes | Serves 2

- 10 ounces (283 g) wild cod (1 large piece or 2 smaller ones)
- ⅓ cup panko bread crumbs
- 1 tablespoon dried oregano
- Zest of 1 lemon
- ½ teaspoon salt
- Pinch freshly ground black
- pepper
- 1 tablespoon olive oil
- 2 tablespoons freshly squeezed lemon juice
- 2 tablespoons white wine
- 1 tablespoon minced fresh parsley

1. Preheat your oven to 350°F (180°C). Place the cod fillet in a baking dish and pat it dry with a paper towel to remove excess moisture. 2. In a small bowl, mix together the panko breadcrumbs, oregano, lemon zest, salt, pepper, and olive oil until well combined. Press the panko mixture evenly onto the top of the cod fillet. 3. In another small bowl, combine the lemon juice and wine, then pour this mixture around the fish in the baking dish. 4. Bake the cod for about 20 minutes, or until it easily flakes with a fork and reaches an internal temperature of 145°F (63°C). 5. Once cooked, garnish the fish with freshly minced parsley and serve immediately.

Per Serving:

calories: 203 | fat: 8g | protein: 23g | carbs: 9g | fiber: 2g | sodium: 149mg

Moroccan-Spiced Sea Bass with Chickpeas and Artichokes

Prep time: 15 minutes | Cook time: 40 minutes | Serves 4

- 1½ teaspoons ground turmeric, divided
- ¾ teaspoon saffron
- ½ teaspoon ground cumin
- ¼ teaspoon kosher salt
- ¼ teaspoon freshly ground black pepper
- 1½ pounds (680 g) sea bass fillets, about ½ inch thick
- 8 tablespoons extra-virgin olive oil, divided
- 8 garlic cloves, divided (4 minced cloves and 4 sliced)
- 6 medium baby portobello mushrooms, chopped
- 1 large carrot, sliced on an angle
- 2 sun-dried tomatoes, thinly sliced (optional)
- 2 tablespoons tomato paste
- 1 (15-ounce / 425-g) can chickpeas, drained and rinsed
- 1½ cups low-sodium vegetable broth
- ¼ cup white wine
- 1 tablespoon ground coriander (optional)
- 1 cup sliced artichoke hearts marinated in olive oil
- ½ cup pitted kalamata olives
- ½ lemon, juiced
- ½ lemon, cut into thin rounds
- 4 to 5 rosemary sprigs or 2 tablespoons dried rosemary
- Fresh cilantro, for garnish

1. In a small mixing bowl, combine 1 teaspoon turmeric and the saffron and cumin. Season with salt and pepper. Season both sides of the fish with the spice mixture. Add 3 tablespoons of olive oil and work the fish to make sure it's well coated with the spices and the olive oil. 2. In a large sauté pan or skillet, heat 2 tablespoons of olive oil over medium heat until shimmering but not smoking. Sear the top side of the sea bass for about 1 minute, or until golden. Remove and set aside. 3. In the same skillet, add the minced garlic and cook very briefly, tossing regularly, until fragrant. Add the mushrooms, carrot, sun-dried tomatoes (if using), and tomato paste. Cook for 3 to 4 minutes over medium heat, tossing frequently, until fragrant. Add the chickpeas, broth, wine, coriander (if using), and the sliced garlic. Stir in the remaining ½ teaspoon ground turmeric. Raise the heat, if needed, and bring to a boil, then lower heat to simmer. Cover part of the way and let the sauce simmer for about 20 minutes, until thickened. 4. Carefully add the seared fish to the skillet. Ladle a bit of the sauce on top of the fish. Add the artichokes, olives, lemon juice and slices, and rosemary sprigs. Cook another 10 minutes or until the fish is fully cooked and flaky. Garnish with fresh cilantro.

Per Serving:

calories: 696 | fat: 41g | protein: 48g | carbs: 37g | fiber: 9g | sodium: 810mg

Chapter 7

Beef, Pork, and Lamb

Chapter 7 Beef, Pork, and Lamb

Beef Brisket with Onions

Prep time: 10 minutes | Cook time: 6 hours | Serves 6

- 1 large yellow onion, thinly sliced
- 2 garlic cloves, smashed and peeled
- 1 first cut of beef brisket (4 pounds / 1.8 kg), trimmed
- of excess fat
- Coarse sea salt
- Black pepper
- 2 cups chicken broth
- 2 tablespoons chopped fresh parsley leaves, for serving

1. Place the onion and garlic at the bottom of the slow cooker, spreading them out evenly. 2. Season the brisket generously with salt and pepper, then position it in the slow cooker, fat-side up. 3. Pour the broth into the slow cooker, covering the onion and garlic around the brisket. Cover with the lid and cook on high for approximately 6 hours, or until the brisket is tender and can be easily pulled apart with a fork. 4. Once cooked, transfer the brisket to a cutting board and slice it thinly against the grain. 5. Serve the sliced brisket with the cooked onion and some of the cooking liquid, garnished with chopped fresh parsley.

Per Serving:
calories: 424 | fat: 16g | protein: 67g | carbs: 4g | fiber: 1g | sodium: 277mg

Roast Pork Tenderloin with Cherry Balsamic Reduction

Prep timePrep Time: 20 minutes | Cook Time: 20 minutes | Serves 2

- 1 cup frozen cherries, thawed
- ⅓ cup balsamic vinegar
- 1 fresh rosemary sprig
- 1 (8-ounce/ 227-g) pork
- tenderloin
- ¼ teaspoon salt
- ⅛ teaspoon freshly ground black pepper
- 1 tablespoon olive oil

1. Combine the cherries and vinegar in a blender and purée until smooth. 2. Pour into a saucepan, add the rosemary sprig, and bring the mixture to a boil. Reduce the heat to medium-low and simmer for 15 minutes, or until it's reduced by half. 3. While the sauce is simmering, preheat the oven to 425°F (220°C) and set the rack in the middle position. 4. Season the pork on all sides with the salt and pepper. 5. Heat the oil in a sauté pan over medium-high heat. Add the pork and sear for 3 minutes, turning often, until it's golden on all sides. 6. Transfer the pork to an oven-safe baking dish and roast for 15 minutes, or until the internal temperature is 145°F(63°C). 7. Let the pork rest for 5 minutes before serving. Serve sliced and topped with the cherry-balsamic sauce.

Per Serving:
calories: 328 | fat: 11g | protein: 21g | carbs: 30g | fiber: 1g | sodium: 386mg

Crispy Pork Milanese with Lemon and Parsley

Prep time: 10 minutes | Cook time: 12 minutes | Serves 4

- 4 (1-inch) boneless pork chops
- Fine sea salt and ground black pepper, to taste
- 2 large eggs
- ¾ cup powdered Parmesan cheese
- Chopped fresh parsley, for garnish
- Lemon slices, for serving

1. Spray the air fryer basket with avocado oil. Preheat the air fryer to 400°F (204°C). 2. Place the pork chops between 2 sheets of plastic wrap and pound them with the flat side of a meat tenderizer until they're ¼ inch thick. Lightly season both sides of the chops with salt and pepper. 3. Lightly beat the eggs in a shallow bowl. Divide the Parmesan cheese evenly between 2 bowls and set the bowls in this order: Parmesan, eggs, Parmesan. Dredge a chop in the first bowl of Parmesan, then dip it in the eggs, and then dredge it again in the second bowl of Parmesan, making sure both sides and all edges are well coated. Repeat with the remaining chops. 4. Place the chops in the air fryer basket and air fry for 12 minutes, or until the internal temperature reaches 145°F (63°C), flipping halfway through. 5. Garnish with fresh parsley and serve immediately with lemon slices. Store leftovers in an airtight container in the refrigerator for up to 3 days. Reheat in a preheated 390°F (199°C) air fryer for 5 minutes, or until warmed through.

Per Serving:
calories: 349 | fat: 14g | protein: 50g | carbs: 3g | fiber: 0g | sodium: 464mg

Grilled Kefta

Prep time: 10 minutes | Cook time: 5 minutes | Serves 4

- 1 medium onion
- ⅓ cup fresh Italian parsley
- 1 pound (454 g) ground beef
- ¼ teaspoon ground cumin
- ¼ teaspoon cinnamon
- 1 teaspoon salt
- ½ teaspoon freshly ground black pepper

1. Preheat a grill or grill pan to high heat. 2. In a food processor, mince the onion and parsley until finely chopped. 3. In a large mixing bowl, combine the ground beef with the minced onion and parsley mixture, ground cumin, cinnamon, salt, and black pepper. Use your hands to mix until well combined. 4. Divide the meat mixture into 6 equal portions, shaping each one into a flat oval patty. 5. Place the patties on the hot grill or grill pan and cook for about 3 minutes on each side, or until they are cooked to your desired doneness.

Per Serving:
calories: 203 | fat: 10g | protein: 24g | carbs: 3g | fiber: 1g | sodium: 655mg

Lamb Stew

Prep time: 20 minutes | Cook time: 2 hours 20 minutes | Serves 6

- 3 carrots, peeled and sliced
- 2 onions, minced
- 2 cups white wine
- ½ cup flat-leaf parsley, chopped
- 2 garlic cloves, minced
- 3 bay leaves
- 1 teaspoon dried rosemary leaves
- ¼ teaspoon nutmeg
- ¼ teaspoon ground cloves
- 2 pounds (907 g) boneless lamb, cut into 1-inch pieces
- ¼ cup olive oil
- 1 package frozen artichoke hearts
- Sea salt and freshly ground pepper, to taste

1. In a plastic bag or shallow dish, combine the carrots, onion, white wine, parsley, garlic, bay leaves, and your choice of seasonings. Mix well to create the marinade. 2. Add the lamb to the marinade, making sure it is fully coated, and refrigerate overnight. 3. When ready to cook, remove the lamb from the marinade, reserving the marinade for later use. Pat the lamb dry with paper towels. 4. Heat olive oil in a large stew pot over medium-high heat. Add the lamb and brown it on all sides, turning frequently to ensure even cooking. 5. Pour the reserved marinade into the stew pot, cover with a lid, and reduce the heat to low. Let it simmer for about 2 hours until the lamb is tender. 6. Add the artichoke hearts to the pot and let it continue to simmer for an additional 20 minutes. Season with sea salt and freshly ground black pepper to taste before serving.

Per Serving:
calories: 399 | fat: 18g | protein: 33g | carbs: 13g | fiber: 3g | sodium: 167mg

One-Pot Pork Loin Dinner

Prep time: 35 minutes | Cook time: 28 minutes | Serves 6

- 1 tablespoon olive oil
- 1 small onion, peeled and diced
- 1 pound (454 g) boneless pork loin, cut into 1" pieces
- ½ teaspoon salt
- ¼ teaspoon ground black pepper
- ½ cup white wine
- 1 cup low-sodium chicken broth
- 1 large rutabaga, peeled and diced
- 1 large turnip, peeled and diced
- 4 small Yukon Gold or red potatoes, quartered
- 4 medium carrots, peeled and diced
- 1 stalk celery, finely diced
- ½ cup sliced leeks, white part only
- ½ teaspoon mild curry powder
- ¼ teaspoon dried thyme
- 2 teaspoons dried parsley
- 3 tablespoons lemon juice
- 2 large Granny Smith apples, peeled, cored, and diced

1. Press the Sauté button on the Instant Pot® and heat the oil. Once hot, add the onion and sauté for about 3 minutes until tender. Add the pork, seasoning it with salt and pepper, and cook for around 5 minutes until the pork begins to brown. Stir in the wine, broth, rutabaga, and turnip, mixing well. Then add potatoes, carrots, celery, leeks, curry powder, thyme, parsley, and lemon juice, stirring to combine everything. Press the Cancel button to stop sautéing. 2. Secure the lid on the Instant Pot®, set the steam release to Sealing, press the Manual button, and set the cooking time to 15 minutes. When the cooking time ends, allow the pressure to release naturally for about 25 minutes. Press the Cancel button once the pressure has fully released. 3. Open the lid and add the diced apples. Press the Sauté button again and simmer for about 5 minutes, or until the apples are tender. Serve hot in large bowls, enjoying the blend of flavors and textures.

Per Serving:
calories: 271 | fat: 4g | protein: 14g | carbs: 30g | fiber: 5g | sodium: 316mg

Red Wine Braised Short Ribs

Prep time: 10 minutes | Cook time: 1 hour 30 minutes to 2 hours| Serves 4

- 1½ pounds (680 g) boneless beef short ribs (if using bone-in, use 3½ pounds)
- 1 teaspoon salt
- ½ teaspoon freshly ground black pepper
- ½ teaspoon garlic powder
- ¼ cup extra-virgin olive oil
- 1 cup dry red wine (such as cabernet sauvignon or merlot)
- 2 to 3 cups beef broth, divided
- 4 sprigs rosemary

1. Preheat the oven to 350°F(180°C). 2. Season the short ribs with salt, pepper, and garlic powder. Let sit for 10 minutes. 3. In a Dutch oven or oven-safe deep skillet, heat the olive oil over medium-high heat. 4. When the oil is very hot, add the short ribs and brown until dark in color, 2 to 3 minutes per side. Remove the meat from the oil and keep warm. 5. Add the red wine and 2 cups beef broth to the Dutch oven, whisk together, and bring to a boil. Reduce the heat to low and simmer until the liquid is reduced to about 2 cups, about 10 minutes. 6. Return the short ribs to the liquid, which should come about halfway up the meat, adding up to 1 cup of remaining broth if needed. Cover and braise until the meat is very tender, about 1½ to 2 hours. 7. Remove from the oven and let sit, covered, for 10 minutes before serving. Serve warm, drizzled with cooking liquid.

Per Serving:
calories: 525 | fat: 37g | protein: 34g | carbs: 5g | fiber: 1g | sodium: 720mg

Flank Steak and Blue Cheese Wraps

Prep time: 20 minutes | Cook time: 0 minutes | Serves 6

- 1 cup leftover flank steak, cut into 1-inch slices
- ¼ cup red onion, thinly sliced
- ¼ cup cherry tomatoes, chopped
- ¼ cup low-salt olives, pitted and chopped
- ¼ cup roasted red bell peppers, drained and coarsely chopped
- ¼ cup blue cheese crumbles
- 6 whole-wheat or spinach wraps
- Sea salt and freshly ground pepper, to taste

1. In a small bowl, combine the flank steak, onion, tomatoes, olives, bell pepper, and blue cheese, mixing until well distributed. 2. Take each wrap and spread ½ cup of the mixture evenly across the center. Roll the wrap halfway, then fold in the ends and continue rolling, just like a burrito. 3. If desired, cut each wrap on a diagonal for presentation, season to taste with salt and pepper, and serve immediately.

Per Serving:
calories: 370 | fat: 26g | protein: 31g | carbs: 1g | fiber: 0g | sodium: 81mg

Spiced Lamb Couscous with Vegetables and Herbs

Prep time: 25 minutes | Cook time: 30 minutes | Serves 8 to 10

- 2 pounds (907 g) boneless lamb meat, cut into 2-inch pieces
- ½ teaspoon dried thyme
- ½ teaspoon dried marjoram
- Sea salt and freshly ground pepper, to taste
- ¼ cup olive oil
- 1 onion, peeled and coarsely chopped
- 1 bulb celeriac, cut in chunks
- 5 cups chicken broth
- 2 zucchini, cut into 1-inch pieces
- 1 cup cooked chickpeas
- 1 cup raisins (optional)
- ¼ teaspoon ground ginger
- ¼ teaspoon ground cinnamon
- ¼ teaspoon ground cardamom
- ¼ teaspoon ground cloves
- ¼ teaspoon ground nutmeg
- 5 cups cooked whole-wheat couscous
- ½ cup fresh cilantro, chopped
- ½ cup fresh mint, chopped
- ½ cup green onions, chopped

1. Season the lamb meat with the thyme, marjoram, sea salt, and freshly ground pepper, and grill in a grill basket for 8–10 minutes, stirring frequently. 2. If you don't have a grill basket, you can also cook the lamb in a heavy skillet. 3. Set aside, but keep warm. 4. Heat the olive oil in a large skillet. 5. Add the onion and celeriac, and cook until tender, stirring frequently. 6. Add the chicken broth, zucchini, chickpeas, raisins, and spices, and simmer 10–20 minutes. 7. To serve, mound the couscous in the middle of a serving platter and arrange the vegetables and meat around the couscous. Garnish with the fresh cilantro, mint, and green onions.

Per Serving:
calories: 442 | fat: 13g | protein: 31g | carbs: 53g | fiber: 9g | sodium: 118mg

Pan-Fried Pork Chops with Peppers and Onions

Prep time: 5 minutes | Cook time: 25 minutes | Serves 4

- 4 (4-ounce / 113-g) pork chops, untrimmed
- 1½ teaspoons salt, divided
- 1 teaspoon freshly ground black pepper, divided
- ½ cup extra-virgin olive oil, divided
- 1 red or orange bell pepper, thinly sliced
- 1 green bell pepper, thinly
- sliced
- 1 small yellow onion, thinly sliced
- 2 teaspoons dried Italian herbs (such as oregano, parsley, or rosemary)
- 2 garlic cloves, minced
- 1 tablespoon balsamic vinegar

1. Season the pork chops evenly with 1 teaspoon of salt and ½ teaspoon of black pepper. 2. Heat ¼ cup of olive oil in a large skillet over medium-high heat. Add the pork chops and fry until they are browned and nearly cooked through, about 4 to 5 minutes per side depending on their thickness. Remove the pork chops from the skillet and cover them to keep warm. 3. Add the remaining ¼ cup of olive oil to the skillet. Over medium-high heat, sauté the sliced peppers, onions, and herbs until tender, about 6 to 8 minutes.

Stir in the garlic, mixing to combine, then return the pork chops to the skillet. Cover the skillet, reduce the heat to low, and cook for an additional 2 to 3 minutes, or until the pork is completely cooked through. 4. Turn off the heat. Use a slotted spoon to transfer the pork chops, peppers, and onions to a serving platter. Add the vinegar to the oil remaining in the skillet and whisk until well combined. Drizzle the vinaigrette over the pork chops and serve them warm.

Per Serving:
calories: 402 | fat: 31g | protein: 26g | carbs: 4g | fiber: 1g | sodium: 875mg

Herb-Crusted Parmesan Filet Mignon

Prep time: 20 minutes | Cook time: 13 minutes | Serves 4

- 1 pound (454 g) filet mignon
- Sea salt and ground black pepper, to taste
- ½ teaspoon cayenne pepper
- 1 teaspoon dried basil
- 1 teaspoon dried rosemary
- 1 teaspoon dried thyme
- 1 tablespoon sesame oil
- 1 small-sized egg, well-whisked
- ½ cup Parmesan cheese, grated

1. Season the filet mignon with salt, black pepper, cayenne pepper, basil, rosemary, and thyme. Brush with sesame oil. 2. Put the egg in a shallow plate. Now, place the Parmesan cheese in another plate. 3. Coat the filet mignon with the egg; then lay it into the Parmesan cheese. Set the air fryer to 360°F (182°C). 4. Cook for 10 to 13 minutes or until golden. Serve with mixed salad leaves and enjoy!

Per Serving:
calories: 252 | fat: 13g | protein: 32g | carbs: 1g | fiber: 0g | sodium: 96mg

Roast Pork Tenderloin

Prep time: 10 minutes | Cook time: 12 minutes | Serves 6

- 2 tablespoons olive oil
- 1 teaspoon Spanish paprika
- 1 teaspoon red wine vinegar
- 1 clove garlic, minced
- ½ teaspoon ground cumin
- ½ teaspoon ground coriander
- ½ teaspoon ginger
- ½ teaspoon freshly ground pepper
- ¼ teaspoon turmeric
- 1 pound (454 g) pork tenderloin
- Sea salt and freshly ground pepper, to taste

1. In a bowl, combine all the ingredients except for the pork tenderloin to create a thick paste. 2. Spread this paste evenly over the pork tenderloin, cover it, and refrigerate for several hours or overnight to allow the flavors to infuse. 3. Preheat a grill to medium heat. Grill the tenderloin for about 10–12 minutes, turning it halfway through. The internal temperature should reach 145°F (63°C) when tested with an instant-read thermometer. 4. Once cooked, transfer the tenderloin to a serving platter and let it rest for 15 minutes before slicing. 5. Season the slices to taste and serve immediately.

Per Serving:
calories: 125 | fat: 6g | protein: 16g | carbs: 1g | fiber: 0g | sodium: 41mg

Crispy Pork and Beef Egg Rolls

Prep time: 30 minutes | Cook time: 7 to 8 minutes per batch | Makes 8 egg rolls

- ¼ pound (113 g) very lean ground beef
- ¼ pound (113 g) lean ground pork
- 1 tablespoon soy sauce
- 1 teaspoon olive oil
- ½ cup grated carrots
- 2 green onions, chopped
- 2 cups grated Napa cabbage
- ¼ cup chopped water

- chestnuts
- ¼ teaspoon salt
- ¼ teaspoon garlic powder
- ¼ teaspoon black pepper
- 1 egg
- 1 tablespoon water
- 8 egg roll wraps
- Oil for misting or cooking spray

1. In a large skillet, brown beef and pork with soy sauce. Remove cooked meat from skillet, drain, and set aside. 2. Pour off any excess grease from skillet. Add olive oil, carrots, and onions. Sauté until barely tender, about 1 minute. 3. Stir in cabbage, cover, and cook for 1 minute or just until cabbage slightly wilts. Remove from heat. 4. In a large bowl, combine the cooked meats and vegetables, water chestnuts, salt, garlic powder, and pepper. Stir well. If needed, add more salt to taste. 5. Beat together egg and water in a small bowl. 6. Fill egg roll wrappers, using about ¼ cup of filling for each wrap. Roll up and brush all over with egg wash to seal. Spray very lightly with olive oil or cooking spray. 7. Place 4 egg rolls in air fryer basket and air fry at 390ºF (199ºC) for 4 minutes. Turn over and cook 3 to 4 more minutes, until golden brown and crispy. 8. Repeat to cook remaining egg rolls.

Per Serving:
calories: 176 | fat: 5g | protein: 11g | carbs: 22g | fiber: 2g | sodium: 339mg

Mediterranean Beef Pita Wraps

Prep timePrep Time: 15 minutes | Cook Time: 10 minutes | Serves 2

For the beef
- 1 tablespoon olive oil
- ½ medium onion, minced
- 2 garlic cloves, minced
For the yogurt sauce
- ⅓ cup plain Greek yogurt
- 1 ounce (28 g) crumbled feta cheese (about 3 tablespoons)
- 1 tablespoon minced fresh parsley
For the sandwiches
- 2 large Greek-style pitas
- ½ cup cherry tomatoes, halved

- 6 ounces (170 g) lean ground beef
- 1 teaspoon dried oregano

- 1 tablespoon minced scallion
- 1 tablespoon freshly squeezed lemon juice
- Pinch salt

- 1 cup diced cucumber
- Salt
- Freshly ground black pepper

Make the beef Heat the olive oil in a sauté pan over medium high-heat. Add the onion, garlic, and ground beef and sauté for 7 minutes, breaking up the meat well. When the meat is no longer pink, drain off any fat and stir in the oregano. Turn off the heat. Make the yogurt sauce In a small bowl, combine the yogurt, feta, parsley, scallion, lemon juice, and salt. To assemble the sandwiches

1. Warm the pitas in the microwave for 20 seconds each. 2. To serve, spread some of the yogurt sauce over each warm pita. Top with the ground beef, cherry tomatoes, and diced cucumber. Season with salt and pepper. Add additional yogurt sauce if desired.

Per Serving:
calories: 541 | fat: 21g | protein: 29g | carbs: 57g | fiber: 4g | sodium: 694mg

Herbed Dijon Lamb Chops

Prep time: 5 minutes | Cook time: 14 minutes | Serves 4

- Oil, for spraying
- 1 tablespoon Dijon mustard
- 2 teaspoons lemon juice
- ½ teaspoon dried tarragon
- ¼ teaspoon salt

- ¼ teaspoon freshly ground black pepper
- 4 (1¼-inch-thick) loin lamb chops

1. Preheat the air fryer to 390ºF (199ºC). Line the air fryer basket with parchment and spray lightly with oil. 2. In a small bowl, mix together the mustard, lemon juice, tarragon, salt, and black pepper. 3. Pat dry the lamb chops with a paper towel. Brush the chops on both sides with the mustard mixture. 4. Place the chops in the prepared basket. You may need to work in batches, depending on the size of your air fryer. 5. Cook for 8 minutes, flip, and cook for another 6 minutes, or until the internal temperature reaches 125ºF (52ºC) for rare, 145ºF (63ºC) for medium-rare, or 155ºF (68ºC) for medium.

Per Serving:
calories: 96 | fat: 4g | protein: 14g | carbs: 0g | fiber: 0g | sodium: 233mg

Herbed Lamb Steaks

Prep time: 30 minutes | Cook time: 15 minutes | Serves 4

- ½ medium onion
- 2 tablespoons minced garlic
- 2 teaspoons ground ginger
- 1 teaspoon ground cinnamon
- 1 teaspoon onion powder

- 1 teaspoon cayenne pepper
- 1 teaspoon salt
- 4 (6 ounces / 170 g) boneless lamb sirloin steaks
- Oil, for spraying

1. In a blender, combine the onion, garlic, ginger, cinnamon, onion powder, cayenne pepper, and salt. Pulse until the onion is finely minced and all ingredients are well mixed. 2. Place the lamb steaks in a large bowl or a zip-top plastic bag, then sprinkle the onion mixture over the steaks. Turn the steaks to coat them evenly with the mixture. Cover the bowl with plastic wrap or seal the bag, and refrigerate for 30 minutes to let the flavors marinate. 3. Preheat the air fryer to 330ºF (166ºC). Line the air fryer basket with parchment paper and spray lightly with oil to prevent sticking. 4. Arrange the lamb steaks in a single layer in the basket, ensuring they do not overlap. You may need to cook them in batches if your air fryer is small. 5. Cook the lamb steaks for 8 minutes, then flip them over and cook for an additional 7 minutes, or until the internal temperature reaches 155ºF (68ºC). Serve hot.

Per Serving:
calories: 255 | fat: 10g | protein: 35g | carbs: 5g | fiber: 1g | sodium: 720mg

Slow-Cooked Mediterranean Pork with Olives

Prep time: 10 minutes | Cook time: 6 to 8 hours | Serves 4

- 1 small onion, sliced
- 4 thick-cut, bone-in pork chops
- 1 cup low-sodium chicken broth
- Juice of 1 lemon
- 2 garlic cloves, minced
- 1 teaspoon sea salt
- 1 teaspoon dried oregano
- 1 teaspoon dried parsley
- ½ teaspoon freshly ground black pepper
- 2 cups whole green olives, pitted
- 1 pint cherry tomatoes

1. Put the onion in a slow cooker and arrange the pork chops on top. 2. In a small bowl, whisk together the chicken broth, lemon juice, garlic, salt, oregano, parsley, and pepper. Pour the sauce over the pork chops. Top with the olives and tomatoes. 3. Cover the cooker and cook for 6 to 8 hours on Low heat.

Per Serving:

calories: 339 | fat: 14g | protein: 42g | carbs: 6g | fiber: 4g | sodium: 708mg

Aromatic Spiced Lamb Chops

Prep time: 30 minutes | Cook time: 15 minutes | Serves 4

- ½ yellow onion, coarsely chopped
- 4 coin-size slices peeled fresh ginger
- 5 garlic cloves
- 1 teaspoon garam masala
- 1 teaspoon ground fennel
- 1 teaspoon ground cinnamon
- 1 teaspoon ground turmeric
- ½ to 1 teaspoon cayenne pepper
- ½ teaspoon ground cardamom
- 1 teaspoon kosher salt
- 1 pound (454 g) lamb sirloin chops

1. In a blender, combine the onion, ginger, garlic, garam masala, fennel, cinnamon, turmeric, cayenne, cardamom, and salt. Pulse until the onion is finely minced and the mixture forms a thick paste, 3 to 4 minutes. 2. Place the lamb chops in a large bowl. Slash the meat and fat with a sharp knife several times to allow the marinade to penetrate better. Add the spice paste to the bowl and toss the lamb to coat. Marinate at room temperature for 30 minutes or cover and refrigerate for up to 24 hours. 3. Place the lamb chops in a single layer in the air fryer basket. Set the air fryer to 325°F (163°C) for 15 minutes, turning the chops halfway through the cooking time. Use a meat thermometer to ensure the lamb has reached an internal temperature of 145°F (63°C) (medium-rare).

Per Serving:

calories: 179 | fat: 7g | protein: 24g | carbs: 4g | fiber: 1g | sodium: 657mg

Cube Steak Roll-Ups

Prep time: 30 minutes | Cook time: 8 to 10 minutes | Serves 4

- 4 cube steaks (6 ounces / 170 g each)
- 1 (16-ounce / 454-g) bottle Italian dressing
- 1 teaspoon salt
- ½ teaspoon freshly ground black pepper
- ½ cup finely chopped yellow onion
- ½ cup finely chopped green bell pepper
- ½ cup finely chopped mushrooms
- 1 to 2 tablespoons oil

1. In a large resealable bag or airtight container, add the steaks and pour in the Italian dressing. Seal the bag, shake to coat evenly, and refrigerate for at least 2 hours to marinate. 2. Remove the steaks from the marinade and place them on a cutting board. Discard the marinade. Season the steaks evenly on both sides with salt and black pepper. 3. In a small bowl, mix together the onion, bell pepper, and mushrooms. Distribute the vegetable mixture evenly over each steak. Roll up the steaks tightly, jelly roll-style, and secure them with toothpicks. 4. Preheat the air fryer to 400°F (204°C). 5. Arrange the rolled steaks in the air fryer basket, making sure they are not overlapping. 6. Cook the steaks for 4 minutes, then flip them and spritz lightly with oil. Continue cooking for an additional 4 to 6 minutes, or until the internal temperature reaches 145°F (63°C). Let the steaks rest for 5 minutes before serving.

Per Serving:

calories: 364 | fat: 20g | protein: 37g | carbs: 7g | fiber: 1g | sodium: 715mg

Balsamic Pork Tenderloin

Prep time: 10 minutes | Cook time: 6 to 8 hours | Serves 6

- 1 small onion, sliced
- 1 (3-pound/ 1.4-kg) pork tenderloin
- 1 cup balsamic vinegar
- ½ cup low-sodium beef broth
- 3 garlic cloves, crushed
- 2 tablespoons capers, undrained
- 1½ teaspoons olive oil
- 1 teaspoon dried rosemary
- 1 teaspoon sea salt
- ½ teaspoon freshly ground black pepper

1. Place the sliced onion at the bottom of the slow cooker, then arrange the pork tenderloin on top of the onions. 2. In a small bowl, whisk together the vinegar, beef broth, minced garlic, capers, olive oil, rosemary, salt, and black pepper until well combined. Pour this mixture evenly over the pork tenderloin. 3. Cover the slow cooker with the lid and cook on Low heat for 6 to 8 hours, until the pork is tender and infused with flavor.

Per Serving:

calories: 281 | fat: 10g | protein: 45g | carbs: 7g | fiber: 0g | sodium: 523mg

Chapter **8**

Poultry

Chapter 8 Poultry

Chicken Avgolemono

Prep time: 10 minutes | Cook time: 50 minutes | Serves 4

- 1½ pounds (680 g) boneless, skinless chicken breasts
- 6 cups chicken broth, as needed
- ¾ cup dried Greek orzo
- 3 large eggs
- Juice of 2 lemons
- Sea salt
- Freshly ground black pepper

1. Place the chicken in a stockpot and add enough broth to cover the chicken by about 1 inch. Bring the broth to a boil over high heat, then reduce the heat to low, cover, and simmer for 30 to 45 minutes, or until the chicken is cooked through. Remove the chicken from the pot and set it aside in a medium bowl. 2. Increase the heat to medium-high to bring the broth back to a boil. Add the orzo and cook for 7 to 10 minutes, or until it is tender. 3. While the orzo is cooking, shred the cooked chicken using two forks. Once the orzo is ready, return the shredded chicken to the pot. 4. In a small bowl, whisk the eggs until frothy, then whisk in the lemon juice. Slowly add 1 cup of hot broth to the egg mixture while continuously whisking to temper the eggs. Pour the egg mixture back into the pot, stirring to combine. Let the soup simmer for another minute, then season with salt and pepper to taste before serving.

Per Serving:
calories: 391 | fat: 9g | protein: 46g | carbs: 29g | fiber: 1g | sodium: 171mg

Tex-Mex Chicken Roll-Ups

Prep time: 10 minutes | Cook time: 14 to 17 minutes | Serves 8

- 2 pounds (907 g) boneless, skinless chicken breasts or thighs
- 1 teaspoon chili powder
- ½ teaspoon smoked paprika
- ½ teaspoon ground cumin
- Sea salt and freshly ground
- black pepper, to taste
- 6 ounces (170 g) Monterey Jack cheese, shredded
- 4 ounces (113 g) canned diced green chiles
- Avocado oil spray

1. Place the chicken breasts in a large zip-top bag or between two sheets of plastic wrap. Use a meat mallet or a heavy skillet to pound the chicken to about ¼ inch thickness for even cooking. 2. In a small bowl, mix together the chili powder, smoked paprika, cumin, and a pinch of salt and black pepper. Evenly sprinkle both sides of the chicken with the seasoning blend. 3. Sprinkle the Monterey Jack cheese over each piece of chicken, followed by the diced green chiles. 4. Roll each chicken piece up tightly from the long side, tucking in the ends as you roll. Secure each roll-up with a toothpick to hold it in place. 5. Preheat the air fryer to 350ºF (177ºC). Lightly spray the outside of each chicken roll-up with avocado oil. Place the chicken in a single layer in the air fryer basket, working in batches if necessary. Cook for 7 minutes, then flip and cook for another 7 to 10 minutes, or until an instant-read thermometer registers 160ºF

(71ºC). 6. Carefully remove the chicken from the air fryer and let it rest for about 5 minutes before serving.

Per Serving:
calories: 220 | fat: 10g | protein: 31g | carbs: 1g | fiber: 0g | sodium: 355mg

Spicy Buffalo Chicken Cheese Bites

Prep time: 5 minutes | Cook time: 8 minutes | Serves 2

- 1 cup shredded cooked chicken
- ¼ cup buffalo sauce
- 1 cup shredded Mozzarella
- cheese
- 1 large egg
- ¼ cup crumbled feta

1. In a large bowl, mix all ingredients except the feta. Cut a piece of parchment to fit your air fryer basket and press the mixture into a ½-inch-thick circle. 2. Sprinkle the mixture with feta and place into the air fryer basket. 3. Adjust the temperature to 400ºF (204ºC) and air fry for 8 minutes. 4. After 5 minutes, flip over the cheese mixture. 5. Allow to cool 5 minutes before cutting into sticks. Serve warm.

Per Serving:
calories: 413 | fat: 25g | protein: 43g | carbs: 3g | fiber: 0g | sodium: 453mg

Braised Turkey Thighs with Fig Balsamic Sauce

Prep time: 15 minutes | Cook time: 14 minutes | Serves 4

- 4 (¾-pound / 340-g) bone-in turkey thighs, skin removed
- 1 large onion, peeled and quartered
- 2 large carrots, peeled and sliced
- ½ stalk celery, finely diced
- ½ cup balsamic vinegar
- 2 tablespoons tomato paste
- 1 cup low-sodium chicken broth
- ½ teaspoon salt
- ¾ teaspoon ground black pepper
- 12 dried figs, cut in half

1. Add the turkey, onion, carrots, and celery to the Instant Pot®. Whisk vinegar, tomato paste, broth, salt, and pepper in a small bowl. Pour into pot. Add figs. Close lid, set steam release to Sealing, press the Manual button, and set time to 14 minutes. When the timer beeps, let pressure release naturally, about 25 minutes. 2. Open the lid. Transfer thighs, carrots, and figs to a serving platter. Tent loosely with aluminum foil and keep warm while you finish the sauce. 3. Strain pan juices. Discard onion and celery. Skim and discard fat. Pour strained sauce over the thighs. Serve immediately.

Per Serving:
calories: 565 | fat: 17g | protein: 68g | carbs: 26g | fiber: 5g | sodium: 685mg

Cauliflower Crust Chicken Pizzas

Prep time: 10 minutes | Cook time: 25 minutes | Serves 2

- 1 (12-ounce / 340-g) bag frozen riced cauliflower
- ⅓ cup shredded Mozzarella cheese
- ¼ cup almond flour
- ¼ grated Parmesan cheese
- 1 large egg
- ½ teaspoon salt
- 1 teaspoon garlic powder
- 1 teaspoon dried oregano
- ¼ cup fresh baby arugula, divided

- 4 tablespoons no-sugar-added marinara sauce, divided
- 4 ounces (113 g) fresh Mozzarella, chopped, divided
- 1 cup cooked chicken breast, chopped, divided
- ½ cup chopped cherry tomatoes, divided

1. Preheat the air fryer to 400ºF (204ºC). Cut 4 sheets of parchment paper to fit the basket of the air fryer. Brush with olive oil and set aside. 2. In a large glass bowl, microwave the cauliflower according to package directions. Place the cauliflower on a clean towel, draw up the sides, and squeeze tightly over a sink to remove the excess moisture. Return the cauliflower to the bowl and add the shredded Mozzarella along with the almond flour, Parmesan, egg, salt, garlic powder, and oregano. Stir until thoroughly combined. 3. Divide the dough into two equal portions. Place one piece of dough on the prepared parchment paper and pat gently into a thin, flat disk 7 to 8 inches in diameter. Air fry for 15 minutes until the crust begins to brown. Let cool for 5 minutes. 4. Transfer the parchment paper with the crust on top to a baking sheet. Place a second sheet of parchment paper over the crust. While holding the edges of both sheets together, carefully lift the crust off the baking sheet, flip it, and place it back in the air fryer basket. The new sheet of parchment paper is now on the bottom. Remove the top piece of paper and air fry the crust for another 15 minutes until the top begins to brown. Remove the basket from the air fryer. 5. Spread 2 tablespoons of the marinara sauce on top of the crust, followed by half the fresh Mozzarella, chicken, cherry tomatoes, and arugula. Air fry for 5 to 10 minutes longer, until the cheese is melted and beginning to brown. Remove the pizza from the oven and let it sit for 10 minutes before serving. Repeat with the remaining ingredients to make a second pizza.

Per Serving:
calories: 655 | fat: 35g | protein: 67g | carbs: 20g | fiber: 7g | sodium: 741mg

Zucchini Marinara Chicken Bake

Prep time: 10 minutes | Cook time: 15 minutes | Serves 4

- 2 large zucchini, trimmed and chopped
- 4 (6-ounce / 170-g) chicken breast halves
- 3 cups marinara sauce

- 1 tablespoon Italian seasoning
- ½ teaspoon salt
- 1 cup shredded mozzarella cheese

1. Place zucchini on the bottom of the Instant Pot®. Place chicken on zucchini. Pour marinara sauce over chicken. Sprinkle with Italian seasoning and salt. 2. Close lid, set steam release to Sealing, press the Poultry button, and cook for the default time of 15 minutes. When the timer beeps, let pressure release naturally for 10 minutes. Quick-release any remaining pressure until the float valve

drops and then open lid. Check chicken using a meat thermometer to ensure the internal temperature is at least 165ºF (74ºC). 3. Sprinkle chicken with cheese. Close lid and let stand on the Keep Warm setting for 5 minutes to allow the cheese to melt. 4. Transfer chicken and zucchini to a serving platter. Serve hot.

Per Serving:
calories: 21 | fat: 13g | protein: 51g | carbs: 21g | fiber: 5g | sodium: 442mg

Turkey Breast in Yogurt Sauce

Prep time: 10 minutes | Cook time: 16 minutes | Serves 6

- 1 cup plain low-fat yogurt
- 1 teaspoon ground turmeric
- 1 teaspoon ground cumin
- 1 teaspoon yellow mustard seeds
- ¼ teaspoon salt
- ½ teaspoon ground black pepper

- 1 pound (454 g) boneless turkey breast, cut into bite-sized pieces
- 1 tablespoon olive oil
- 1 (1-pound / 454-g) bag frozen baby peas and pearl onions, thawed

1. In a large bowl, combine yogurt, turmeric, cumin, mustard seeds, salt, and black pepper. Add the turkey to the bowl and stir until all pieces are well coated in the marinade. Cover and refrigerate for 4 hours to allow the flavors to develop. 2. Press the Sauté button on the Instant Pot® and heat the oil. Add the marinated turkey along with the yogurt mixture to the pot. Press the Cancel button, then close the lid and set the steam release to Sealing. Press the Manual button and set the cooking time to 8 minutes. Once the timer beeps, quick-release the pressure and carefully open the lid. 3. Stir in the peas and onions. Press the Cancel button, then press the Sauté button again and simmer for about 8 minutes, or until the sauce thickens to your desired consistency. Serve the dish hot.

Per Serving:
calories: 146 | fat: 6g | protein: 17g | carbs: 7g | fiber: 1g | sodium: 554mg

Harissa Yogurt Chicken Thighs

Prep time: 5 minutes | Cook time: 25 minutes | Serves 4

- ½ cup plain Greek yogurt
- 2 tablespoons harissa
- 1 tablespoon lemon juice
- ½ teaspoon kosher salt

- ¼ teaspoon freshly ground black pepper
- 1½ pounds (680 g) boneless, skinless chicken thighs

1. In a mixing bowl, combine the yogurt, harissa, lemon juice, salt, and black pepper. Add the chicken thighs and mix until thoroughly coated. Let the chicken marinate in the refrigerator for at least 15 minutes, or up to 4 hours for deeper flavor. 2. Preheat your oven to 425ºF (220ºC). Line a baking sheet with parchment paper or foil for easy cleanup. Remove the chicken thighs from the marinade and place them in a single layer on the prepared baking sheet. Roast for 20 minutes, flipping the chicken halfway through cooking to ensure even browning. 3. After roasting, set the oven to broil. Broil the chicken for 2 to 3 minutes, or until it turns golden brown in spots. Serve immediately while hot.

Per Serving:
calories: 190 | fat: 10g | protein: 24g | carbs: 1g | fiber: 0g | sodium: 230mg

Citrus and Spice Chicken

Prep time: 15 minutes | Cook time: 17 minutes | Serves 8

- 2 tablespoons olive oil
- 3 pounds (1.4 kg) boneless, skinless chicken thighs
- 1 teaspoon smoked paprika
- ½ teaspoon salt
- ⅛ teaspoon ground cinnamon
- ⅛ teaspoon ground ginger
- ⅛ teaspoon ground nutmeg
- ½ cup golden raisins
- ½ cup slivered almonds
- 1 cup orange juice
- ⅛ cup lemon juice
- ⅛ cup lime juice
- 1 pound (454 g) carrots, peeled and chopped
- 2 tablespoons water
- 1 tablespoon arrowroot powder

1. Press the Sauté button on the Instant Pot® and add the oil. Once hot, add the chicken thighs and fry for about 2 minutes on each side until they are browned. 2. Add the paprika, salt, cinnamon, ginger, nutmeg, raisins, almonds, orange juice, lemon juice, lime juice, and carrots to the pot. Press the Cancel button to stop sautéing. 3. Secure the lid, set the steam release to Sealing, press the Manual button, and set the cooking time to 10 minutes. Once the timer beeps, let the pressure release naturally for 5 minutes, then quick-release any remaining pressure until the float valve drops. Carefully open the lid and check the internal temperature of the chicken using a meat thermometer, ensuring it reaches at least 165°F (74°C). 4. Use a slotted spoon to remove the chicken thighs, carrots, and raisins from the pot, and transfer them to a serving platter. Press the Cancel button. 5. In a small bowl, whisk together water and arrowroot to create a slurry. Add the slurry to the liquid in the Instant Pot®, stirring to combine. Press the Sauté button, then press the Adjust button to change the temperature to Less, and let the sauce simmer uncovered for about 3 minutes until thickened. Pour the sauce over the chicken and serve immediately.

Per Serving:
calories: 332 | fat: 14g | protein: 36g | carbs: 14g | fiber: 3g | sodium: 337mg

Balsamic Tomato Basil Chicken Thighs

Prep time: 15 minutes | Cook time: 17 minutes | Serves 6

- 1 pound (454 g) boneless, skinless chicken thighs
- ¼ teaspoon salt
- ¼ teaspoon ground black pepper
- ¼ teaspoon Italian seasoning
- 3 tablespoons olive oil
- 1 medium white onion, peeled and chopped
- 1 medium red bell pepper,
- seeded and chopped
- 2 cloves garlic, peeled and minced
- 4 medium tomatoes, seeded and diced
- ½ cup red wine
- ¼ cup balsamic vinegar
- ½ cup grated Parmesan cheese
- ¼ cup chopped fresh basil

1. Season chicken on both sides with salt, black pepper, and Italian seasoning. Press the Sauté button on the Instant Pot® and heat oil. Add chicken and brown well on both sides, about 4 minutes per side. Transfer chicken to a plate and set aside. 2. Add onion and bell pepper to the Instant Pot®. Cook until just tender, about 2 minutes. Add garlic and cook until fragrant, about 30 seconds.

Stir in tomatoes and wine, and scrape any brown bits from the bottom of the pot. Press the Cancel button. 3. Stir in chicken and balsamic vinegar. Close lid, set steam release to Sealing, press the Manual button, and set time to 6 minutes. When the timer beeps, let pressure release naturally, about 15 minutes. Press the Cancel button and open lid. Top with cheese and basil, and serve hot.

Per Serving:
calories: 239 | fat: 13g | protein: 20g | carbs: 8g | fiber: 1g | sodium: 447mg

Chicken in Mango Chutney

Prep time: 10 minutes | Cook time: 6 to 8 hours | Serves 2

- 12 ounces (340 g) boneless, skinless chicken thighs, cut into 1-inch pieces
- ½ cup thinly sliced red onion
- 1 cup canned mango or peaches, drained and diced
- 2 tablespoons golden raisins
- 2 tablespoons apple cider
- vinegar
- 1 teaspoon minced fresh ginger
- ¼ teaspoon red pepper flakes
- 1 teaspoon curry powder
- ¼ teaspoon ground cinnamon
- ⅛ teaspoon sea salt

1. Add all the ingredients to the slow cooker and gently stir to ensure everything is well combined. 2. Cover with the lid and cook on Low heat for 6 to 8 hours. The chutney should be thick and sweet while the chicken should be tender and fully cooked through by the end of the cooking time.

Per Serving:
calories: 278 | fat: 8g | protein: 35g | carbs: 17g | fiber: 3g | sodium: 320mg

Herbed Garlic Chicken with Wine Sauce and Couscous

Prep time: 10 minutes | Cook time: 3½ hours | Serves 4

- 1 whole chicken, 3½ to 4 pounds(1.6 to 1.8 kg), cut into 6 to 8 pieces and patted dry
- Coarse sea salt
- Black pepper
- 1 tablespoon extra-virgin olive oil
- 1 medium yellow onion, halved and thinly sliced
- 6 cloves garlic, halved
- 2 teaspoons dried thyme
- 1 cup dry white wine
- ⅓ cup all-purpose flour
- 1 cup uncooked couscous
- ¼ chopped fresh parsley

1. Season the chicken with salt and pepper. 2. In a large skillet, heat the oil over medium-high heat. Add the chicken skin-side down and cook in batches until the skin is golden brown, about 4 minutes. Turn and cook an additional 2 minutes. 3. Add the onion, garlic, and thyme to the slow cooker. 4. Top the contents of slow cooker with chicken, skin-side up, in a tight layer. 5. In a small bowl, whisk together the wine and the flour until smooth, and add to the slow cooker. 6. Cover and cook until the chicken is tender, about 3½ hours on high or 7 hours on low. 7. Cook the couscous according to package instructions. 8. Serve the chicken and sauce hot over the couscous, sprinkled with parsley.

Per Serving:
calories: 663 | fat: 38g | protein: 46g | carbs: 21g | fiber: 1g | sodium: 166mg

Chicken Cutlets with Greek Salsa

Prep time: 15 minutes | Cook time: 15 minutes | Serves 2

- 2 tablespoons olive oil, divided
- ¼ teaspoon salt, plus additional to taste
- Zest of ½ lemon
- Juice of ½ lemon
- 8 ounces (227 g) chicken cutlets, or chicken breast sliced through the middle to make 2 thin pieces
- 1 cup cherry or grape tomatoes, halved or quartered (about 4 ounces / 113 g)
- ½ cup minced red onion (about ⅓ medium onion)
- 1 medium cucumber, peeled, seeded and diced (about 1 cup)
- 5 to 10 pitted Greek olives, minced (more or less depending on size and your taste)
- 1 tablespoon minced fresh parsley
- 1 tablespoon minced fresh oregano
- 1 tablespoon minced fresh mint
- 1 ounce (28 g) crumbled feta cheese
- 1 tablespoon red wine vinegar

1. In a medium bowl, mix together 1 tablespoon of olive oil, salt, lemon zest, and lemon juice. Add the chicken pieces, coating them well, and let them marinate while you prepare the salsa. 2. In a small bowl, combine the tomatoes, onion, cucumber, olives, parsley, oregano, mint, feta cheese, and red wine vinegar. Toss lightly to mix. Cover and refrigerate the salsa for at least 30 minutes to allow the flavors to meld. Taste and adjust seasoning with salt or additional herbs as needed before serving. 3. To cook the chicken, heat the remaining 1 tablespoon of olive oil in a large nonstick skillet over medium-high heat. Add the marinated chicken pieces, cooking for 3 to 6 minutes on each side, depending on the thickness. Avoid flipping the chicken until it naturally releases from the pan, which indicates it's ready to turn. 4. Once the chicken is cooked through, top it with the chilled salsa and serve immediately.

Per Serving:
calories: 357 | fat: 23g | protein: 31g | carbs: 8g | fiber: 2g | sodium: 202mg

Moroccan Chicken Stew with Green Olives and Couscous

Prep time: 15 minutes | Cook time: 4 hours | Serves 4

- 1 (28-ounce / 794-g) can diced tomatoes, drained
- 1 cup chicken stock
- 1 large yellow onion, sliced
- 1 garlic clove, minced
- 1 teaspoon ground cumin
- 1 teaspoon paprika
- ½ teaspoon ground turmeric
- 1 tablespoon olive oil
- 1 (3-pound / 1.4-kg) skinless
- quartered chicken
- ½ teaspoon black pepper
- ¼ teaspoon sea salt
- ½ cup red wine
- ½ cup pitted green olives
- Zest of 1 lemon
- 2 cups hot cooked couscous
- ¼ cup sliced almonds, toasted

1. Place the tomatoes, stock, onion, and garlic into the slow cooker. Sprinkle in the cumin, paprika, and turmeric. 2. Heat a large skillet over medium-high heat. Add the olive oil and swirl to coat the pan. 3. Sprinkle the chicken with the pepper and salt. Add the chicken to pan. Cook the chicken about 8 minutes, browning on all sides. Place in the slow cooker. 4. Pour the wine into the skillet, scraping the pan with a wooden spoon to loosen the flavorful browned bits on the bottom. Pour the liquid into the slow cooker. 5. Cover and cook on high for 4 hours. At 30 minutes before the end of the cooking time, stir in the olives and lemon zest. 6. Remove the chicken from the slow cooker, place on a plate, and cool. Remove the meat from the bones and return it to the slow cooker. Discard bones. 7. Serve the chicken stew hot over the couscous, and sprinkle with the toasted almonds.

Per Serving:
calories: 630 | fat: 15g | protein: 83g | carbs: 34g | fiber: 7g | sodium: 487mg

Chicken with Artichokes

Prep time: 10 minutes | Cook time: 20 minutes | Serves 4

- 1 cup chicken broth
- 2 tablespoons all-purpose flour
- 4 tablespoons olive oil, divided
- 1½ teaspoons grated lemon zest
- 2 tablespoons lemon juice, divided
- 3 cloves garlic, minced, divided
- 4 (6-ounce / 170-g) skinless, boneless chicken breast halves
- ¼ teaspoon salt
- ¼ teaspoon freshly ground black pepper
- 2 shallots, thinly sliced
- 1 tablespoon chopped fresh rosemary
- 2 ounces (57 g) pancetta, finely chopped
- ½ cup dry sherry
- 2 cups artichoke hearts, quartered frozen (thawed), or canned (drained and rinsed)
- 4 teaspoons chopped fresh flat-leaf parsley, divided

1. In a small bowl, whisk together the broth and flour until smooth. Set aside. 2. In a medium bowl, mix together 1 tablespoon of olive oil, lemon zest, 4 teaspoons of lemon juice, and 1 clove of minced garlic. Add the chicken pieces and turn them to coat well. Let the chicken marinate at room temperature for 30 minutes. 3. After marinating, drain the chicken and discard the marinade. Season the chicken evenly with salt and black pepper. Heat 2 tablespoons of olive oil in a large skillet over medium-high heat. Add the chicken and cook for about 5 minutes per side, until browned and fully cooked through. Transfer the cooked chicken to a plate. 4. Reduce the heat to medium and add the remaining 1 tablespoon of olive oil to the skillet. Add the shallots, rosemary, and pancetta, cooking until the shallots are softened, about 3 minutes. Add the remaining 2 cloves of minced garlic and cook, stirring constantly, for an additional 30 seconds. 5. Pour in the sherry, stirring well, and cook until it has mostly evaporated, about 4 minutes. Stir in the broth and flour mixture, and bring the sauce to a near boil. Add the artichoke hearts, cooking for about 1 more minute until the sauce thickens. Stir in the remaining 2 teaspoons of lemon juice and 2 teaspoons of chopped parsley. Return the chicken to the skillet, letting it cook for another 1 to 2 minutes until heated through. Serve the chicken hot, garnished with the remaining parsley.

Per Serving:
calories: 498 | fat: 27g | protein: 48g | carbs: 15g | fiber: 5g | sodium: 806mg

Turkey Meatloaf

- 8 ounces (227 g) sliced mushrooms
- 1 small onion, coarsely chopped
- 2 cloves garlic
- 1½ pounds (680 g) 85% lean ground turkey
- 2 eggs, lightly beaten
- 1 tablespoon tomato paste
- ¼ cup almond meal
- 2 tablespoons almond milk
- 1 tablespoon dried oregano
- 1 teaspoon salt
- ½ teaspoon freshly ground black pepper
- 1 Roma tomato, thinly sliced

1. Preheat your air fryer to 350°F (177°C). Lightly coat a round baking pan with olive oil and set it aside. 2. In a food processor with a metal blade attachment, combine the mushrooms, onion, and garlic. Pulse until the vegetables are finely chopped, then transfer the mixture to a large mixing bowl. 3. Add the ground turkey, eggs, tomato paste, almond meal, milk, oregano, salt, and black pepper to the bowl. Mix gently until everything is well combined, taking care not to overmix. Transfer the mixture to the prepared baking pan and shape it into a loaf. Arrange the tomato slices on top of the loaf. 4. Place the pan in the preheated air fryer and cook for about 50 minutes, or until the meatloaf is browned and an instant-read thermometer inserted into the center reads 165°F (74°C). Once cooked, remove the meatloaf from the air fryer and allow it to rest for about 10 minutes before slicing. Serve warm.

Per Serving:
calories: 353 | fat: 20g | protein: 38g | carbs: 7g | fiber: 2g | sodium: 625mg

Air-Fried Pesto Chicken Parm

- 2 large eggs
- 1 tablespoon water
- Fine sea salt and ground black pepper, to taste
- 1 cup powdered Parmesan cheese (about 3 ounces / 85 g)
- 2 teaspoons Italian seasoning
- 4 (5-ounce / 142-g) boneless, skinless chicken breasts or thighs,
- pounded to ¼ inch thick
- 1 cup pesto
- 1 cup shredded Mozzarella cheese (about 4 ounces / 113 g)
- Finely chopped fresh basil, for garnish (optional)
- Grape tomatoes, halved, for serving (optional)

1. Spray the air fryer basket with avocado oil. Preheat the air fryer to 400°F (204°C). 2. Crack the eggs into a shallow baking dish, add the water and a pinch each of salt and pepper, and whisk to combine. In another shallow baking dish, stir together the Parmesan and Italian seasoning until well combined. 3. Season the chicken breasts well on both sides with salt and pepper. Dip one chicken breast in the eggs and let any excess drip off, then dredge both sides of the breast in the Parmesan mixture. Spray the breast with avocado oil and place it in the air fryer basket. Repeat with the remaining 3 chicken breasts. 4. Air fry the chicken in the air fryer for 20 minutes, or until the internal temperature reaches 165°F (74°C) and the breading is golden brown, flipping halfway through. 5. Dollop each chicken breast with ¼ cup of the pesto and top with the Mozzarella. Return the breasts to the air fryer and cook for 3 minutes, or until the cheese is melted. Garnish with basil and serve with halved grape tomatoes on the side, if desired. 6. Store leftovers in an airtight container in the refrigerator for up to 4 days. Reheat in a preheated 400°F (204°C) air fryer for 5 minutes, or until warmed through.

Per Serving:
calories: 631 | fat: 45g | protein: 52g | carbs: 4g | fiber: 0g | sodium: 607mg

Asian-Style Hoisin Turkey Burgers

- Olive oil
- 1 pound (454 g) lean ground turkey
- ¼ cup whole-wheat bread crumbs
- ¼ cup hoisin sauce
- 2 tablespoons soy sauce
- 4 whole-wheat buns

1. Spray the air fryer basket lightly with olive oil. 2. In a large bowl, mix together the turkey, bread crumbs, hoisin sauce, and soy sauce. 3. Form the mixture into 4 equal patties. Cover with plastic wrap and refrigerate the patties for 30 minutes. 4. Place the patties in the air fryer basket in a single layer. Spray the patties lightly with olive oil. 5. Air fry at 370°F (188°C) for 10 minutes. Flip the patties over, lightly spray with olive oil, and cook until golden brown, an additional 5 to 10 minutes. 6. Place the patties on buns and top with your choice of low-calorie burger toppings like sliced tomatoes, onions, and cabbage slaw.

Per Serving:
calories: 330 | fat: 13g | protein: 26g | carbs: 29g | fiber: 3g | sodium: 631mg

Roasted Lemon Chicken with Artichokes and Crispy Kale

Prep time: 15 minutes | Cook time: 35 minutes | Serves 4

- 3 tablespoons extra-virgin olive oil, divided
- 2 tablespoons lemon juice
- Zest of 1 lemon
- 2 garlic cloves, minced
- 2 teaspoons dried rosemary
- ½ teaspoon kosher salt
- ¼ teaspoon freshly ground black pepper
- 1½ pounds (680 g) boneless, skinless chicken breast
- 2 (14-ounce / 397-g) cans artichoke hearts, drained
- 1 bunch (about 6 ounces / 170 g) lacinato kale, stemmed and torn or chopped into pieces

1. In a large bowl or zip-top bag, combine 2 tablespoons of the olive oil, the lemon juice, lemon zest, garlic, rosemary, salt, and black pepper. Mix well and then add the chicken and artichokes. Marinate for at least 30 minutes, and up to 4 hours in the refrigerator. 2. Preheat the oven to 350ºF (180ºC). Line a baking sheet with parchment paper or foil. Remove the chicken and artichokes from the marinade and spread them in a single layer on the baking sheet. Roast for 15 minutes, turn the chicken over, and roast another 15 minutes. Remove the baking sheet and put the chicken, artichokes, and juices on a platter or large plate. Tent with foil to keep warm. 3. Change the oven temperature to broil. In a large bowl, combine the kale with the remaining 1 tablespoon of the olive oil. Arrange the kale on the baking sheet and broil until golden brown in spots and as crispy as you like, about 3 to 5 minutes. Place the kale on top of the chicken and artichokes.

Per Serving:

calories: 430 | fat: 16g | protein: 46g | carbs: 29g | fiber: 19g | sodium: 350mg

Chicken Skewers

Prep time: 10 minutes | Cook time: 7 minutes | Serves 4

- ¼ cup olive oil
- Zest of 1 lemon
- Juice of 2 lemons
- 2 tablespoons dried oregano
- 1 tablespoon dried thyme
- 2 garlic cloves, minced
- Sea salt
- Freshly ground black pepper
- 3 pounds (1.4 kg) boneless, skinless chicken breasts, cut into 2-inch cubes

1. In a large bowl, combine the olive oil, lemon zest, lemon juice, oregano, thyme, and minced garlic. Season generously with salt and black pepper, then stir until well mixed. Add the chicken pieces to the bowl, tossing until they are well coated in the marinade. Cover the bowl and refrigerate for 20 to 30 minutes to allow the flavors to develop. 2. After marinating, remove the chicken from the refrigerator and thread the pieces onto skewers, using about 4 to 5 pieces per skewer. 3. Heat a cast-iron skillet over medium-high heat. Working in batches, add about 3 skewers to the skillet at a time and cook, turning frequently, for 5 to 7 minutes or until the chicken is thoroughly cooked and reaches an internal temperature of 165ºF (74ºC). Repeat with the remaining skewers. Serve hot and enjoy.

Per Serving:

calories: 504 | fat: 19g | protein: 76g | carbs: 4g | fiber: 1g | sodium: 214mg

Chapter 9

Snacks and Appetizers

Chapter 9 Snacks and Appetizers

Dijon Salmon Niçoise with Chive Vinaigrette

Prep time: 10 minutes | Cook time: 20 minutes | Serves 4

- 1 pound (454 g) baby or fingerling potatoes
- ½ pound (227 g) green beans
- 6 tablespoons olive oil
- 4 (4-ounce / 113-g) salmon fillets
- ¼ teaspoon freshly ground black pepper
- 2 teaspoons Dijon mustard
- 3 tablespoons red wine vinegar
- 1 tablespoon, plus 1 teaspoon finely chopped fresh chives
- 1 head romaine lettuce, sliced cross-wise
- 2 hard-boiled eggs, quartered
- ¼ cup Niçoise or other small black olives
- 1 cup cherry tomatoes, quartered

1. Put potatoes in a large saucepan and add cold water to cover. Bring the water to a boil, then reduce the heat to maintain a simmer and cook for 12 to 15 minutes, until fork-tender. Drain and set aside until cool enough to handle, then cut into cubes. Set aside. 2. Meanwhile, bring a medium saucepan of water to a boil. Add the green beans and cook for 3 minutes. Drain and rinse with cold water to stop the cooking. Set aside. 3. In a large skillet, heat 1 tablespoon of the olive oil over medium-high heat. Season the salmon with pepper. Add the salmon to the pan and cook for 4 to 5 minutes on each side. Transfer to a platter; keep warm. 4. In a small bowl, whisk together the mustard, vinegar, 1 tablespoon of chives, and remaining 5 tablespoons olive oil. 5. Divide the lettuce evenly among four plates. Add 1 salmon fillet to each plate. Divide the potatoes, green beans, eggs, olives, and tomatoes among the plates and drizzle with the dressing. 6.Sprinkle with the remaining 1 teaspoon chives and serve.

Per Serving:
1 cup: calories: 398 | fat: 25g | protein: 15g | carbs: 30g | fiber: 8g | sodium: 173mg

Spicy Roasted Potatoes

Prep time: 20 minutes | Cook time: 25 minutes | Serves 5

- 1½ pounds (680 g) red potatoes or gold potatoes
- 3 tablespoons garlic, minced
- 1½ teaspoons salt
- ¼ cup extra-virgin olive oil
- ½ cup fresh cilantro,
- chopped
- ½ teaspoon freshly ground black pepper
- ¼ teaspoon cayenne pepper
- 3 tablespoons lemon juice

1. Begin by setting the oven to 450°F (235ºC) to heat up. 2. Give the potatoes a thorough scrub and dry them off with a towel. 3. Chop the potatoes into ½-inch cubes and transfer them to a mixing bowl. 4. Sprinkle in the garlic, salt, and drizzle with olive oil, then toss everything together to ensure the potatoes are fully coated. 5. Spread the potatoes evenly on a baking sheet and slide them into the oven to roast for 25 minutes. Halfway through, use a spatula to flip them, then continue roasting until the edges turn golden and crispy. 6. Once done, take the potatoes out of the oven and let them rest on the sheet for about 5 minutes. 7. Use a spatula to lift the potatoes off the sheet and into a separate bowl. 8. Stir in the cilantro, black pepper, cayenne, and a squeeze of lemon juice, tossing to combine everything evenly. 9. Serve immediately while warm.

Per Serving:
calories: 203 | fat: 11g | protein: 3g | carbs: 24g | fiber: 3g | sodium: 728mg

Sumac-Spiced Red Lentil Dip

Prep time: 5 minutes | Cook time: 20 minutes | Serves 6 to 8

- 1 cup red lentils, picked through and rinsed
- 1 teaspoon ground sumac
- ½ teaspoon salt
- Pita chips, warm pita bread, or raw vegetables, for serving

1. In a medium saucepan, combine the lentils, sumac, and 2 cups water. Bring the water to a boil. Reduce the heat to maintain a simmer and cook for 15 minutes, or until the lentils are softened and most of the water has been absorbed. Stir in the salt and cook until the lentils have absorbed all the water, about 5 minutes more. 2. Serve with pita chips, warm pita bread, or as a dip for raw vegetables.

Per Serving:
1 cup: calories: 162 | fat: 1g | protein: 11g | carbs: 30g | fiber: 9g | sodium: 219mg

Citrus-Infused Melon Salad

Prep time: 5 minutes | Cook time: 0 minutes | Serves 4

- 2 cups cubed melon, such as Crenshaw, Sharlyn, or honeydew
- 2 cups cubed cantaloupe
- ½ cup freshly squeezed
- orange juice
- ¼ cup freshly squeezed lime juice
- 1 tablespoon orange zest

1. In a large bowl, combine the melon cubes. In a small bowl, whisk together the orange juice, lime juice, and orange zest and pour over the fruit. 2. Cover and refrigerate for at least 4 hours, stirring occasionally. Serve chilled.

Per Serving:
calories: 80 | fat: 0g | protein: 2g | carbs: 20g | fiber: 2g | sodium: 30mg

Tuna Croquettes

Prep time: 40 minutes | Cook time: 25 minutes | Makes 36 croquettes

- 6 tablespoons extra-virgin olive oil, plus 1 to 2 cups
- 5 tablespoons almond flour, plus 1 cup, divided
- 1¼ cups heavy cream
- 1 (4 ounces / 113 g) can olive oil-packed yellowfin tuna
- 1 tablespoon chopped red onion
- 2 teaspoons minced capers
- ½ teaspoon dried dill
- ¼ teaspoon freshly ground black pepper
- 2 large eggs
- 1 cup panko breadcrumbs (or a gluten-free version)

1. Heat 6 tablespoons of olive oil in a large skillet over medium-low heat. Add 5 tablespoons of almond flour and cook, stirring constantly, until the mixture forms a smooth paste and the flour slightly browns, about 2 to 3 minutes. 2. Raise the heat to medium-high and gradually whisk in the heavy cream, continuing to stir until the sauce thickens and becomes smooth, about 4 to 5 minutes. 3. Remove from heat and mix in the tuna, red onion, capers, dill, and pepper. 4. Transfer the mixture to a well-oiled 8-inch square baking dish and let it cool to room temperature. Once cooled, cover and refrigerate for at least 4 hours or overnight. 5. For the croquettes, prepare three bowls: beat the eggs in one, add the remaining almond flour to another, and place the panko in the third. Line a baking sheet with parchment paper. 6. Scoop about a tablespoon of the chilled mixture and roll it in the almond flour to coat. Shake off the excess and shape the mixture into an oval. 7. Dip each croquette into the beaten egg and coat it lightly with panko before placing it on the prepared baking sheet. Repeat until all the dough is used. 8. In a small saucepan, heat 1 to 2 cups of olive oil over medium-high heat, making sure the oil is about 1 inch deep. Adjust the amount of oil depending on the size of your pan, adding more for each batch. 9. To check if the oil is ready, drop a pinch of panko into the oil. If it sizzles, it's hot enough; if it sinks, wait a little longer. Fry the croquettes in batches of 3 to 4, depending on your pan size, until golden brown, using a slotted spoon to remove them. Adjust the oil temperature as needed to prevent burning, lowering the heat if the croquettes brown too quickly.

Per Serving:

2 croquettes: calories: 271 | fat: 26g | protein: 5g | carbs: 6g | fiber: 1g | sodium: 89mg

Herb-Infused Steamed Artichokes with Lemon Garlic Dip

Prep time: 10 minutes | Cook time: 10 minutes | Serves 6

- 3 medium artichokes with stems cut off
- 1 medium lemon, halved
- 1 cup water
- ¼ cup lemon juice
- ⅓ cup extra-virgin olive oil
- 1 clove garlic, peeled and minced
- ¼ teaspoon salt
- 1 teaspoon chopped fresh oregano
- 1 teaspoon chopped fresh rosemary
- 1 teaspoon chopped fresh flat-leaf parsley
- 1 teaspoon fresh thyme leaves

1. Run artichokes under running water, making sure water runs between leaves to flush out any debris. Slice off top ⅓ of artichoke and pull away any tough outer leaves. Rub all cut surfaces with lemon. 2. Add water and lemon juice to the Instant Pot®, then add rack. Place artichokes upside down on rack. Close lid, set steam release to Sealing, press the Manual button, and set time to 10 minutes. When the timer beeps, let pressure release naturally, about 20 minutes. 3. Press the Cancel button and open lid. Remove artichokes, transfer to a cutting board, and slice in half. Place halves on a serving platter. 4. In a small bowl, combine oil, garlic, salt, oregano, rosemary, parsley, and thyme. Drizzle half of mixture over artichokes, then serve remaining mixture in a small bowl for dipping. Serve warm.

Per Serving:

calories: 137 | fat: 13g | protein: 2g | carbs: 7g | fiber: 4g | sodium: 158mg

Greens Chips with Curried Yogurt Sauce

Prep time: 10 minutes | Cook time: 5 to 6 minutes | Serves 4

- 1 cup low-fat Greek yogurt
- 1 tablespoon freshly squeezed lemon juice
- 1 tablespoon curry powder
- ½ bunch curly kale, stemmed, ribs removed and discarded, leaves cut into 2-
- to 3-inch pieces
- ½ bunch chard, stemmed, ribs removed and discarded, leaves cut into 2- to 3-inch pieces
- 1½ teaspoons olive oil

1. In a small bowl, mix the yogurt, lemon juice, and curry powder until smooth, then set aside. 2. In a large bowl, combine the kale and chard with olive oil, massaging the oil into the leaves with your hands to help soften the fibers, making the chips tender once cooked. 3. Working in batches, air fry the greens at 390ºF (199ºC) for 5 to 6 minutes, shaking the basket halfway through to ensure even crisping. Serve the crispy greens with the yogurt dipping sauce on the side.

Per Serving:

calories: 98 | fat: 4g | protein: 7g | carbs: 13g | fiber: 4g | sodium: 186mg

Quick Garlic Mushrooms

Prep time: 10 minutes | Cook time: 10 minutes | Serves 4 to 6

- 2 pounds (907 g) cremini mushrooms, cleaned
- 3 tablespoons unsalted butter
- 2 tablespoons garlic, minced
- ½ teaspoon salt
- ½ teaspoon freshly ground black pepper

1. Slice each mushroom in half from stem to top and place them in a bowl. 2. Heat a large sauté pan or skillet over medium heat. 3. Melt the butter in the pan and add the garlic, cooking for about 2 minutes while stirring occasionally. 4. Add the mushrooms and salt to the pan, tossing them in the garlic butter mixture. Cook for 7 to 8 minutes, stirring every 2 minutes to ensure even cooking. 5. Transfer the cooked mushrooms to a serving dish and sprinkle with black pepper before serving.

Per Serving:

calories: 183 | fat: 9g | protein: 9g | carbs: 10g | fiber: 3g | sodium: 334mg

Crispy Five-Spice Air-Fried Chicken Wings

Prep time: 30 minutes | Cook time: 13 to 15 minutes | Serves 4

- 2 pounds (907 g) chicken wings
- ½ cup Asian-style salad dressing
- 2 tablespoons Chinese five-spice powder

1. Cut off wing tips and discard or freeze for stock. Cut remaining wing pieces in two at the joint. 2. Place wing pieces in a large sealable plastic bag. Pour in the Asian dressing, seal bag, and massage the marinade into the wings until well coated. Refrigerate for at least an hour. 3. Remove wings from bag, drain off excess marinade, and place wings in air fryer basket. 4. Air fry at 360°F (182°C) for 13 to 15 minutes or until juices run clear. About halfway through cooking time, shake the basket or stir wings for more even cooking. 5. Transfer cooked wings to plate in a single layer. Sprinkle half of the Chinese five-spice powder on the wings, turn, and sprinkle other side with remaining seasoning.

Per Serving:
calories: 357 | fat: 12g | protein: 51g | carbs: 9g | fiber: 2g | sodium: 591mg

Tirokafteri (Spicy Feta and Yogurt Dip)

Prep time: 10 minutes | Cook time: 0 minutes | Serves 8

- 1 teaspoon red wine vinegar
- 1 small green chili, seeded and sliced
- 2 teaspoons extra virgin
- olive oil
- 9 ounces (255 g) full-fat feta
- ¾ cup full-fat Greek yogurt

1. In a food processor, blend together the vinegar, chili, and olive oil until smooth. 2. In a small bowl, mash the feta and Greek yogurt with a fork until they form a smooth paste. Stir in the pepper mixture and mix until fully combined. 3. Cover the bowl and refrigerate for at least 1 hour before serving. This dip can be stored in the fridge, covered, for up to 3 days.

Per Serving:
calories: 109 | fat: 8g | protein: 6g | carbs: 4g | fiber: 0g | sodium: 311mg

Greek Street Tacos

Prep time: 10 minutes | Cook time: 3 minutes | Makes 8 small tacos

- 8 small flour tortillas (4-inch diameter)
- 8 tablespoons hummus
- 4 tablespoons crumbled feta cheese
- 4 tablespoons chopped kalamata or other olives (optional)
- Olive oil for misting

1. Spoon 1 tablespoon of hummus or tapenade onto the center of each tortilla. Top with 1 teaspoon of feta crumbles and 1 teaspoon of chopped olives, if desired. 2. Moisten the edges of the tortilla with water using your finger or a small spoon. 3. Fold the tortilla in half to form a half-moon shape, gently pressing the center, then firmly press the edges to seal in the filling. 4. Lightly mist both sides of the tortilla with olive oil. 5. Arrange the filled tortillas in the air fryer basket, placing them close together but not overlapping. 6. Air fry at 390ºF (199ºC) for 3 minutes, or until they are lightly browned and crispy.

Per Serving:
1 taco: calories: 127 | fat: 4g | protein: 4g | carbs: 19g | fiber: 1g | sodium: 292mg

Manchego Crackers

Prep time: 15 minutes | Cook time: 15 minutes | Makes 40 crackers

- 4 tablespoons butter, at room temperature
- 1 cup finely shredded Manchego cheese
- 1 cup almond flour
- 1 teaspoon salt, divided
- ¼ teaspoon freshly ground black pepper
- 1 large egg

1. Beat the butter and shredded cheese together with an electric mixer until smooth and fully blended. 2. In a separate small bowl, mix the almond flour with ½ teaspoon of salt and pepper. Gradually add this dry mixture to the cheese, stirring until the dough forms into a ball. 3. Place the dough on a piece of parchment or plastic wrap and roll it into a log about 1½ inches thick. Tightly wrap and chill for at least 1 hour. 4. Preheat your oven to 350°F (180°C) and line two baking sheets with parchment paper or silicone mats. 5. To make the egg wash, whisk together the egg and remaining ½ teaspoon of salt in a small bowl. 6. After the dough has chilled, slice it into rounds about ¼ inch thick and arrange them on the prepared baking sheets. 7. Brush the tops of each round with the egg wash and bake for 12 to 15 minutes, or until golden and crispy. Let the crackers cool on a wire rack. 8. Serve the crackers warm, or once fully cooled, store them in an airtight container in the refrigerator for up to a week.

Per Serving:
2 crackers: calories: 73 | fat: 7g | protein: 3g | carbs: 1g | fiber: 1g | sodium: 154mg

Crispy Lemon-Pepper Air-Fried Drumsticks

Prep time: 30 minutes | Cook time: 30 minutes | Serves 2

- 2 teaspoons freshly ground coarse black pepper
- 1 teaspoon baking powder
- ½ teaspoon garlic powder
- 4 chicken drumsticks (4 ounces / 113 g each)
- Kosher salt, to taste
- 1 lemon

1. In a small bowl, stir together the pepper, baking powder, and garlic powder. Place the drumsticks on a plate and sprinkle evenly with the baking powder mixture, turning the drumsticks so they're well coated. Let the drumsticks stand in the refrigerator for at least 1 hour or up to overnight. 2. Sprinkle the drumsticks with salt, then transfer them to the air fryer, standing them bone-end up and leaning against the wall of the air fryer basket. Air fry at 375ºF (191°C) until cooked through and crisp on the outside, about 30 minutes. 3. Transfer the drumsticks to a serving platter and finely grate the zest of the lemon over them while they're hot. Cut the lemon into wedges and serve with the warm drumsticks.

Per Serving:
calories: 438 | fat: 24g | protein: 48g | carbs: 6g | fiber: 2g | sodium: 279mg

Cheese-Stuffed Dates

Prep time: 10 minutes | Cook time: 10 minutes
| Serves 4

- 2 ounces (57 g) low-fat cream cheese, at room temperature
- 2 tablespoons sweet pickle relish
- 1 tablespoon low-fat plain Greek yogurt
- 1 teaspoon finely chopped fresh chives
- ¼ teaspoon kosher salt
- ⅛ teaspoon ground black pepper
- Dash of hot sauce
- 2 tablespoons pistachios, chopped
- 8 Medjool dates, pitted and halved

1. In a small bowl, combine the cream cheese, relish, yogurt, chives, salt, pepper, and hot sauce, stirring until smooth. 2. Place the pistachios on a clean plate. Transfer the cream cheese mixture into a resealable plastic bag and snip off one corner. Pipe the mixture into the date halves, then gently press the tops into the pistachios to coat.

Per Serving:
calories: 196 | fat: 4g | protein: 3g | carbs: 41g | fiber: 4g | sodium: 294mg

Baked Spinach Ricotta Bites with Basil

Prep time: 15 minutes | Cook time: 2 minutes |
Serves 4

- 1½ tablespoons extra virgin olive oil
- 1 garlic clove
- 9 ounces (255 g) fresh baby leaf spinach, washed
- 3 spring onions (white parts only), thinly sliced
- 9 ounces (255 g) ricotta, drained
- 1¾ ounces (50 g) grated Parmesan cheese
- 2 tablespoons chopped fresh basil
- ¾ teaspoon salt, divided
- ¼ teaspoon plus a pinch of freshly ground black pepper, divided
- 4½ tablespoons plus ⅓ cup unseasoned breadcrumbs, divided
- 1 egg

1. Preheat the oven to 400°F (205°C). Line a large baking pan with parchment paper. 2. Add the olive oil and garlic clove to a large pan over medium heat. When the oil begins to shimmer, add the spinach and sauté, tossing continuously, until the spinach starts to wilt, then add the spring onions. Continue tossing and sautéing until most of the liquid has evaporated, about 6 minutes, then transfer the spinach and onion mixture to a colander to drain and cool for 10 minutes. 3. When the spinach mixture has cooled, discard the garlic clove and squeeze the spinach to remove as much of the liquid as possible. Transfer the spinach mixture to a cutting board and finely chop. 4. Combine the ricotta, Parmesan, basil, ½ teaspoon of the salt, and ¼ teaspoon of the black pepper in a large bowl. Use a fork to mash the ingredients together, then add the spinach and continue mixing until the ingredients are combined. Add 4½ tablespoons of the breadcrumbs and mix until all ingredients are well combined. 5. In a small bowl, whisk the egg with the remaining ¼ teaspoon salt and a pinch of the black pepper. Place the remaining ⅓ cup of breadcrumbs on a small plate. Scoop out 1 tablespoon of the spinach mixture and roll it into a smooth ball, then dip it in the egg mixture and then roll it in the breadcrumbs. Place the ball on the prepared baking pan and continue the process with the remaining spinach mixture. 6. Bake for 16–20 minutes or until the balls turn a light golden brown. Remove the balls from the oven and serve promptly. Store covered in the refrigerator for up to 1 day. (Reheat before serving.)

Per Serving:
calories: 311 | fat: 19g | protein: 18g | carbs: 18g | fiber: 3g | sodium: 684mg

Heart-Healthy Nut and Fruit Trail Mix

Prep time: 15 minutes | Cook time: 30 minutes
| Serves 10

- 1 cup raw almonds
- 1 cup walnut halves
- 1 cup pumpkin seeds
- 1 cup dried apricots, cut into thin strips
- 1 cup dried cherries, roughly
- chopped
- 1 cup golden raisins
- 2 tablespoons extra-virgin olive oil
- 1 teaspoon salt

1. Preheat the oven to 300°F(150°C). Line a baking sheet with aluminum foil. 2. In a large bowl, combine the almonds, walnuts, pumpkin seeds, apricots, cherries, and raisins. Pour the olive oil over all and toss well with clean hands. Add salt and toss again to distribute. 3. Pour the nut mixture onto the baking sheet in a single layer and bake until the fruits begin to brown, about 30 minutes. Cool on the baking sheet to room temperature. 4. Store in a large airtight container or zipper-top plastic bag.

Per Serving:
calories: 346 | fat: 20g | protein: 8g | carbs: 39g | fiber: 5g | sodium: 240mg

Mascarpone-Stuffed Dates with Toasted Pecans

Prep time: 15 minutes | Cook time: 10 minutes
| Serves 12 to 15

- 1 cup pecans, shells removed
- 1 (8-ounce / 227-g)
- container mascarpone cheese
- 20 Medjool dates

1. Preheat the oven to 350°F(180°C). Put the pecans on a baking sheet and bake for 5 to 6 minutes, until lightly toasted and aromatic. Take the pecans out of the oven and let cool for 5 minutes. 2. Once cooled, put the pecans in a food processor fitted with a chopping blade and chop until they resemble the texture of bulgur wheat or coarse sugar. 3. Reserve ¼ cup of ground pecans in a small bowl. Pour the remaining chopped pecans into a larger bowl and add the mascarpone cheese. 4. Using a spatula, mix the cheese with the pecans until evenly combined. 5. Spoon the cheese mixture into a piping bag. 6. Using a knife, cut one side of the date lengthwise, from the stem to the bottom. Gently open and remove the pit. 7. Using the piping bag, squeeze a generous amount of the cheese mixture into the date where the pit used to be. Close up the date and repeat with the remaining dates. 8. Dip any exposed cheese from the stuffed dates into the reserved chopped pecans to cover it up. 9. Set the dates on a serving plate; serve immediately or chill in the fridge until you are ready to serve.

Per Serving:
calories: 253 | fat: 4g | protein: 2g | carbs: 31g | fiber: 4g | sodium: 7mg

Stuffed Cucumber Cups

Prep time: 5 minutes | Cook time: 0 minutes | Serves 2

- 1 medium cucumber (about 8 ounces / 227 g, 8 to 9 inches long)
- ½ cup hummus (any flavor) or white bean dip
- 4 or 5 cherry tomatoes, sliced in half
- 2 tablespoons fresh basil, minced

1. Cut off both ends of the cucumber (about ½ inch from each side) and slice it into 1-inch thick pieces. 2. Using a paring knife or spoon, carefully scoop out the seeds from each cucumber slice to create a small cup, making sure not to cut all the way through. 3. Spoon about 1 tablespoon of hummus or bean dip into each cucumber cup. 4. Garnish each with a cherry tomato half and a light sprinkle of freshly minced basil.

Per Serving:
calories: 135 | fat: 6g | protein: 6g | carbs: 16g | fiber: 5g | sodium: 242mg

Pesto-Stuffed Cucumber Boats

Prep time: 10 minutes | Cook time: 0 minutes | Serves 4 to 6

- 3 medium cucumbers
- ¼ teaspoon salt
- 1 packed cup fresh basil leaves
- 1 garlic clove, minced
- ¼ cup walnut pieces
- ¼ cup grated Parmesan cheese
- ¼ cup extra-virgin olive oil
- ½ teaspoon paprika

1. Cut each cucumber in half lengthwise and again in half crosswise to make 4 stocky pieces. Use a spoon to remove the seeds and hollow out a shallow trough in each piece. Lightly salt each piece and set aside on a platter. 2. In a blender or food processor, combine the basil, garlic, walnuts, Parmesan cheese, and olive oil and blend until smooth. 3. Use a spoon to spread pesto into each cucumber "boat" and sprinkle each with paprika. Serve.

Per Serving:
calories: 143 | fat: 14g | protein: 3g | carbs: 4g | fiber: 1g | sodium: 175mg

Spanish Home Fries with Spicy Tomato Sauce

Prep time: 5 minutes | Cook time: 1 hour | Serves 6

- 4 russet potatoes, peeled, cut into large dice
- ¼ cup olive oil plus 1 tablespoon, divided
- ½ cup crushed tomatoes
- 1½ teaspoons red wine
- 1 teaspoon hot smoked
- paprika
- 1 serrano chile, seeded and chopped
- ½ teaspoon salt
- ¼ teaspoon freshly ground black pepper

1. Preheat the oven to 425°F (220°C). 2. In a large bowl, toss the potatoes with ¼ cup of olive oil, then spread them evenly on a baking sheet. Season with salt and pepper, and roast for 50 to 60 minutes, flipping once halfway through, until the potatoes are golden and crispy. 3. While the potatoes are roasting, prepare the sauce by blending the tomatoes, remaining 1 tablespoon olive oil, wine, paprika, chile, salt, and pepper in a food processor or blender until smooth. 4. Serve the hot potatoes with the sauce on the side for dipping or drizzled over the top.

Per Serving:
calories: 201 | fat: 11g | protein: 3g | carbs: 25g | fiber: 4g | sodium: 243mg

Mediterranean Pita Pizza with Feta and Olives

Prep time: 15 minutes | Cook time: 10 minutes | Serves 4

- 4 (6-inch) whole-wheat pitas
- 1 tablespoon extra-virgin olive oil
- ½ cup hummus
- ½ bell pepper, julienned
- ½ red onion, julienned
- ¼ cup olives, pitted and
- chopped
- ¼ cup crumbled feta cheese
- ¼ teaspoon red pepper flakes
- ¼ cup fresh herbs, chopped (mint, parsley, oregano, or a mix)

1. Preheat the broiler to low. Line a baking sheet with parchment paper or foil. 2. Place the pitas on the prepared baking sheet and brush both sides with the olive oil. Broil 1 to 2 minutes per side until starting to turn golden brown. 3. Spread 2 tablespoons hummus on each pita. Top the pitas with bell pepper, onion, olives, feta cheese, and red pepper flakes. Broil again until the cheese softens and starts to get golden brown, 4 to 6 minutes, being careful not to burn the pitas. 4. Remove from broiler and top with the herbs.

Per Serving:
calories: 185 | fat: 11g | protein: 5g | carbs: 17g | fiber: 3g | sodium: 285mg

No-Mayo Tuna Salad Cucumber Bites

Prep time: 5 minutes | Cook time: 0 minutes | Serves 3

- 1 (5-ounce / 142-g) can water-packed tuna, drained
- ⅓ cup full-fat Greek yogurt
- ½ teaspoon extra virgin olive oil
- 1 tablespoon finely chopped spring onion (white parts only)
- 1 tablespoon chopped fresh dill
- Pinch of coarse sea salt
- ¼ teaspoon freshly ground black pepper
- 1 medium cucumber, cut into 15 (¼-inch) thick slices
- 1 teaspoon red wine vinegar

1. In a medium bowl, mix together the tuna, yogurt, olive oil, spring onion, dill, sea salt, and black pepper until well combined. 2. Arrange the cucumber slices on a plate and drizzle the vinegar over them. 3. Spoon a heaping teaspoon of the tuna salad onto each cucumber slice. 4. Serve immediately. Store any leftover tuna salad mixture in the refrigerator, covered, for up to 1 day.

Per Serving:
calories: 80 | fat: 3g | protein: 11g | carbs: 4g | fiber: 1g | sodium: 131mg

Chapter 10

Salads

Classic Caprese Salad with Oregano Drizzle

Prep time: 5 minutes | Cook time: 0 minutes | Serves 2

- 2 firm medium tomatoes (any variety), cut into ¼-inch slices
- ¼ teaspoon kosher salt
- 8 fresh basil leaves
- 7 ounces (198 g) fresh

- mozzarella, cut into ¼-inch slices
- ¼ teaspoon dried oregano
- 3 teaspoons extra virgin olive oil

1. Place the sliced tomatoes on a cutting board and sprinkle them with the kosher salt. Set aside. 2. Arrange 4 basil leaves in a circular pattern on a large, round serving plate. (Tear the leaves into 2 pieces if they're large.) 3. Assemble the tomato slices and mozzarella slices on top of the basil leaves, alternating a tomato slice and then a mozzarella slice, adding a basil leaf between every 3–4 slices of tomato and mozzarella. 4. Sprinkle the oregano over the top and then drizzle the olive oil over the entire salad. Serve promptly. (This salad is best served fresh.)

Per Serving:
calories: 361 | fat: 24g | protein: 28g | carbs: 8g | fiber: 2g | sodium: 313mg

Mediterranean Salad with Bulgur

Prep time: 27 minutes | Cook time: 12 minutes | Serves 4

- 1 cup water
- ½ cup dried bulgur
- 1 (9-ounce / 255-g) bag chopped romaine lettuce
- 1 English cucumber, cut into ¼-inch-thick slices
- 1 red bell pepper, chopped
- ½ cup raw hulled pumpkin seeds

- 20 kalamata olives, pitted and halved lengthwise
- ¼ cup extra-virgin olive oil
- Juice of 1 small orange
- Juice of 1 small lemon
- ¼ teaspoon dried oregano
- Sea salt
- Freshly ground black pepper

1. In a medium saucepan, bring the water and bulgur to a boil over medium heat. Once boiling, reduce the heat to low, cover, and cook until the bulgur is tender, about 12 minutes. Drain any excess liquid, fluff with a fork, and set aside. 2. In a medium bowl, combine the lettuce, cucumber, bell pepper, cooked bulgur, pumpkin seeds, and olives. Toss gently and set aside. 3. In a small bowl, whisk together the olive oil, orange juice, lemon juice, and oregano. Season with salt and black pepper to taste. 4. Pour 3 tablespoons of the dressing over the salad and toss to coat. Taste and add more dressing, salt, or black pepper as needed before serving.

Per Serving:
calories: 322 | fat: 23g | protein: 8g | carbs: 24g | fiber: 6g | sodium: 262mg

Tossed Green Mediterranean Salad

Prep time: 15 minutes | Cook time: 0 minutes | Serves 4

- 1 medium head romaine lettuce, washed, dried, and chopped into bite-sized pieces
- 2 medium cucumbers, peeled and sliced
- 3 spring onions (white parts only), sliced
- ½ cup finely chopped fresh

- dill
- ⅓ cup extra virgin olive oil
- 2 tablespoons fresh lemon juice
- ¼ teaspoon fine sea salt
- 4 ounces (113 g) crumbled feta
- 7 Kalamata olives, pitted

1. In a large bowl, combine the lettuce, cucumber, spring onions, and dill. Toss everything together until evenly mixed. 2. In a small bowl, whisk the olive oil and lemon juice until well combined. Drizzle the dressing over the salad, toss again, then sprinkle with sea salt. 3. Top the salad with feta and olives, and gently toss once more. Serve immediately for the best flavor. (This salad is best enjoyed fresh.)

Per Serving:
calories: 284 | fat: 25g | protein: 7g | carbs: 10g | fiber: 5g | sodium: 496mg

Mediterranean Greek Salad with Lemon-Oregano Dressing

Prep time: 15 minutes | Cook time: 15 minutes | Serves 8

- ½ red onion, thinly sliced
- ¼ cup extra-virgin olive oil
- 3 tablespoons fresh lemon juice or red wine vinegar
- 1 clove garlic, minced
- 1 teaspoon chopped fresh oregano or ½ teaspoon dried
- ½ teaspoon ground black pepper
- ¼ teaspoon kosher salt
- 4 tomatoes, cut into large chunks

- 1 large English cucumber, peeled, seeded (if desired), and diced
- 1 large yellow or red bell pepper, chopped
- ½ cup pitted kalamata or Niçoise olives, halved
- ¼ cup chopped fresh flat-leaf parsley
- 4 ounces (113 g) Halloumi or feta cheese, cut into ½' cubes

1. In a medium bowl, soak the onion in enough water to cover for 10 minutes. 2. In a small bowl, combine the oil, lemon juice or vinegar, garlic, oregano, black pepper, and salt. 3. Drain the onion and add to a large bowl with the tomatoes, cucumber, bell pepper, olives, and parsley. Gently toss to mix the vegetables. 4. Pour the vinaigrette over the salad. Add the cheese and toss again to distribute. 5. Serve immediately, or chill for up to 30 minutes.

Per Serving:
calories: 190 | fat: 16g | protein: 5g | carbs: 8g | fiber: 2g | sodium: 554mg

Citrus Nectarine Spinach-Arugula Salad

Prep time: 15 minutes | Cook time: 0 minutes | Serves 6

- 1 (7-ounce / 198-g) package baby spinach and arugula blend
- 3 tablespoons fresh lemon juice
- 5 tablespoons olive oil
- ⅛ teaspoon salt
- Pinch (teaspoon) sugar
- Freshly ground black pepper, to taste
- ½ red onion, thinly sliced
- 3 ripe nectarines, pitted and sliced into wedges
- 1 cucumber, peeled, seeded, and sliced
- ½ cup crumbled feta cheese

1. Place the spinach-arugula blend in a large bowl. 2. In a small bowl, whisk together the lemon juice, olive oil, salt, and sugar and season with pepper. Taste and adjust the seasonings. 3. Add the dressing to the greens and toss. Top with the onion, nectarines, cucumber, and feta. 4. Serve immediately.

Per Serving:
1 cup: calories: 178 | fat: 14g | protein: 4g | carbs: 11g | fiber: 2g | sodium: 193mg

Asparagus Salad

Prep time: 10 minutes | Cook time: 0 minutes | Serves 4

- 1 pound (454 g) asparagus
- Sea salt and freshly ground pepper, to taste
- 4 tablespoons olive oil
- 1 tablespoon balsamic vinegar
- 1 tablespoon lemon zest

1. Roast the asparagus, or if preferred, use a vegetable peeler to shave it into thin strips. 2. Season the asparagus to taste with salt and pepper. 3. Drizzle with olive oil and vinegar, sprinkle with lemon zest, and serve immediately.

Per Serving:
calories: 146 | fat: 14g | protein: 3g | carbs: 5g | fiber: 3g | sodium: 4mg

Citrus Avocado Salad

Prep time: 5 minutes | Cook time: 0 minutes | Serves 2

- ½ medium orange (any variety), peeled and cut into bite-sized chunks
- 1 medium tangerine, peeled and sectioned
- ½ medium white grapefruit, peeled and cut into bite-
For the Dressing:
- 3 tablespoons extra virgin olive oil
- 1 tablespoon fresh lemon juice
- sized chunks
- 2 thin slices red onion
- 1 medium avocado, peeled, pitted, and sliced
- Pinch of freshly ground black pepper
- ½ teaspoon ground cumin
- ½ teaspoon coarse sea salt
- Pinch of freshly ground black pepper

1. Prepare the dressing by mixing the olive oil, lemon juice, cumin, sea salt, and black pepper in a small jar or bowl. Whisk

or shake to combine thoroughly. 2. In a medium bowl, toss the orange, tangerine, and grapefruit segments together, then layer the sliced onion on top. Drizzle half of the dressing over the salad. 3. Arrange the avocado slices on top of the salad, then drizzle with the remaining dressing and sprinkle with a pinch of black pepper. 4. Toss gently just before serving. (This salad is best enjoyed fresh, but can be stored in the refrigerator for up to 1 day.)

Per Serving:
calories: 448 | fat: 36g | protein: 4g | carbs: 35g | fiber: 11g | sodium: 595mg

Tomato Caper Sicilian Salad

Prep time: 5 minutes | Cook time: 0 minutes | Serves 2

- 2 tablespoons extra virgin olive oil
- 1 tablespoon red wine vinegar
- 2 medium tomatoes (preferably beefsteak variety), sliced
- ½ medium red onion, thinly sliced
- 2 tablespoons capers, drained
- 6 green olives, halved
- 1 teaspoon dried oregano
- Pinch of fine sea salt

1. Make the dressing by combining the olive oil and vinegar in a small bowl. Use a fork to whisk until the mixture thickens slightly. Set aside. 2. Arrange the sliced tomatoes on a large plate and then scatter the onions, capers, and olives over the tomatoes. 3. Sprinkle the oregano and sea salt over the top, then drizzle the dressing over the salad. Serve promptly. (This salad is best served fresh, but can be stored covered in the refrigerator for up to 1 day.)

Per Serving:
calories: 169 | fat: 15g | protein: 2g | carbs: 8g | fiber: 3g | sodium: 336mg

Arugula Spinach Salad with Shaved Parmesan

Prep time: 10 minutes | Cook time: 2 minutes | Serves 3

- 3 tablespoons raw pine nuts
- 3 cups arugula
- 3 cups baby leaf spinach
- 5 dried figs, pitted and chopped
- 2½ ounces (71 g) shaved Parmesan cheese
- For the Dressing:
- 4 teaspoons balsamic vinegar
- 1 teaspoon Dijon mustard
- 1 teaspoon honey
- 5 tablespoons extra virgin olive oil

1. Toast the pine nuts in a small pan over low heat for about 2 minutes, stirring frequently until they start to brown. Immediately remove from the heat and set aside in a small bowl to cool. 2. To make the dressing, mix the balsamic vinegar, Dijon mustard, and honey in a small bowl. Gradually whisk in the olive oil until the dressing is smooth and emulsified. 3. In a large bowl, combine the arugula and spinach. Arrange the figs, Parmesan cheese, and toasted pine nuts on top. Drizzle with the dressing and toss gently to coat everything evenly. Serve immediately. (This salad is best enjoyed fresh.)

Per Serving:
calories: 416 | fat: 35g | protein: 10g | carbs: 18g | fiber: 3g | sodium: 478mg

Sumac-Spiced Pita Bread Salad

Prep time: 10 minutes | Cook time: 0 minutes | Serves 4

For the Dressing:
- ½ cup lemon juice
- ½ cup olive oil
- 1 small clove garlic, minced
- 1 teaspoon salt
- ½ teaspoon ground sumac
- ¼ teaspoon freshly ground black pepper

For the Salad:
- 2 cups shredded romaine lettuce
- 1 large or 2 small cucumbers, seeded and diced
- 2 medium tomatoes, diced
- ½ cup chopped fresh flat-leaf parsley leaves
- ¼ cup chopped fresh mint leaves
- 1 small green bell pepper, diced
- 1 bunch scallions, thinly sliced
- 2 whole-wheat pita bread rounds, toasted and broken into quarter-sized pieces
- Ground sumac for garnish

1. To make the dressing, whisk together the lemon juice, olive oil, garlic, salt, sumac, and pepper in a small bowl. 2. To make the salad, in a large bowl, combine the lettuce, cucumber, tomatoes, parsley, mint, bell pepper, scallions, and pita bread. Toss to combine. Add the dressing and toss again to coat well. 3. Serve immediately sprinkled with sumac.

Per Serving:
calories: 359 | fat: 27g | protein: 6g | carbs: 29g | fiber: 6g | sodium: 777mg

Peach and Tomato Summer Salad

Prep time: 15 minutes | Cook time: 0 minutes | Serves 2

- 2 ripe peaches, pitted and sliced into wedges
- 2 ripe tomatoes, cut into wedges
- ½ red onion, thinly sliced
- Sea salt and freshly ground pepper, to taste
- 3 tablespoons olive oil
- 1 tablespoon lemon juice

1. Toss the peaches, tomatoes, and red onion in a large bowl. Season to taste. 2. Add the olive oil and lemon juice, and gently toss. Serve at room temperature.

Per Serving:
calories: 272 | fat: 21g | protein: 3g | carbs: 22g | fiber: 4g | sodium: 8mg

Wilted Kale Salad

Prep time: 10 minutes | Cook time: 5 minutes | Serves 4

- 2 heads kale
- 1 tablespoon olive oil, plus 1 teaspoon
- 2 cloves garlic, minced
- 1 cup cherry tomatoes,
- sliced
- Sea salt and freshly ground pepper, to taste
- Juice of 1 lemon

1. Wash and dry the kale thoroughly. 2. Tear the kale into small, bite-sized pieces. 3. Heat 1 tablespoon of olive oil in a large skillet over medium heat. Add the garlic and cook for about a minute until fragrant. 4. Add the kale to the skillet and cook just until it wilts, stirring occasionally. 5. Add the tomatoes and cook until they soften and release their juices. 6. Remove the skillet from the heat and transfer the kale and tomatoes to a bowl. 7. Season with sea salt and freshly ground black pepper. Drizzle with the remaining olive oil and a squeeze of lemon juice. Serve immediately and enjoy!

Per Serving:
calories: 153 | fat: 6g | protein: 10g | carbs: 23g | fiber: 9g | sodium: 88mg

Lemony Quinoa Salad with Zucchini, Mint, and Pistachios

Prep time: 20 to 30 minutes | Cook time: 20 minutes | Serves 4

For the Quinoa:
- 1½ cups water
- 1 cup quinoa
- ¼ teaspoon kosher salt

For the Salad:
- 2 tablespoons extra-virgin olive oil
- 1 zucchini, thinly sliced into rounds
- 6 small radishes, sliced
- 1 shallot, julienned
- ¾ teaspoon kosher salt
- ¼ teaspoon freshly ground
- black pepper
- 2 garlic cloves, sliced
- Zest of 1 lemon
- 2 tablespoons lemon juice
- ¼ cup fresh mint, chopped
- ¼ cup fresh basil, chopped
- ¼ cup pistachios, shelled and toasted

Make the Quinoa: Bring the water, quinoa, and salt to a boil in a medium saucepan. Reduce to a simmer, cover, and cook for 10 to 12 minutes. Fluff with a fork. Make the Salad: 1. Heat the olive oil in a large skillet or sauté pan over medium-high heat. Add the zucchini, radishes, shallot, salt, and black pepper, and sauté for 7 to 8 minutes. Add the garlic and cook 30 seconds to 1 minute more. 2. In a large bowl, combine the lemon zest and lemon juice. Add the quinoa and mix well. Add the cooked zucchini mixture and mix well. Add the mint, basil, and pistachios and gently mix.

Per Serving:
calories: 220 | fat: 12g | protein: 6g | carbs: 25g | fiber: 5g | sodium: 295mg

Fruited Chicken Salad

Prep time: 10 minutes | Cook time: 0 minutes | Serves 2

- 2 cups chopped cooked chicken breast
- 2 Granny Smith apples, peeled, cored, and diced
- ½ cup dried cranberries
- ¼ cup diced red onion
- ¼ cup diced celery
- 2 tablespoons honey Dijon mustard
- 1 tablespoon olive oil mayonnaise
- ½ teaspoon salt
- ¼ teaspoon freshly ground black pepper

1. In a medium bowl, mix together the chicken, apples, cranberries, onion, and celery until well combined. 2. In a small bowl, whisk together the mustard, mayonnaise, salt, and pepper until smooth and fully blended. 3. Pour the dressing over the chicken mixture and stir until everything is evenly coated.

Per Serving:
calories: 384 | fat: 9g | protein: 45g | carbs: 28g | fiber: 7g | sodium: 638mg

Greek Potato Salad

Prep time: 15 minutes | Cook time: 15 to 18 minutes | Serves 6

- 1½ pounds (680 g) small red or new potatoes
- ½ cup olive oil
- ⅓ cup red wine vinegar
- 1 teaspoon fresh Greek oregano
- 4 ounces (113 g) feta cheese, crumbled, if desired, or 4 ounces (113 g) grated
- Swiss cheese (for a less salty option)
- 1 green bell pepper, seeded and chopped (1¼ cups)
- 1 small red onion, halved and thinly sliced (generous 1 cup)
- ½ cup Kalamata olives, pitted and halved

1. Place the potatoes in a large pot and add enough water to fully submerge them. Bring to a boil and cook until the potatoes are tender, about 15 to 18 minutes. Once done, drain the water and allow the potatoes to cool until they are manageable. 2. While the potatoes are cooling, prepare the dressing by whisking together olive oil, vinegar, and oregano in a large mixing bowl. 3. Once the potatoes have cooled slightly, cut them into 1-inch cubes and add them to the bowl with the dressing. Toss well to coat. Then, add in the chopped bell pepper, onion, cheese, and olives. Gently mix everything together. Let the salad rest for about 30 minutes before serving to allow the flavors to meld.

Per Serving:
calories: 315 | fat: 23g | protein: 5g | carbs: 21g | fiber: 3g | sodium: 360mg

Pistachio Quinoa Salad with Pomegranate Citrus Vinaigrette

Prep time: 15 minutes | Cook time: 15 minutes | Serves 6

For the Quinoa:
- 1½ cups water
- 1 cup quinoa
- ¼ teaspoon kosher salt
- For the Dressing:
- 1 cup extra-virgin olive oil
- ½ cup pomegranate juice
- ½ cup freshly squeezed orange juice

For the Salad:
- 3 cups baby spinach
- ½ cup fresh parsley, coarsely chopped
- ½ cup fresh mint, coarsely chopped
- Approximately ¾ cup

- 1 small shallot, minced
- 1 teaspoon pure maple syrup
- 1 teaspoon za'atar
- ½ teaspoon ground sumac
- ½ teaspoon kosher salt
- ¼ teaspoon freshly ground black pepper

- pomegranate seeds, or 2 pomegranates
- ¼ cup pistachios, shelled and toasted
- ¼ cup crumbled blue cheese

Make the Quinoa: Bring the water, quinoa, and salt to a boil in a small saucepan. Once boiling, reduce the heat, cover, and simmer for 10 to 12 minutes until the quinoa is tender. Fluff with a fork and set aside.
Make the Dressing: 1. In a medium bowl, whisk together the olive oil, pomegranate juice, orange juice, shallot, maple syrup, za'atar, sumac, salt, and black pepper until smooth. 2. Pour about ½ cup of the dressing into a large bowl. Store the remaining dressing in a glass jar or airtight container in the refrigerator for up to 2 weeks. Let the dressing come to room temperature before using.

Make the Salad: 3. Add the spinach, parsley, and mint to the bowl with the dressing and toss gently to combine. 4. Add the cooked quinoa and toss again to combine. 5. Add the pomegranate seeds, or if using whole pomegranates: Cut the pomegranates in half. Fill a large bowl with water and place the cut side of the pomegranate down in the water. Tap the back with a wooden spoon to release the seeds into the water. Repeat with the remaining pomegranates. Skim off the white pith and drain the seeds before adding them to the salad. 6. Add the pistachios and cheese, then toss gently to combine.

Per Serving:
calories: 300 | fat: 19g | protein: 8g | carbs: 28g | fiber: 5g | sodium: 225mg

Lemon-Garlic Cabbage and Carrot Slaw

Prep time: 10 minutes | Cook time: 0 minutes | Serves 3

- ½ medium head cabbage, thinly sliced, rinsed, and drained
- 3 medium carrots, peeled and shredded
- 4 tablespoons extra virgin olive oil
- 3 tablespoons fresh lemon juice
- ½ teaspoon salt
- ¼ teaspoon freshly ground black pepper
- 1 garlic clove, minced
- 8 Kalamata olives, pitted

1. Place the cabbage and carrots in a large bowl and toss. 2. In a jar or small bowl, combine the olive oil, lemon juice, salt, black pepper, and garlic. Whisk or shake to combine. 3. Pour the dressing over the salad and toss. (Note that it will reduce in volume.) 4. Scatter the olives over the salad just before serving. Store covered in the refrigerator for up to 2 days.

Per Serving:
calories: 237 | fat: 19g | protein: 3g | carbs: 16g | fiber: 6g | sodium: 570mg

Lemon-Dijon Shrimp Endive Salad

Prep time: 15 minutes | Cook time: 2 minutes | Serves 4

- ¼ cup olive oil
- 1 small shallot, minced
- 1 tablespoon Dijon mustard
- Juice and zest of 1 lemon
- Sea salt and freshly ground pepper, to taste
- 2 cups salted water
- 14 shrimp, peeled and deveined
- 1 head endive
- ½ cup tart green apple, diced
- 2 tablespoons toasted walnuts

1. For the vinaigrette, whisk together the first five ingredients in a small bowl until creamy and emulsified. 2. Refrigerate for at least 2 hours for best flavor. 3. In a small pan, boil salted water. Add the shrimp and cook 1–2 minutes, or until the shrimp turns pink. Drain and cool under cold water. 4. To assemble the salad, wash and break the endive. Place on serving plates and top with the shrimp, green apple, and toasted walnuts. 5. Drizzle with the vinaigrette before serving.

Per Serving:
calories: 194 | fat: 16g | protein: 6g | carbs: 8g | fiber: 5g | sodium: 191mg

Garden Salad with Sardine Fillets

- ½ cup olive oil
- Juice of 1 medium lemon
- 1 teaspoon Dijon mustard
- Sea salt and freshly ground pepper, to taste
- 4 medium tomatoes, diced
- 1 large cucumber, peeled and diced
- 1 pound (454 g) arugula,
- trimmed and chopped
- 1 small red onion, thinly sliced
- 1 small bunch flat-leaf parsley, chopped
- 4 whole sardine fillets packed in olive oil, drained and chopped

1. For the dressing, whisk together olive oil, lemon juice, and mustard, then season with sea salt and pepper. Set aside. 2. In a large bowl, combine all the vegetables with the parsley and toss to mix. Top with the sardine fillets. 3. Just before serving, drizzle the dressing over the salad and toss lightly.

Per Serving:
calories: 226 | fat: 20g | protein: 5g | carbs: 9g | fiber: 3g | sodium: 66mg

Hearts of Palm Salad with Avocado and Yellow Tomatoes

- 2 (14-ounce / 397-g) cans hearts of palm, drained and cut into ½-inch-thick slices
- 1 avocado, cut into ½-inch pieces
- 1 cup halved yellow cherry tomatoes
- ½ small shallot, thinly sliced
- ¼ cup coarsely chopped
- flat-leaf parsley
- 2 tablespoons low-fat mayonnaise
- 2 tablespoons extra-virgin olive oil
- ¼ teaspoon salt
- ⅛ teaspoon freshly ground black pepper

1. In a large bowl, toss the hearts of palm, avocado, tomatoes, shallot, and parsley. 2. In a small bowl, whisk the mayonnaise, olive oil, salt, and pepper, then mix into the large bowl.

Per Serving:
calories: 192 | fat: 15g | protein: 5g | carbs: 14g | fiber: 7g | sodium: 841mg

Mediterranean Tuna and Olive Salad

- ¼ cup olive oil
- 3 tablespoons white wine vinegar
- 1 teaspoon salt
- 1 cup pitted green olives
- 1 medium red bell pepper, seeded and diced
- 1 small clove garlic, minced
- 2 (6-ounce / 170-g) cans or jars tuna in olive oil, well drained
- Several leaves curly green or red lettuce

1. In a large bowl, whisk together the olive oil, vinegar, and salt. 2. Add the olives, bell pepper, and garlic to the dressing and toss to

coat. Stir in the tuna, cover, and chill in the refrigerator for at least 1 hour to let the flavors meld. 3. To serve, line a serving bowl with the lettuce leaves and spoon the salad on top. Serve chilled.

Per Serving:
calories: 339 | fat: 24g | protein: 25g | carbs: 4g | fiber: 2g | sodium: 626mg

Marinated Greek Veggie Salad with Goat Cheese

- ½ cup white wine vinegar
- 1 small garlic clove, minced
- 1 teaspoon crumbled dried Greek oregano
- ½ teaspoon salt
- ¼ teaspoon freshly ground black pepper
- 2 Persian cucumbers, sliced thinly
- 4 to 6 long, skinny red or yellow banana peppers or other mild peppers
- 1 medium red onion, cut into rings
- 1 pint mixed small heirloom tomatoes, halved
- 2 ounces (57 g) crumbled goat cheese or feta

1. In a large, nonreactive (glass, ceramic, or plastic) bowl, whisk together the vinegar, garlic, oregano, salt, and pepper. Add the cucumbers, peppers, and onion and toss to mix. Cover and refrigerate for at least 1 hour. 2. Add the tomatoes to the bowl and toss to coat. Serve topped with the cheese.

Per Serving:
calories: 98 | fat: 4g | protein: 4g | carbs: 13g | fiber: 3g | sodium: 460mg

No-Mayo Florence Tuna Salad

- 4 cups spring mix greens
- 1 (15-ounce / 425-g) can cannellini beans, drained
- 2 (5-ounce / 142-g) cans water-packed, white albacore tuna, drained (I prefer Wild Planet brand)
- ⅔ cup crumbled feta cheese
- ½ cup thinly sliced sun-dried tomatoes
- ¼ cup sliced pitted kalamata olives
- ¼ cup thinly sliced scallions, both green and white parts
- 3 tablespoons extra-virgin olive oil
- ½ teaspoon dried cilantro
- 2 or 3 leaves thinly chopped fresh sweet basil
- 1 lime, zested and juiced
- Kosher salt
- Freshly ground black pepper

1. In a large bowl, toss together the greens, beans, tuna, feta cheese, tomatoes, olives, and scallions. 2. Drizzle in the olive oil, followed by the cilantro, basil, and freshly squeezed lime juice. Add a little zest from the lime as well. 3. Season the salad with salt and pepper to taste, then give everything a good mix. Serve immediately and enjoy the vibrant flavors!

Per Serving:
1 cup: calories: 355 | fat: 19g | protein: 22g | carbs: 25g | fiber: 8g | sodium: 744mg

Bacalhau and Black-Eyed Pea Salad

Prep time: 10 minutes | Cook time: 10 minutes | Serves 4

- 1 pound (454 g) bacalhau (salt cod) fillets
- ¼ cup olive oil, plus 1 tablespoon, divided
- 3 tablespoons white wine vinegar
- 1 teaspoon salt
- ¼ teaspoon freshly ground black pepper
- 1 (15-ounce / 425-g) can black-eyed peas, drained and rinsed
- 1 small yellow onion, halved and thinly sliced crosswise
- 1 small clove garlic, minced
- ¼ cup chopped fresh flat-leaf parsley leaves, divided

1. Rinse the cod under cold running water to remove any excess salt. Place the fish in a large nonreactive pot, cover it with water, and refrigerate, making sure to change the water several times over the next 24 hours. 2. After 24 hours, drain the water, refill the pot with fresh water, and gently bring the cod to a simmer. Cook until the fish flakes easily with a fork, which should take around 7 to 10 minutes, depending on the thickness of the fillets. Once cooked, drain the cod and set it aside to cool. 3. In a small bowl, whisk together olive oil, vinegar, salt, and pepper to create the dressing. 4. In a large bowl, combine beans, onion, garlic, and ¾ of the parsley. Add the dressing and toss until everything is well coated. Gently fold in the cooled salt cod, cover the bowl, and refrigerate for at least 2 hours to let the flavors meld. Let the salad sit at room temperature for 30 minutes before serving. 5. Serve the salad garnished with the remaining parsley. Enjoy the chilled, flavorful dish!

Per Serving:

calories: 349 | fat: 18g | protein: 32g | carbs: 16g | fiber: 4g | sodium: 8mg

Roasted Cauliflower Salad with Tahini-Yogurt Dressing

Prep time: 10 minutes | Cook time: 35 minutes | Serves 8 to 10

- 10 cups cauliflower florets (1- to 2-inch florets, from 1 to 2 heads)
- 1½ tablespoons olive oil
- ¾ teaspoon kosher salt, divided
- ½ cup walnuts
- ½ cup yogurt
- ¼ cup tahini, at room temperature
- ¼ cup lemon juice, plus more to taste
- ¼ cup water
- 1 tablespoon honey
- ¼ cup chopped fresh dill
- 1 tablespoon minced shallot

1. Preheat your oven to 450°F (235°C). 2. On a large baking sheet, toss the cauliflower with olive oil and ¼ teaspoon of salt. Spread it out in a single layer and roast for about 30 minutes, or until the cauliflower is tender and browned on the edges. Once done, transfer the roasted cauliflower to a large bowl and set aside to cool while preparing the rest of the salad. 3. In a skillet over medium heat, toast the walnuts for about 5 minutes, until fragrant and golden. Chop them roughly and set aside. 4. In a blender or food processor, blend together the yogurt, tahini, lemon juice, water, and honey until smooth. If the dressing is too thick, add extra water, one tablespoon at a time, to reach the desired consistency. 5. Toss the cooled cauliflower with dill, shallot, and the remaining ½ teaspoon salt. Pour the dressing over the cauliflower and toss to coat. 6. Serve at room temperature, topped with the toasted walnuts for crunch. Enjoy!

Per Serving:

calories: 153 | fat: 10g | protein: 6g | carbs: 12g | fiber: 4g | sodium: 249mg

Roasted Cauliflower Arugula Salad with Pomegranate and Pine Nuts

Prep time: 20 minutes | Cook time: 20 minutes | Serves 4

- 1 head cauliflower, trimmed and cut into 1-inch florets
- 2 tablespoons extra-virgin olive oil, plus more for drizzling (optional)
- 1 teaspoon ground cumin
- ½ teaspoon kosher salt
- ¼ teaspoon freshly ground black pepper
- 5 ounces (142 g) arugula
- ⅓ cup pomegranate seeds
- ¼ cup pine nuts, toasted

1. Preheat the oven to 425°F (220°C). Line a baking sheet with parchment paper or foil. 2. In a large bowl, combine the cauliflower, olive oil, cumin, salt, and black pepper. Spread in a single layer on the prepared baking sheet and roast for 20 minutes, tossing halfway through. 3. Divide the arugula among 4 plates. Top with the cauliflower, pomegranate seeds, and pine nuts. 4. Serve with a simple drizzle of olive oil.

Per Serving:

calories: 190 | fat: 14g | protein: 6g | carbs: 16g | fiber: 6g | sodium: 210mg

Chapter *11*

Pizzas, Wraps, and Sandwiches

Chapter 11 Pizzas, Wraps, and Sandwiches

Classic Mozzarella Basil Margherita Pizza

Prep time: 10 minutes | Cook time: 10 minutes | Serves 4

- All-purpose flour, for dusting
- 1 pound (454 g) premade pizza dough
- 1 (15-ounce / 425-g) can crushed San Marzano tomatoes, with their juices
- 2 garlic cloves
- 1 teaspoon Italian seasoning
- Pinch sea salt, plus more as needed
- 1½ teaspoons olive oil, for drizzling
- 10 slices mozzarella cheese
- 12 to 15 fresh basil leaves

1. Preheat the oven to 475ºF (245ºC). 2. On a floured surface, roll out the dough to a 12-inch round and place it on a lightly floured pizza pan or baking sheet. 3. In a food processor, combine the tomatoes with their juices, garlic, Italian seasoning, and salt and process until smooth. Taste and adjust the seasoning. 4. Drizzle the olive oil over the pizza dough, then spoon the pizza sauce over the dough and spread it out evenly with the back of the spoon, leaving a 1-inch border. Evenly distribute the mozzarella over the pizza. 5. Bake until the crust is cooked through and golden, 8 to 10 minutes. Remove from the oven and let sit for 1 to 2 minutes. Top with the basil right before serving.

Per Serving:
calories: 570 | fat: 21g | protein: 28g | carbs: 66g | fiber: 4g | sodium: 570mg

Ras Al Hanout Lamb Flatbread with Pine Nuts and Mint

Prep time: 10 minutes | Cook time: 20 minutes | Serves 4

- 1⅓ cups plain Greek yogurt
- Juice of 1½ lemons, divided
- 1¼ teaspoons salt, divided
- 1 pound (454 g) ground lamb
- 1 medium red onion, diced
- 1 clove garlic, minced
- 1 tablespoon ras al hanout
- ¼ cup chopped fresh mint
- leaves
- Freshly ground black pepper
- 4 Middle Eastern-style flatbread rounds
- 2 tablespoons toasted pine nuts
- 16 cherry tomatoes, halved
- 2 tablespoons chopped cilantro

1. Preheat the oven to 450°F(235ºC). 2. In a small bowl, stir together the yogurt, the juice of ½ lemon, and ¼ teaspoon salt. 3. Heat a large skillet over medium-high heat. Add the lamb and cook, stirring frequently, until browned, about 5 minutes. Drain any excess rendered fat from the pan and then stir in the onion and garlic and cook, stirring, until softened, about 3 minutes more. Stir in the ras al hanout, mint, the remaining teaspoon of salt, and pepper. 4. Place the flatbread rounds on a baking sheet (or two if necessary) and top with the lamb mixture, pine nuts, and tomatoes, dividing equally. Bake in the preheated oven until the crust is golden brown and the tomatoes have softened, about 10 minutes. Scatter the cilantro over the flatbreads and squeeze the remaining lemon juice over them. Cut into wedges and serve dolloped with the yogurt sauce.

Per Serving:
calories: 463 | fat: 22g | protein: 34g | carbs: 34g | fiber: 3g | sodium: 859mg

Roasted Vegetable Bocadillo with Romesco Sauce

Prep time: 10 minutes | Cook time: 20 minutes | Serves 4

- 2 small yellow squash, sliced lengthwise
- 2 small zucchini, sliced lengthwise
- 1 medium red onion, thinly sliced
- 4 large button mushrooms, sliced
- 2 tablespoons olive oil
- 1 teaspoon salt, divided
- ½ teaspoon freshly ground black pepper, divided
- 2 roasted red peppers from a jar, drained
- 2 tablespoons blanched almonds
- 1 tablespoon sherry vinegar
- 1 small clove garlic
- 4 crusty multigrain rolls
- 4 ounces (113 g) goat cheese, at room temperature
- 1 tablespoon chopped fresh basil

1. Preheat your oven to 400°F (205ºC). 2. In a medium bowl, toss the yellow squash, zucchini, onion, and mushrooms with olive oil, ½ teaspoon of salt, and ¼ teaspoon of pepper. Spread the mixture evenly on a large baking sheet. Roast the vegetables for 20 minutes, or until they are softened and slightly caramelized. 3. While the vegetables are roasting, make the sauce by blending the roasted peppers, almonds, vinegar, garlic, the remaining ½ teaspoon of salt, and the remaining ¼ teaspoon of pepper in a food processor. Process until smooth and creamy. 4. Cut the rolls in half and spread ¼ of the goat cheese on the bottom of each roll. Layer the roasted vegetables on top of the cheese, dividing them evenly between the rolls. Top with freshly chopped basil. Spread the roasted red pepper sauce over the top half of the rolls. 5. Serve immediately while the rolls are warm and the sauce is fresh. Enjoy this tasty, veggie-packed sandwich!

Per Serving:
calories: 379 | fat: 21g | protein: 17g | carbs: 32g | fiber: 4g | sodium: 592mg

Kale and Cannellini Bean Pizza

Prep time: 11 minutes | Cook time: 14 to 19 minutes | Serves 4

- ¾ cup whole-wheat pastry flour
- ½ teaspoon low-sodium baking powder
- 1 tablespoon olive oil, divided
- 1 cup chopped kale
- 2 cups chopped fresh baby spinach
- 1 cup canned no-salt-added cannellini beans, rinsed and drained
- ½ teaspoon dried thyme
- 1 piece low-sodium string cheese, torn into pieces

1. In a small bowl, mix the pastry flour and baking powder until well combined. 2. Add ¼ cup of water and 2 teaspoons of olive oil. Mix until a dough forms. 3. On a floured surface, press or roll the dough into a 7-inch round. Set aside while you cook the greens. 4. In a baking pan, mix the kale, spinach, and remaining teaspoon of the olive oil. Air fry at 350ºF (177ºC) for 3 to 5 minutes, until the greens are wilted. Drain well. 5. Put the pizza dough into the air fryer basket. Top with the greens, cannellini beans, thyme, and string cheese. Air fry for 11 to 14 minutes, or until the crust is golden brown and the cheese is melted. Cut into quarters to serve.

Per Serving:
calories: 181 | fat: 6g | protein: 8g | carbs: 27g | fiber: 6g | sodium: 103mg

Herbed Tuna Bocadillo with Piquillo Peppers

Prep time: 5 minutes | Cook time: 20 minutes | Serves 4

- 2 tablespoons olive oil, plus more for brushing
- 1 medium onion, finely chopped
- 2 leeks, white and tender green parts only, finely chopped
- 1 teaspoon chopped thyme
- ½ teaspoon dried marjoram
- ½ teaspoon salt
- ¼ teaspoon freshly ground black pepper
- 3 tablespoons sherry vinegar
- 1 carrot, finely diced
- 2 (8-ounce / 227-g) jars Spanish tuna in olive oil
- 4 crusty whole-wheat sandwich rolls, split
- 1 ripe tomato, grated on the large holes of a box grater
- 4 piquillo peppers, cut into thin strips

1. Heat 2 tablespoons olive oil in a medium skillet over medium heat. Add the onion, leeks, thyme, marjoram, salt, and pepper. Stir frequently until the onions are softened, about 10 minutes. Stir in the vinegar and carrot and cook until the liquid has evaporated, 5 minutes. Transfer the mixture to a bowl and let cool to room temperature or refrigerate for 15 minutes or so. 2. In a medium bowl, combine the tuna, along with its oil, with the onion mixture, breaking the tuna chunks up with a fork. 3. Brush the rolls lightly with oil and toast under the broiler until lightly browned, about 2 minutes. Spoon the tomato pulp onto the bottom half of each roll, dividing equally and spreading it with the back of the spoon. Divide the tuna mixture among the rolls and top with the piquillo pepper slices. Serve immediately.

Per Serving:
calories: 416 | fat: 18g | protein: 35g | carbs: 30g | fiber: 5g | sodium: 520mg

Dill Salmon Salad Wraps

Prep time: 10 minutes |Cook time: 10 minutes| Serves:6

- 1 pound (454 g) salmon filet, cooked and flaked, or 3 (5-ounce / 142-g) cans salmon
- ½ cup diced carrots (about 1 carrot)
- ½ cup diced celery (about 1 celery stalk)
- 3 tablespoons chopped fresh dill
- 3 tablespoons diced red onion (a little less than ⅛ onion)
- 2 tablespoons capers
- 1½ tablespoons extra-virgin olive oil
- 1 tablespoon aged balsamic vinegar
- ½ teaspoon freshly ground black pepper
- ¼ teaspoon kosher or sea salt
- 4 whole-wheat flatbread wraps or soft whole-wheat tortillas

1. In a large bowl, combine the salmon, carrots, celery, dill, red onion, capers, olive oil, vinegar, black pepper, and sea salt. Mix everything together thoroughly. 2. Take the flatbreads and evenly distribute the salmon salad onto each one. Fold up the bottom of the flatbread, then roll it tightly into a wrap. Serve immediately.

Per Serving:
calories: 185 | fat: 8g | protein: 17g | carbs: 12g | fiber: 2g | sodium: 237mg

Open-Faced Eggplant Parmesan Sandwich

Prep time: 10 minutes | Cook time: 10 minutes | Serves 2

- 1 small eggplant, sliced into ¼-inch rounds
- Pinch sea salt
- 2 tablespoons olive oil
- Sea salt and freshly ground pepper, to taste
- 2 slices whole-grain bread, thickly cut and toasted
- 1 cup marinara sauce (no added sugar)
- ¼ cup freshly grated, low-fat Parmesan cheese

1. Preheat the broiler to high heat. 2. Sprinkle salt on both sides of the eggplant slices and let sit for 20 minutes to draw out any bitterness. 3. Rinse the eggplant slices under cold water and pat them dry with a paper towel. 4. Brush both sides of the eggplant with olive oil, and season with sea salt and freshly ground black pepper. 5. Arrange the eggplant slices on a sheet pan and broil for about 4 minutes, or until crispy. Flip and broil the other side until golden and crisp. 6. Lay the slices of toasted bread on a separate sheet pan. Spoon marinara sauce generously onto each slice of bread. Layer the crispy eggplant on top. 7. Sprinkle half of the cheese over the eggplant, then add another spoonful of marinara sauce. 8. Top with the remaining cheese. 9. Place the sandwiches under the broiler for about 2 minutes, until the cheese is melted and bubbly. 10. Carefully transfer the sandwiches to plates using a spatula and serve immediately.

Per Serving:
calories: 355 | fat: 19g | protein: 10g | carbs: 38g | fiber: 13g | sodium: 334mg

Chicken and Goat Cheese Pizza

Prep time: 10 minutes | Cook time: 10 minutes | Serves 4

- All-purpose flour, for dusting
- 1 pound (454 g) premade pizza dough
- 2 tablespoons olive oil
- 1 cup shredded cooked
- chicken
- 3 ounces (85 g) goat cheese, crumbled
- Sea salt
- Freshly ground black pepper

1. Preheat the oven to 475°F (245°C). 2. Roll out the pizza dough on a floured surface to about a 12-inch round. Transfer it to a pizza pan or baking sheet that's lightly floured. Drizzle olive oil over the dough, spreading it evenly across the surface. 3. Top the dough with the cooked chicken and crumbled goat cheese. 4. Bake the pizza for 8 to 10 minutes, or until the crust is golden and the cheese is melted. 5. Season with sea salt and freshly ground black pepper. Slice and serve!

Per Serving:
calories: 555 | fat: 23g | protein: 24g | carbs: 60g | fiber: 2g | sodium: 660mg

Hummus Cucumber Basil Sandwiches

Prep time: 10 minutes | Cook time: 0 minutes | Serves 2

- Cucumber Basil Sandwiches
- 4 slices whole-grain bread
- ¼ cup hummus
- 1 large cucumber, thinly sliced
- 4 whole basil leaves

1. Spread the hummus on 2 slices of bread, and layer the cucumbers onto it. Top with the basil leaves and close the sandwiches. 2. Press down lightly and serve immediately.

Per Serving:
calories: 209 | fat: 5g | protein: 9g | carbs: 32g | fiber: 6g | sodium: 275mg

Vegetable Pita Sandwiches

Prep time: 15 minutes | Cook time: 9 to 12 minutes | Serves 4

- 1 baby eggplant, peeled and chopped
- 1 red bell pepper, sliced
- ½ cup diced red onion
- ½ cup shredded carrot
- 1 teaspoon olive oil
- ⅓ cup low-fat Greek yogurt
- ½ teaspoon dried tarragon
- 2 low-sodium whole-wheat pita breads, halved crosswise

1. In a baking pan, combine the eggplant, red bell pepper, red onion, carrot, and olive oil. Toss to coat evenly, then transfer the vegetable mixture to the air fryer basket. Roast at 390°F (199°C) for 7 to 9 minutes, stirring once halfway through, until the vegetables are tender. Drain any excess moisture if needed. 2. In a small bowl, mix the yogurt and tarragon together until well blended. 3. Stir the yogurt-tarragon mixture into the roasted vegetables until evenly coated. 4. Stuff each pita pocket with one-fourth of the vegetable mixture. Place the stuffed pitas in the air fryer and cook for 2 to 3 minutes, or until the bread is crispy and golden. Serve immediately.

Per Serving:
calories: 115 | fat: 2g | protein: 4g | carbs: 22g | fiber: 6g | sodium: 90mg

Anchovy Burrata Panini with Herbed Focaccia

Prep time: 5 minutes | Cook time: 8 minutes | Serves 4

- 8 ounces (227 g) burrata cheese, chilled and sliced
- 1 pound (454 g) whole-wheat herbed focaccia, cut crosswise into 4 rectangles and split horizontally
- 1 can anchovy fillets packed in oil, drained
- 8 slices tomato, sliced
- 2 cups arugula
- 1 tablespoon olive oil

1. Divide the cheese evenly among the bottom halves of the focaccia rectangles. Top each with 3 or 4 anchovy fillets, 2 slices of tomato, and ½ cup arugula. Place the top halves of the focaccia on top of the sandwiches. 2. To make the panini, heat a skillet or grill pan over high heat and brush with the olive oil. 3. Place the sandwiches in the hot pan and place another heavy pan, such as a cast-iron skillet, on top to weigh them down. Cook for about 3 to 4 minutes, until crisp and golden on the bottom, and then flip over and repeat on the second side, cooking for an additional 3 to 4 minutes until golden and crisp. Slice each sandwich in half and serve hot.

Per Serving:
calories: 596 | fat: 30g | protein: 27g | carbs: 58g | fiber: 5g | sodium: 626mg

Barbecue Chicken Pita Pizza

Prep time: 5 minutes | Cook time: 5 to 7 minutes per batch | Makes 4 pizzas

- 1 cup barbecue sauce, divided
- 4 pita breads
- 2 cups shredded cooked chicken
- 2 cups shredded Mozzarella
- cheese
- ½ small red onion, thinly sliced
- 2 tablespoons finely chopped fresh cilantro

1. Start by measuring ½ cup of barbecue sauce into a small cup. Spread 2 tablespoons of this sauce evenly on each pita. 2. In a medium bowl, combine the remaining ½ cup of barbecue sauce with the shredded chicken. Mix well. Spoon ½ cup of the chicken mixture onto each pita. Sprinkle ½ cup of mozzarella cheese over the chicken. Add the red onion on top of each pizza. 3. Place one pizza in the air fryer basket and air fry at 400°F (204°C) for 5 to 7 minutes, or until the cheese is melted and bubbly. Repeat with the other pizzas. 4. Once all the pizzas are cooked, finish by sprinkling fresh cilantro on top for a burst of flavor and color. Serve immediately and enjoy your barbecue chicken pita pizzas!

Per Serving:
calories: 530 | fat: 19g | protein: 40g | carbs: 47g | fiber: 2g | sodium: 672mg

Sautéed Mushroom, Onion, and Pecorino Romano Panini

Prep time: 10 minutes | Cook time: 20 minutes | Serves 4

- 3 tablespoons olive oil, divided
- 1 small onion, diced
- 10 ounces (283 g) button or cremini mushrooms, sliced
- ½ teaspoon salt
- ¼ teaspoon freshly ground black pepper
- 4 crusty Italian sandwich rolls
- 4 ounces (113 g) freshly grated Pecorino Romano

1. Heat 1 tablespoon of olive oil in a skillet over medium-high heat. Add the onion and sauté, stirring occasionally, for about 3 minutes, or until it starts to soften. Add the mushrooms, season with salt and pepper, and cook for about 7 minutes, stirring occasionally, until the mushrooms release their moisture and become tender. 2. To assemble the panini, preheat a skillet or grill pan over high heat and brush it with the remaining 1 tablespoon of olive oil. Lightly brush the inside of the rolls with the other tablespoon of olive oil. Divide the mushroom mixture evenly between the rolls, and top each with ¼ of the grated cheese. 3. Place the sandwiches in the hot skillet, and use a heavy pan (like a cast-iron skillet) to weigh them down. Grill for about 3 to 4 minutes, until the bottom is golden and crispy. Flip the sandwiches over and grill the other side for an additional 3 to 4 minutes until crisp and golden. Slice each panini in half and serve immediately while hot.

Per Serving:

calories: 348 | fat: 20g | protein: 14g | carbs: 30g | fiber: 2g | sodium: 506mg

Pesto Chicken English Muffin Pizzas

Prep time: 5 minutes | Cook time: 10 minutes | Serves 4

- 2 cups shredded cooked chicken
- ¾ cup pesto
- 4 English muffins, split
- 2 cups shredded Mozzarella cheese

1. In a medium bowl, toss the chicken with the pesto. Place one-eighth of the chicken on each English muffin half. Top each English muffin with ¼ cup of the Mozzarella cheese. 2. Put four pizzas at a time in the air fryer and air fry at 350ºF (177ºC) for 5 minutes. Repeat this process with the other four pizzas.

Per Serving:

calories: 617 | fat: 36g | protein: 45g | carbs: 29g | fiber: 3g | sodium: 544mg

Chapter **12**

Desserts

Chapter 12 Desserts

Date and Honey Almond Milk Ice Cream

Prep time: 10 minutes | Cook time: 5 minutes | Serves 4

- ¾ cup (about 4 ounces/ 113 g) pitted dates
- ¼ cup honey
- ½ cup water
- 2 cups cold unsweetened almond milk
- 2 teaspoons vanilla extract

1. In a small saucepan, combine the dates and water, bringing it to a boil over high heat. Once boiling, remove the pan from the heat, cover it, and let the dates soak for 15 minutes. 2. In a blender, combine the soaked dates, almond milk, the soaking water, honey, and vanilla extract. Blend until the mixture is completely smooth. 3. Cover the blender and refrigerate the mixture for at least 1 hour to chill. 4. Pour the chilled mixture into an electric ice cream maker and freeze according to the manufacturer's instructions. 5. Serve the ice cream immediately or transfer it to a freezer-safe container, freezing it for at least 4 hours or until firm. Enjoy it frozen!

Per Serving:
calories: 106 | fat: 2g | protein: 1g | carbs: 23g | fiber: 3g | sodium: 92mg

Lemon Almond Pistachio Biscotti

Prep time: 5 minutes | Cook time: 1 hour 20 minutes | Serves 12

- 2 cups almond flour or hazelnut flour
- ½ packed cup flax meal
- ½ teaspoon baking soda
- ½ teaspoon ground nutmeg
- ½ teaspoon vanilla powder or 1½ teaspoons unsweetened vanilla extract
- ¼ teaspoon salt
- 1 tablespoon fresh lemon zest
- 2 large eggs
- 2 tablespoons extra-virgin olive oil
- 1 tablespoon unsweetened almond extract
- 1 teaspoon apple cider vinegar or fresh lemon juice
- Optional: low-carb sweetener, to taste
- ⅔ cup unsalted pistachio nuts

1. Preheat the oven to 285°F (140°C) fan assisted or 320°F (160°C) conventional. Line one or two baking trays with parchment paper. 2. In a bowl, mix the almond flour, flax meal, baking soda, nutmeg, vanilla, salt, and lemon zest. Add the eggs, olive oil, almond extract, vinegar, and optional sweetener. Mix well until a dough forms, then mix in the pistachio nuts. 3. Form the dough into a low, wide log shape, about 8 × 5 inches (20 × 13 cm). Place in the oven and bake for about 45 minutes. Remove from oven and let cool for 15 to 20 minutes. Using a sharp knife, cut into 12 slices. 4. Reduce the oven temperature to 250°F (120°C) fan assisted or 285°F (140°C) conventional. Lay the slices very carefully in a flat layer on the lined trays. Bake for 15 to 20 minutes, flip over, and bake for 15 to 20 minutes. 5. Remove from the oven and let the biscotti cool

down completely to fully crisp up. Store in a sealed jar for up to 2 weeks.

Per Serving:
calories: 196 | fat: 17g | protein: 7g | carbs: 7g | fiber: 4g | sodium: 138mg

Dried Fruit Compote

Prep time: 15 minutes | Cook time: 8 minutes | Serves 6

- 8 ounces (227 g) dried apricots, quartered
- 8 ounces (227 g) dried peaches, quartered
- 1 cup golden raisins
- 1½ cups orange juice
- 1 cinnamon stick
- 4 whole cloves

1. Add all the ingredients to the Instant Pot® and stir to combine. Close the lid, set the steam release valve to Sealing, press the Manual button, and set the timer for 3 minutes. When the timer goes off, let the pressure release naturally for about 20 minutes. Once done, press Cancel and open the lid. 2. Remove and discard the cinnamon stick and cloves. Press the Sauté button and let the mixture simmer for 5 to 6 minutes. Serve warm, or let it cool, cover, and refrigerate for up to a week.

Per Serving:
calories: 258 | fat: 0g | protein: 4g | carbs: 63g | fiber: 5g | sodium: 7mg

Grilled Fruit Skewers with Honey Vanilla Labneh

Prep time: 15 minutes | Cook time: 10 minutes | Serves 2

- ⅔ cup prepared labneh, or, if making your own, ⅔ cup full-fat plain Greek yogurt
- 2 tablespoons honey
- 1 teaspoon vanilla extract
- Pinch salt
- 3 cups fresh fruit cut into 2-inch chunks (pineapple, cantaloupe, nectarines, strawberries, plums, or mango)

1. If making your own labneh, place a colander over a bowl and line it with cheesecloth. Place the Greek yogurt in the cheesecloth and wrap it up. Put the bowl in the refrigerator and let sit for at least 12 to 24 hours, until it's thick like soft cheese. 2. Mix honey, vanilla, and salt into labneh. Stir well to combine and set it aside. 3. Heat the grill to medium (about 300°F/ 150°C) and oil the grill grate. Alternatively, you can cook these on the stovetop in a heavy grill pan (cast iron works well). 4. Thread the fruit onto skewers and grill for 4 minutes on each side, or until fruit is softened and has grill marks on each side. 5. Serve the fruit with labneh to dip.

Per Serving:
calories: 292 | fat: 6g | protein: 5g | carbs: 60g | fiber: 4g | sodium: 131mg

Cinnamon Grilled Peaches with Honey Yogurt

Prep time: 5 minutes | Cook time: 30 minutes | Serves 4

- 4 ripe peaches, halved and pitted
- 2 tablespoons olive oil
- 1 teaspoon ground cinnamon, plus extra for
- topping
- 2 cups plain full-fat Greek yogurt
- ¼ cup honey, for drizzling

1. Preheat the oven to 350°F (180°C). 2. Place the peaches in a baking dish, cut-side up. 3. In a small bowl, stir together the olive oil and cinnamon, then brush the mixture over the peach halves. 4. Bake the peaches for about 30 minutes, until they are soft. 5. Top the peaches with the yogurt and drizzle them with the honey, then serve.

Per Serving:

calories: 259 | fat: 11g | protein: 6g | carbs: 38g | fiber: 3g | sodium: 57mg

Honey-Grilled Pineapple and Watermelon

Prep time: 10 minutes | Cook time: 7 minutes | Serves 4

- 8 fresh pineapple rings, rind removed
- 8 watermelon triangles, with rind
- 1 tablespoon honey
- ½ teaspoon freshly ground black pepper

1. Preheat an outdoor grill or a grill pan over high heat. 2. Drizzle the fruit slices with honey and sprinkle one side of each piece with pepper. Grill for 5 minutes, turn, and grill for another 2 minutes. Serve.

Per Serving:

calories: 244 | fat: 1g | protein: 4g | carbs: 62g | fiber: 4g | sodium: 7mg

Apple and Brown Rice Pudding

Prep time: 10 minutes | Cook time: 20 minutes | Serves 6

- 2 cups almond milk
- 1 cup long-grain brown rice
- ½ cup golden raisins
- 1 Granny Smith apple, peeled, cored, and chopped
- ¼ cup honey
- 1 teaspoon vanilla extract
- ½ teaspoon ground cinnamon

1. Add all ingredients to the Instant Pot® and stir to combine. Close the lid, set the steam release valve to Sealing, press the Manual button, and set the timer for 20 minutes. 2. When the timer sounds, allow the pressure to release naturally for 15 minutes, then quick-release any remaining pressure. Press Cancel and open the lid. Serve warm or at room temperature.

Per Serving:

calories: 218 | fat: 2g | protein: 3g | carbs: 51g | fiber: 4g | sodium: 54mg

Creamy Blueberry Panna Cotta

Prep time: 5 minutes | Cook time: 0 minutes | Serves 6

- 1 tablespoon gelatin powder
- 2 tablespoons water
- 2 cups goat's cream, coconut cream, or heavy whipping cream
- 2 cups wild blueberries,
- fresh or frozen, divided
- ½ teaspoon vanilla powder or 1½ teaspoons unsweetened vanilla extract
- Optional: low-carb sweetener, to taste

1. In a bowl, sprinkle the gelatin powder over the cold water. Set aside to let it bloom. 2. Place the goat's cream, half of the blueberries, and the vanilla in a blender and process until smooth and creamy. Alternatively, use an immersion blender. 3. Pour the blueberry cream into a saucepan. Gently heat; do not boil. Scrape the gelatin into the hot cream mixture together with the sweetener, if using. Mix well until all the gelatin has dissolved. 4. Divide among 6 (4-ounce / 113-g) jars or serving glasses and fill them about two-thirds full, leaving enough space for the remaining blueberries. Place in the fridge for 3 to 4 hours, or until set. 5. When the panna cotta has set, evenly distribute the remaining blueberries among the jars. Serve immediately or store in the fridge for up to 4 days.

Per Serving:

calories: 172 | fat: 15g | protein: 2g | carbs: 8g | fiber: 2g | sodium: 19mg

Refreshing Cucumber Lime Popsicles

Prep time: 5 minutes | Cook time: 0 minutes | Serves 4 to 6

- 2 cups cold water
- 1 cucumber, peeled
- ¼ cup honey
- Juice of 1 lime
-

1. In a blender, purée the water, cucumber, honey, and lime juice. Pour into popsicle molds, freeze, and enjoy on a hot summer day!

Per Serving:

calories: 49 | fat: 0g | protein: 0g | carbs: 13g | fiber: 0g | sodium: 3mg

Grilled Stone Fruit

Prep time: 15 minutes | Cook time: 6 minutes | Serves 2

- 2 peaches, halved and pitted
- 2 plums, halved and pitted
- 3 apricots, halved and pitted
- ½ cup low-fat ricotta cheese
- 2 tablespoons honey

1. Preheat the grill to medium heat. 2. Lightly oil the grates or spray with cooking spray. 3. Place the fruit cut side down on the grill, cooking for 2–3 minutes per side, until tender and lightly charred. 4. Serve the grilled fruit warm, topped with ricotta cheese and a drizzle of honey. Enjoy!

Per Serving:

calories: 263 | fat: 6g | protein: 10g | carbs: 48g | fiber: 4g | sodium: 63mg

Chocolate Hazelnut Energy Truffles

Prep time: 5 minutes | Cook time: 50 minutes | Makes 12 truffles

Filling:
- 1¾ cups blanched hazelnuts, divided
- ½ cup coconut butter
- 4 tablespoons butter or ¼ cup virgin coconut oil
- ¼ cup collagen powder

- ¼ cup raw cacao powder
- 1 teaspoon vanilla powder or cinnamon
- Optional: low-carb sweetener, to taste

Chocolate Coating:
- 2½ ounces (71 g) 100% dark chocolate
- 1 ounce (28 g) cacao butter
- Pinch of salt

1. Preheat the oven to 285°F (140°C) fan assisted or 320°F (160°C) conventional. 2. To make the filling: Spread the hazelnuts on a baking tray and roast for 40 to 50 minutes, until lightly golden. Remove from the oven and let cool for a few minutes. 3. Place 1 cup of the roasted hazelnuts in a food processor. Process for 1 to 2 minutes, until chunky. Add the coconut butter, butter, collagen powder, cacao powder, vanilla, and sweetener, if using. Process again until well combined. Place the dough in the fridge to set for 1 hour. 4. Reserve 12 hazelnuts for filling and crumble the remaining hazelnuts unto small pieces. 5. To make the chocolate coating: Line a baking tray with parchment. Melt the dark chocolate and cacao butter in a double boiler, or use a heatproof bowl placed over a small saucepan filled with 1 cup of water, placed over medium heat. Remove from the heat and let cool to room temperature before using for coating. Alternatively, use a microwave and melt in short 10- to 15-second bursts until melted, stirring in between. 6. Remove the dough from the fridge and use a spoon to scoop about 1 ounce (28 g) of the dough. Press one whole hazelnut into the center and use your hands to wrap the dough around to create a truffle. Place in the freezer for about 15 minutes. 7. Gently pierce each very cold truffle with a toothpick or a fork. Working one at a time, hold the truffle over the melted chocolate and spoon the chocolate over it to coat completely. Turn the toothpick as you work until the coating is solidified. Place the coated truffles on the lined tray and drizzle any remaining coating over them. Before they become completely solid, roll them in the chopped nuts. Refrigerate the coated truffles for at least 15 minutes to harden. 8. Keep refrigerated for up to 1 week or freeze for up to 3 months.

Per Serving:
calories: 231 | fat: 22g | protein: 4g | carbs: 8g | fiber: 4g | sodium: 3mg

Avocado-Orange Fruit Salad

Prep time: 10 minutes | Cook time: 0 minutes | Serves 5 to 6

- 2 large Gala apples, chopped
- 2 oranges, segmented and chopped
- ⅓ cup sliced almonds
- ½ cup honey

- 1 tablespoon extra-virgin olive oil
- ½ teaspoon grated orange zest
- 1 large avocado, semi-ripened, medium diced

1. In a large bowl, combine the apples, oranges, and almonds, mixing them gently. 2. In a separate small bowl, whisk together the honey, oil, and orange zest until well combined. 3. Drizzle the orange mixture over the fruit salad and toss to coat. Add the avocado, and gently toss everything together one final time.

Per Serving:
calories: 296 | fat: 12g | protein: 3g | carbs: 51g | fiber: 7g | sodium: 4mg

Balsamic Cherry Ricotta with a Hint of Black Pepper

Prep time: 10 minutes | Cook time: 0 minutes | Serves 4

- 1 cup (8 ounces/ 227 g) ricotta
- 2 tablespoons honey
- 1 teaspoon vanilla extract
- 3 cups pitted sweet cherries

- (thawed if frozen), halved
- 1½ teaspoons aged balsamic vinegar
- Pinch of freshly ground black pepper

1. In a food processor, combine the ricotta, honey, and vanilla and process until smooth. Transfer the mixture to a medium bowl, cover, and refrigerate for 1 hour. 2. In a small bowl, combine the cherries, vinegar, and pepper and stir to mix well. Chill along with the ricotta mixture. 3. To serve, spoon the ricotta mixture into 4 serving bowls or glasses. Top with the cherries, dividing them equally and spooning a bit of the accumulated juice over the top of each bowl. Serve chilled.

Per Serving:
calories: 236 | fat: 5g | protein: 7g | carbs: 42g | fiber: 1g | sodium: 93mg

Honey Roasted Plums with Nutty Crumble and Yogurt

Prep time: 5 minutes | Cook time: 25 minutes | Serves 4

- ¼ cup honey
- ¼ cup freshly squeezed orange juice
- 4 large plums, halved and pitted
- ¼ cup whole-wheat pastry flour
- 1 tablespoon pure maple

- sugar
- 1 tablespoon nuts, coarsely chopped (your choice; I like almonds, pecans, and walnuts)
- 1½ teaspoons canola oil
- ½ cup plain Greek yogurt

1. Preheat the oven to 400°F (205°C). Combine the honey and orange juice in a square baking dish. Place the plums, cut-side down, in the dish. Roast about 15 minutes, and then turn the plums over and roast an additional 10 minutes, or until tender and juicy. 2. In a medium bowl, combine the flour, maple sugar, nuts, and canola oil and mix well. Spread on a small baking sheet and bake alongside the plums, tossing once, until golden brown, about 5 minutes. Set aside until the plums have finished cooking. 3. Serve the plums drizzled with pan juices and topped with the nut crumble and a dollop of yogurt.

Per Serving:
calories: 175 | fat: 3g | protein: 4g | carbs: 36g | fiber: 2g | sodium: 10mg

Grilled Stone Fruit with Honey Whipped Ricotta

Prep time: 10 minutes |Cook time: 10 minutes| Serves: 4

- Nonstick cooking spray
- 4 peaches or nectarines (or 8 apricots or plums), halved and pitted
- 2 teaspoons extra-virgin olive oil
- ¾ cup whole-milk ricotta
- cheese
- 1 tablespoon honey
- ¼ teaspoon freshly grated nutmeg
- 4 sprigs mint, for garnish (optional)

1. Spray the cold grill or a grill pan with nonstick cooking spray. Heat the grill or grill pan to medium heat. 2. Place a large, empty bowl in the refrigerator to chill. 3. Brush the fruit all over with the oil. Place the fruit cut-side down on the grill or pan and cook for 3 to 5 minutes, or until grill marks appear. (If you're using a grill pan, cook in two batches.) Using tongs, turn the fruit over. Cover the grill (or the grill pan with aluminum foil) and cook for 4 to 6 minutes, until the fruit is easily pierced with a sharp knife. Set aside to cool. 4. Remove the bowl from the refrigerator and add the ricotta. Using an electric beater, beat the ricotta on high for 2 minutes. Add the honey and nutmeg and beat for 1 more minute. Divide the warm (or room temperature) fruit among 4 serving bowls, top with the ricotta mixture, and a sprig of mint (if using) and serve.

Per Serving:
calories: 180 | fat: 9g | protein: 7g | carbs: 21g | fiber: 3g | sodium: 39mg

Light and Lemony Olive Oil Cupcakes

Prep time: 10 minutes | Cook time: 24 minutes | Serves 18

- 2 cups all-purpose flour
- 4 teaspoons baking powder
- 1 cup granulated sugar
- 1 cup extra virgin olive oil
- 2 eggs
- 7 ounces (198 g) 2% Greek

Glaze:
- 1 tablespoon lemon juice
- 5 tablespoons powdered
- yogurt
- 1 teaspoon pure vanilla extract
- 4 tablespoons fresh lemon juice
- Zest of 2 lemons

- sugar

1. Begin by heating your oven to 350°F (180°C). Prepare a muffin tin by lining a 12-cup section with cupcake liners and a separate 6-cup section with more liners. Set these aside for later use. 2. In a medium-sized mixing bowl, whisk together the flour and baking powder. Put this mixture aside for now. 3. In a larger bowl, blend together the sugar and olive oil until the mixture is smooth and creamy. Add the eggs one at a time, stirring thoroughly after each addition. Follow this by incorporating the Greek yogurt, vanilla extract, lemon juice, and zest. Continue mixing until everything is evenly combined. 4. Gradually add the flour mixture to the wet ingredients, ½ cup at a time, ensuring you stir continuously so the batter stays smooth. 5. Spoon the batter into the prepared cupcake liners, filling each about two-thirds full. Bake for 22 to 25 minutes, or until a toothpick inserted into the center of a cupcake comes out clean. 6. While the cupcakes are baking, prepare the glaze by whisking together lemon juice and powdered sugar in a small bowl until smooth. Set this aside. 7. Once the cupcakes are done, allow them to cool in the pan for about 5 minutes. Afterward, carefully remove them from the pans and transfer to a wire rack to cool completely. 8. Once the cupcakes are fully cooled, drizzle the lemon glaze over the tops. Store the cupcakes in the refrigerator, where they will stay fresh for up to 4 days.

Per Serving:
calories: 225 | fat: 13g | protein: 3g | carbs: 25g | fiber: 1g | sodium: 13mg

Fresh Figs with Chocolate Sauce

Prep time: 5 minutes | Cook time: 0 minutes | Serves 4

- ¼ cup honey
- 2 tablespoons cocoa powder
- 8 fresh figs

1. In a small bowl, mix together the honey and cocoa powder until smooth, forming a syrup. 2. Slice the figs in half and arrange them cut side up. Drizzle the honey-cocoa syrup over the figs. Serve immediately and enjoy!

Per Serving:
calories: 112 | fat: 1g | protein: 1g | carbs: 30g | fiber: 3g | sodium: 3mg

Peaches Poached in Rose Water

Prep time: 15 minutes | Cook time: 1 minute | Serves 6

- 1 cup water
- 1 cup rose water
- ¼ cup wildflower honey
- 8 green cardamom pods, lightly crushed
- 1 teaspoon vanilla bean
- paste
- 6 large yellow peaches, pitted and quartered
- ½ cup chopped unsalted roasted pistachio meats

1. Add water, rose water, honey, cardamom, and vanilla to the Instant Pot® and whisk until well combined. Add the peaches and stir gently. Close the lid, set the steam release valve to Sealing, press the Manual button, and set the timer for 1 minute. 2. Once the timer beeps, quick-release the pressure until the float valve drops. Press Cancel and open the lid. Let the peaches sit for 10 minutes. Using a slotted spoon, carefully remove the peaches from the poaching liquid. 3. Peel the skins off the peach slices and arrange them on a plate. Garnish with pistachios. Serve warm or at room temperature.

Per Serving:
calories: 145 | fat: 3g | protein: 2g | carbs: 28g | fiber: 2g | sodium: 8mg

Poached Apricots and Pistachios with Greek Yogurt

Prep time: 2 minutes | Cook time: 18 minutes | Serves 4

- ½ cup orange juice
- 2 tablespoons brandy
- 2 tablespoons honey
- ¾ cup water
- 1 cinnamon stick

- 12 dried apricots
- ⅓ cup 2% Greek yogurt
- 2 tablespoons mascarpone cheese
- 2 tablespoons shelled pistachios

1. In a saucepan over medium heat, combine the orange juice, brandy, honey, and water, stirring to mix. Add the cinnamon stick and bring the mixture to a gentle simmer. 2. Once the honey has fully dissolved, stir in the apricots. Bring to a boil, then cover, reduce the heat to low, and simmer for 15 minutes. 3. While the apricots are simmering, mix the Greek yogurt and mascarpone cheese in a small bowl until smooth. Set this aside for later. 4. After 15 minutes, uncover the saucepan, add the pistachios, and let it simmer for another 3 minutes. Remove from heat once done. 5. To serve, divide the yogurt-mascarpone mixture into 4 bowls, topping each with 3 apricots, a few pistachios, and a teaspoon of the syrup. The apricots and syrup can be stored in a jar at room temperature for up to 1 month.

Per Serving:

calories: 146 | fat: 3g | protein: 4g | carbs: 28g | fiber: 4g | sodium: 62mg

Pumpkin-Ricotta Cheesecake

Prep time: 25 minutes | Cook time: 45 minutes | Serves 10 to 12

- 1 cup almond flour
- ½ cup butter, melted
- 1 (14½-ounce / 411-g) can pumpkin purée
- 8 ounces (227 g) cream cheese, at room temperature
- ½ cup whole-milk ricotta cheese

- ½ to ¾ cup sugar-free sweetener
- 4 large eggs
- 2 teaspoons vanilla extract
- 2 teaspoons pumpkin pie spice
- Whipped cream, for garnish (optional)

1. Preheat your oven to 350°F (180°C) and line the bottom of a 9-inch springform pan with parchment paper. 2. In a small bowl, mix the almond flour and melted butter together using a fork until fully combined. Press this mixture evenly into the bottom of the prepared pan using your fingers. 3. In a large bowl, use an electric mixer on medium speed to beat together the pumpkin purée, cream cheese, ricotta, and sweetener until smooth and well combined. 4. Add the eggs one by one, beating well after each addition. Stir in the vanilla and pumpkin pie spice until just incorporated. 5. Pour the pumpkin mixture over the crust and bake for 40 to 45 minutes, or until the filling is set. 6. Let the cheesecake cool to room temperature, then refrigerate for at least 6 hours before serving. 7. Serve chilled, optionally topping with whipped cream for extra indulgence.

Per Serving:

calories: 230 | fat: 21g | protein: 6g | carbs: 5g | fiber: 1g | sodium: 103mg

Chapter 13

Pasta

Chapter 13 Pasta

Bowtie Pesto Pasta Salad with Spinach and Tomatoes

Prep time: 5 minutes | Cook time: 4 minutes | Serves 8

- 1 pound (454 g) whole-wheat bowtie pasta
- 4 cups water
- 1 tablespoon extra-virgin olive oil
- 2 cups halved cherry tomatoes
- 2 cups baby spinach
- ½ cup chopped fresh basil
- ½ cup prepared pesto
- ½ teaspoon ground black pepper
- ½ cup grated Parmesan cheese

1. Add pasta, water, and olive oil to the Instant Pot®. Close lid, set steam release to Sealing, press the Manual button, and set time to 4 minutes. 2. When the timer beeps, quick-release the pressure until the float valve drops and open lid. Drain off any excess liquid. Allow pasta to cool to room temperature, about 30 minutes. Stir in tomatoes, spinach, basil, pesto, pepper, and cheese. Refrigerate for 2 hours. Stir well before serving.

Per Serving:
calories: 360 | fat: 13g | protein: 16g | carbs: 44g | fiber: 7g | sodium: 372mg

Rotini with Walnut Pesto, Peas, and Cherry Tomatoes

Prep time: 10 minutes | Cook time: 4 minutes | Serves 8

- 1 cup packed fresh basil leaves
- ⅓ cup chopped walnuts
- ¼ cup grated Parmesan cheese
- ¼ cup plus 1 tablespoon extra-virgin olive oil, divided
- 1 clove garlic, peeled
- 1 tablespoon lemon juice
- ¼ teaspoon salt
- 1 pound (454 g) whole-wheat rotini pasta
- 4 cups water
- 1 pint cherry tomatoes
- 1 cup fresh or frozen green peas
- ½ teaspoon ground black pepper

1. In a food processor, combine the basil and walnuts. Pulse about 12 times, or until finely chopped. Add the cheese, ¼ cup of oil, garlic, lemon juice, and salt, and pulse 10 more times, or until the mixture forms a rough paste. Set aside in the refrigerator until ready to use. 2. In the Instant Pot®, combine the pasta, water, and remaining 1 tablespoon of oil. Close the lid, set the steam release valve to Sealing, press the Manual button, and set the timer for 4 minutes. 3. Once the timer goes off, quick-release the pressure until the float valve drops, then open the lid. Drain any excess liquid and allow the pasta to cool to room temperature, about 30 minutes. Stir in the basil mixture, ensuring the pasta is well coated. Add the

tomatoes, peas, and pepper, and toss to combine. Refrigerate for 2 hours before serving, stirring well before serving.

Per Serving:
calories: 371 | fat: 15g | protein: 12g | carbs: 47g | fiber: 7g | sodium: 205mg

Spicy Lemon Broccoli Pasta Salad

Prep time: 10 minutes | Cook time: 10 minutes | Serves 2

- 8 ounces (227 g) whole-wheat pasta
- 2 cups broccoli florets
- 1 cup carrots, peeled and shredded
- ¼ cup plain Greek yogurt
- Juice of 1 lemon
- 1 teaspoon red pepper flakes
- Sea salt and freshly ground pepper, to taste

1. Cook the pasta according to the package directions for al dente and drain well. 2. When the pasta is cool, combine it with the veggies, yogurt, lemon juice, and red pepper flakes in a large bowl, and stir thoroughly to combine. 3. Taste for seasoning, and add sea salt and freshly ground pepper as needed. 4. This dish can be served at room temperature or chilled.

Per Serving:
calories: 473 | fat: 2g | protein: 22g | carbs: 101g | fiber: 13g | sodium: 101mg

Penne with Tuna and Green Olives

Prep time: 5 minutes | Cook time: 5 minutes | Serves 4

- 2 tablespoons olive oil
- 3 garlic cloves, minced
- ½ cup green olives
- ½ teaspoon salt
- ¼ teaspoon freshly ground black pepper
- 2 (6-ounce / 170-g) cans tuna in olive oil (don't drain
- off the oil)
- ½ teaspoon wine vinegar
- 12 ounces (340 g) penne pasta, cooked according to package directions
- 2 tablespoons chopped flat-leaf parsley

1. In a medium skillet, warm the olive oil over medium heat. Add the garlic and sauté for 2 to 3 minutes, stirring frequently, until the garlic becomes golden and fragrant. Toss in the olives, season with salt and pepper, and add the tuna with its oil. Stir well and let everything cook together for another 1 to 2 minutes, allowing the flavors to meld. Remove from heat and drizzle in the vinegar, giving it one last stir to combine. 2. Add the cooked pasta to the skillet, tossing it thoroughly with the sauce to coat the noodles. Serve right away, topped with a sprinkle of chopped parsley for a fresh finish.

Per Serving:
calories: 511 | fat: 22g | protein: 31g | carbs: 52g | fiber: 1g | sodium: 826mg

Greek Spaghetti with Meat Sauce

- 1 pound (454 g) spaghetti
- 4 cups water
- 3 tablespoons olive oil, divided
- 1 medium white onion, peeled and diced
- ½ pound (227 g) lean ground veal
- ½ teaspoon salt
- ¼ teaspoon ground black pepper
- ¼ cup white wine
- ½ cup tomato sauce
- 1 cinnamon stick
- 2 bay leaves
- 1 clove garlic, peeled
- ¼ cup grated aged myzithra or Parmesan cheese

1. Begin by adding the pasta, water, and 1 tablespoon of oil into the Instant Pot®. Secure the lid, set the steam release valve to Sealing, select the Manual button, and cook for 4 minutes. Once the timer goes off, perform a quick-release of the pressure until the float valve drops. Open the lid, drain the pasta, and press Cancel. Set the pasta aside for now. 2. Switch to the Sauté function and heat the remaining 2 tablespoons of oil. Add the onion and cook, stirring occasionally, until softened and fragrant, about 3 minutes. Toss in the veal and break it up as it cooks, stirring frequently, until it turns golden brown, roughly 5 minutes. Season with salt and pepper, then add the wine and tomato sauce. Stir everything together until well mixed. 3. Toss in the cinnamon stick, bay leaves, and garlic, mixing everything until fragrant. Press Cancel, secure the lid again, set the steam release valve to Sealing, and set the Manual timer to 5 minutes. Once done, quick-release the pressure and open the lid. Discard the cinnamon stick and bay leaves. 4. To serve, place the cooked pasta in a large serving bowl. Sprinkle with cheese and top with the meat sauce. Serve immediately, enjoying the rich, comforting flavors.

Per Serving:
calories: 447 | fat: 15g | protein: 18g | carbs: 60g | fiber: 4g | sodium: 394mg

Whole-Wheat Puttanesca Spaghetti

- 1 pound (454 g) dried whole-wheat spaghetti
- ⅓ cup olive oil
- 5 garlic cloves, minced or pressed
- 4 anchovy fillets, chopped
- ½ teaspoon red pepper flakes
- 1 teaspoon salt
- ½ teaspoon freshly ground black pepper
- 1 (28-ounce / 794-g) can tomato purée
- 1 pint cherry tomatoes, halved
- ½ cup pitted green olives, halved
- 2 tablespoons drained capers
- ¾ cup coarsely chopped basil

1. Cook the pasta according to the package instructions. 2. Meanwhile, heat the oil in a large skillet over medium-high heat. Add the garlic, anchovies, red pepper flakes, salt, and pepper. Cook, stirring frequently, until the garlic just begins to turn golden brown, 2 to 3 minutes. Add the tomato purée, olives, cherry tomatoes, and capers and let the mixture simmer, reducing the heat if necessary, and stirring occasionally, until the pasta is done, about 10 minutes. 3. Drain the pasta in a colander and then add it to the sauce, tossing

with tongs until the pasta is well coated. Serve hot, garnished with the basil.

Per Serving:
calories: 464 | fat: 17g | protein: 12g | carbs: 70g | fiber: 12g | sodium: 707mg

Whole-Wheat Capellini with Sardines, Olives, and Manchego

- 1 (7-ounce / 198-g) jar Spanish sardines in olive oil, chopped (reserve the oil)
- 1 medium onion, diced
- 4 cloves garlic, minced
- 2 medium tomatoes, sliced
- 1 pound (454 g) whole-
- wheat capellini pasta, cooked according to package instructions
- 1 cup pitted, chopped cured black olives, such as Kalamata
- 3 ounces (85 g) freshly grated manchego cheese

1. In a large skillet, heat the olive oil from the sardines over medium-high heat. Add the onion and garlic, sautéing for about 5 minutes until soft and fragrant. Add the tomatoes and sardines, cooking for an additional 2 minutes, stirring occasionally to combine the flavors. 2. Add the cooked and drained pasta to the skillet and toss it well in the sauce, making sure the noodles are evenly coated. 3. Stir in the olives, then serve the pasta immediately, topped with a generous sprinkle of grated cheese for added richness.

Per Serving:
calories: 307 | fat: 11g | protein: 8g | carbs: 38g | fiber: 6g | sodium: 433mg

Avgolemono

- 6 cups chicken stock
- ½ cup orzo
- 1 tablespoon olive oil
- 12 ounces (340 g) cooked chicken breast, shredded
- ½ teaspoon salt
- ½ teaspoon ground black
- pepper
- ¼ cup lemon juice
- 2 large eggs
- 2 tablespoons chopped fresh dill
- 1 tablespoon chopped fresh flat-leaf parsley

1. Pour the stock, orzo, and olive oil into the Instant Pot®. Close the lid, set the steam release valve to Sealing, press the Manual button, and cook for 3 minutes. Once the timer sounds, perform a quick-release of the pressure until the float valve drops. Open the lid and stir in the chicken, salt, and pepper, mixing well. 2. In a medium bowl, whisk together the lemon juice and eggs. Gradually whisk in the hot cooking liquid from the Instant Pot®, adding ¼ cup at a time, until you've incorporated 1 cup of liquid. Quickly pour the egg mixture into the soup and stir thoroughly. Let the soup sit on the Keep Warm setting for 10 minutes, stirring occasionally. 3. After 10 minutes, stir in the fresh dill and parsley. Serve the soup immediately, enjoying its creamy, zesty flavors.

Per Serving:
calories: 193 | fat: 5g | protein: 21g | carbs: 15g | fiber: 1g | sodium: 552mg

Rotini Pasta in Red Wine Marinara Sauce

Prep time: 10 minutes | Cook time: 25 minutes | Serves 6

- 1 pound (454 g) rotini
- 4 cups water
- 1 tablespoon olive oil
- ½ medium yellow onion, peeled and diced
- 3 cloves garlic, peeled and minced
- 1 (15-ounce / 425-g) can crushed tomatoes
- ½ cup red wine
- 1 teaspoon sugar
- 2 tablespoons chopped fresh basil
- ½ teaspoon salt
- ¼ teaspoon ground black pepper

1. Add pasta and water to the Instant Pot®. Close lid, set steam release to Sealing, press the Manual button, and set time to 4 minutes. When the timer beeps, quick-release the pressure until the float valve drops and open the lid. Press the Cancel button. Drain pasta and set aside. 2. Clean pot and return to machine. Press the Sauté button and heat oil. Add onion and cook until it begins to caramelize, about 10 minutes. Add garlic and cook 30 seconds. Add tomatoes, red wine, and sugar, and simmer for 10 minutes. Add basil, salt, pepper, and pasta. Serve immediately.

Per Serving:

calories: 320 | fat: 4g | protein: 10g | carbs: 59g | fiber: 4g | sodium: 215mg

Lemon Garlic Shrimp Fettuccine

Prep time: 10 minutes | Cook time: 10 minutes | Serves 4 to 6

- 8 ounces (227 g) fettuccine pasta
- ¼ cup extra-virgin olive oil
- 3 tablespoons garlic, minced
- 1 pound (454 g) large shrimp (21-25), peeled and deveined
- ⅓ cup lemon juice
- 1 tablespoon lemon zest
- ½ teaspoon salt
- ½ teaspoon freshly ground black pepper

1. Bring a large pot of salted water to a boil. Add the fettuccine and cook for 8 minutes. 2. In a large saucepan over medium heat, cook the olive oil and garlic for 1 minute. 3. Add the shrimp to the saucepan and cook for 3 minutes on each side. Remove the shrimp from the pan and set aside. 4. Add the lemon juice and lemon zest to the saucepan, along with the salt and pepper. 5. Reserve ½ cup of the pasta water and drain the pasta. 6. Add the pasta water to the saucepan with the lemon juice and zest and stir everything together. Add the pasta and toss together to evenly coat the pasta. Transfer the pasta to a serving dish and top with the cooked shrimp. Serve warm.

Per Serving:

calories: 615 | fat: 17g | protein: 33g | carbs: 89g | fiber: 4g | sodium: 407mg

Chapter **14**

Staples, Sauces, Dips, and Dressings

Chapter 14 Staples, Sauces, Dips, and Dressings

Slow-Cooked Brown Onion Masala Base

Prep time: 20 minutes | Cook time: 6½ hours | Makes 4 cups

- 2 tablespoons rapeseed oil
- 6 onions, finely diced
- 8 garlic cloves, finely chopped
- 1¾ pounds (794 g) canned plum tomatoes
- 3-inch piece fresh ginger, grated
- 1 teaspoon salt
- 1½ teaspoons turmeric
- Handful fresh coriander stalks, finely chopped
- 3 fresh green chiles, finely chopped
- 1 teaspoon chili powder
- 1 teaspoon ground cumin seeds
- 1 cup hot water
- 2 teaspoons garam masala

1. Preheat the slow cooker on high (or to the sauté setting, if you have it). Then add the oil and let it heat. Add the onions and cook for a few minutes until they start to brown. Make sure you brown the onions well so you get a deep, flavorsome base. 2. Add the garlic and continue to cook on high for about 10 minutes. 3. Add the tomatoes, ginger, salt, turmeric, coriander stalks, chopped chiles, chili powder, cumin seeds, and water. 4. Cover the slow cooker and cook on low for 6 hours. 5. Remove the lid and stir. Let the masala cook for another 30 minutes uncovered to reduce a little. 6. Add the garam masala after the masala has cooked. 7. Use right away, or freeze it in small tubs or freezer bags. Just defrost what you need, when you need it.

Per Serving:
calories: 286 | fat: 8g | protein: 7g | carbs: 52g | fiber: 8g | sodium: 656mg

Garlic-Rosemary Infused Olive Oil

Prep time: 5 minutes | Cook time: 45 minutes | Makes 1 cup

- 1 cup extra-virgin olive oil
- 4 large garlic cloves, smashed
- 4 (4- to 5-inch) sprigs rosemary

1. In a medium skillet, combine the olive oil, garlic, and rosemary sprigs. Cook over low heat, stirring occasionally, for 30 to 45 minutes, or until the garlic is very tender and fragrant. Be careful not to let the oil heat too much, as it may cause the garlic to burn and develop a bitter taste. 2. Once the garlic and rosemary have infused the oil, remove the skillet from the heat and let it cool slightly. Use a slotted spoon to remove the garlic and rosemary, then pour the infused oil into a glass container. Let it cool completely before sealing with a lid. Store the oil at room temperature for up to 3 months.

Per Serving:
⅛ cup: calories: 241 | fat: 27g | protein: 0g | carbs: 1g | fiber: 0g | sodium: 1mg

Maltese Sun-Dried Tomato Mushroom Vinaigrette

Prep time: 10 minutes | Cook time: 5 minutes | Serves 4

- ⅓ cup olive oil (use a combination of olive oil and sun-dried tomato oil, if they were packed in oil)
- 8 ounces (227 g) mushrooms, sliced
- 3 tablespoons red wine
- vinegar
- Freshly ground black pepper, to taste
- ½ cup sun-dried tomatoes, drained (if they are packed in oil, reserve the oil) and chopped

1. In a medium skillet, heat 2 tablespoons of the olive oil (or mixed olive oil and sun-dried tomato packing oil) over high heat. Add the mushrooms and cook, stirring, until they have released their liquid. 2. Add vinegar and season with pepper. Remove from the heat and add the remaining oil and the sun-dried tomatoes.

Per Serving:
1 cup: calories: 190 | fat: 18g | protein: 3g | carbs: 6g | fiber: 2g | sodium: 21mg

Creamy Ginger-Lime Peanut Sauce

Prep time: 5 minutes | Cook time: 0 minutes | Serves 4

- ⅓ cup peanut butter
- ¼ cup hot water
- 2 tablespoons soy sauce
- 2 tablespoons rice vinegar
- Juice of 1 lime
- 1 teaspoon minced fresh ginger
- 1 teaspoon minced garlic
- 1 teaspoon black pepper

1. In a blender container, combine the peanut butter, hot water, soy sauce, vinegar, lime juice, ginger, garlic, and pepper. Blend until smooth. 2. Use immediately or store in an airtight container in the refrigerator for a week or more.

Per Serving:
calories: 408 | fat: 33g | protein: 16g | carbs: 18g | fiber: 5g | sodium: 2525mg

Vinaigrette

Prep time: 5 minutes | Cook time: 0 minutes | Serves 4

- 2 tablespoons balsamic vinegar
- 2 large garlic cloves, minced
- 1 teaspoon dried rosemary,
- crushed
- ¼ teaspoon freshly ground black pepper
- ¼ cup olive oil

1. In a small bowl, combine the vinegar, garlic, rosemary, and pepper. Slowly add the olive oil while whisking constantly until the mixture emulsifies. Transfer to an airtight container and refrigerate for up to 3 days.

Per Serving:
1 cup: calories: 129 | fat: 1g | protein: 3g | carbs: 0g | fiber: 0g | sodium: 2mg

Red Pepper Chimichurri

Prep time: 10 minutes | Cook time: 0 minutes | Serves 4

- 1 garlic clove, minced
- 3 tablespoons olive oil
- 1 tablespoon red wine vinegar or sherry vinegar
- ¼ teaspoon freshly ground black pepper
- 1 shallot, finely chopped
- 1 large red bell pepper,
- roasted, peeled, seeded, and finely chopped (about 1 cup)
- 3 tablespoons capers, rinsed
- 3 tablespoons chopped fresh parsley
- ½ teaspoon red pepper flakes

1. In a small bowl, combine all the ingredients and stir until fully blended.

Per Serving:
calories: 113 | fat: 10g | protein: 1g | carbs: 5g | fiber: 1g | sodium: 157mg

White Bean Dip with Garlic and Herbs

Prep time: 10 minutes | Cook time: 30 minutes | Serves 16

- 1 cup dried white beans, rinsed and drained
- 3 cloves garlic, peeled and crushed
- 8 cups water
- ¼ cup extra-virgin olive oil
- ¼ cup chopped fresh flat-leaf parsley
- 1 tablespoon chopped fresh oregano
- 1 tablespoon chopped fresh tarragon
- 1 teaspoon chopped fresh thyme leaves
- 1 teaspoon grated lemon zest
- ¼ teaspoon salt
- ¼ teaspoon ground black pepper

1. In the Instant Pot®, combine the beans and garlic, stirring to mix evenly. Add water, then close the lid, set the steam release valve to Sealing, press the Manual button, and cook for 30 minutes. 2. Once the timer goes off, let the pressure release naturally for about 20 minutes. Open the lid and check that the beans are tender. Press Cancel, drain any excess water, and transfer the beans and garlic to a food processor. Add olive oil and pulse until smooth, leaving some small chunks. 3. Add the parsley, oregano, tarragon, thyme, lemon zest, salt, and pepper, pulsing 3 to 5 times to combine. Transfer the mixture to a storage container and refrigerate for at least 4 hours or overnight. Serve chilled or at room temperature.

Per Serving:
calories: 47 | fat: 3g | protein: 1g | carbs: 3g | fiber: 1g | sodium: 38mg

Quick Almond Flour Sandwich Bread

Prep time: 5 minutes | Cook time: 2 minutes | Serves 1

- 3 tablespoons almond flour
- 1 tablespoon extra-virgin olive oil
- 1 large egg
- ½ teaspoon dried rosemary,
- oregano, basil, thyme, or garlic powder (optional)
- ¼ teaspoon baking powder
- ⅛ teaspoon salt

1. In a microwave-safe ramekin, combine the almond flour, olive oil, egg, rosemary (if using), baking powder, and salt. Mix well with a fork. 2. Microwave for 90 seconds on high. 3. Slide a knife around the edges of ramekin and flip to remove the bread. 4. Slice in half with a serrated knife if you want to use it to make a sandwich.

Per Serving:
calories: 354 | fat: 33g | protein: 12g | carbs: 6g | fiber: 3g | sodium: 388mg

Olive Mint Vinaigrette

Prep time: 5 minutes | Cook time: 0 minutes | Makes ½ cup

- ¼ cup white wine vinegar
- ¼ teaspoon honey
- ¼ teaspoon kosher salt
- ¼ teaspoon freshly ground black pepper
- ¼ cup extra-virgin olive oil
- ¼ cup olives, pitted and minced
- 2 tablespoons fresh mint, minced

1. In a bowl, combine the vinegar, honey, salt, and black pepper, whisking until the mixture is smooth. Gradually pour in the olive oil while continuing to whisk until the dressing emulsifies. 2. Add the olives and fresh mint, tossing gently to combine. If you have any leftovers, store them in an airtight container in the refrigerator for up to 5 days.

Per Serving:
2 tablespoons: calories: 135 | fat: 15g | protein: 0g | carbs: 1g | fiber: 0g | sodium: 135mg

Lemon Herb Chermoula Sauce

Prep time: 10 minutes | Cook time: 0 minutes | Makes about 1½ cups

- 2¼ cups fresh cilantro leaves
- 8 garlic cloves, minced
- 1½ teaspoons ground cumin
- 1½ teaspoons paprika
- ½ teaspoon cayenne pepper
- ½ teaspoon table salt
- 6 tablespoons lemon juice (2 lemons)
- ¾ cup extra-virgin olive oil

1. Pulse cilantro, garlic, cumin, paprika, cayenne, and salt in food processor until cilantro is coarsely chopped, about 10 pulses. Add lemon juice and pulse briefly to combine. Transfer mixture to medium bowl and slowly whisk in oil until incorporated and mixture is emulsified. Cover and let sit at room temperature for at least 30 minutes to allow flavors to meld. (Sauce can be refrigerated for up to 2 days; bring to room temperature before serving.)

Per Serving:
¼ cup: calories: 253 | fat: 27g | protein: 1g | carbs: 3g | fiber: 1g | sodium: 199mg

Parsley-Mint Sauce

Prep time: 5 minutes | Cook time: 0 minutes | Serves 6

- ½ cup fresh flat-leaf parsley
- 1 cup fresh mint leaves
- 2 garlic cloves, minced
- 2 scallions (green onions), chopped
- 2 tablespoons pomegranate molasses
- ¼ cup olive oil
- 1 tablespoon fresh lemon juice

1. Place all ingredients in a blender and blend until smooth and well combined. Transfer the mixture to an airtight container and refrigerate until needed. This can be stored in the fridge for up to 1 day.

Per Serving:
calories: 90 | fat: 9g | protein: 1g | carbs: 2g | fiber: 0g | sodium: 5mg

Roasted Harissa

Prep time: 5 minutes | Cook time: 15 minutes | Makes ¾ cup

- 1 red bell pepper
- 2 small fresh red chiles, or more to taste
- 4 garlic cloves, unpeeled
- ½ teaspoon ground coriander
- ½ teaspoon ground cumin
- ½ teaspoon ground caraway
- 1 tablespoon fresh lemon juice
- ½ teaspoon salt

1. Preheat the broiler to high. 2. Arrange the bell pepper, chiles, and garlic on a baking sheet and broil for 6 to 8 minutes. Flip the vegetables and broil for an additional 5 to 6 minutes, or until the pepper and chiles are soft and slightly blackened. Remove from the broiler and allow to cool until they are manageable. Discard the stems, skins, and seeds from the pepper and chiles, and peel the papery skin off the garlic. 3. Transfer the peeled peppers, chiles, and garlic to a blender or food processor. Add the coriander, cumin, caraway, lemon juice, and salt, and blend until smooth. 4. Store in an airtight container in the refrigerator for up to 3 days, covering the sauce with a ¼-inch layer of oil to preserve its freshness.

Per Serving:
calories: 28 | fat: 0g | protein: 1g | carbs: 6g | fiber: 1g | sodium: 393mg

Zesty Cucumber Yogurt Dressing

Prep time: 5 minutes | Cook time: 0 minutes | Serves 2

- 1½ cups plain, unsweetened, full-fat Greek yogurt
- 1 cucumber, seeded and peeled
- ½ lemon, juiced and zested
- 1 tablespoon dried, minced garlic
- ½ tablespoon dried dill
- 2 teaspoons dried oregano
- Salt

1. In a food processor, combine the yogurt, cucumber, lemon juice, garlic, dill, oregano, and a pinch of salt and process until smooth. Adjust the seasonings as needed and transfer to a serving bowl.

Per Serving:
calories: 209 | fat: 10g | protein: 18g | carbs: 14g | fiber: 2g | sodium: 69mg

Zesty Mint Walnut Pesto

Prep time: 5 minutes | Cook time: 0 minutes | Makes about 1 cup

- 1 tablespoon toasted walnuts
- 2 cups packed fresh mint leaves
- 1 clove garlic
- 1 tablespoon lemon juice
- ½ teaspoon lemon zest
- ¼ teaspoon salt
- ⅔ cup olive oil
- ½ cup grated Pecorino cheese

1. Place the walnuts, mint, and garlic in a food processor and pulse to mince finely. Add the lemon juice, lemon zest, and salt and pulse to grind to a paste. 2. With the processor running, add the olive oil in a thin stream. Process until the mixture is well combined. 3. Add the cheese and pulse to combine.

Per Serving:
calories: 113 | fat: 12g | protein: 3g | carbs: 1g | fiber: 0g | sodium: 234mg

Appendix 1: Measurement Conversion Chart

VOLUME EQUIVALENTS(DRY)

US STANDARD	METRIC (APPROXIMATE)
1/8 teaspoon	0.5 mL
1/4 teaspoon	1 mL
1/2 teaspoon	2 mL
3/4 teaspoon	4 mL
1 teaspoon	5 mL
1 tablespoon	15 mL
1/4 cup	59 mL
1/2 cup	118 mL
3/4 cup	177 mL
1 cup	235 mL
2 cups	475 mL
3 cups	700 mL
4 cups	1 L

VOLUME EQUIVALENTS(LIQUID)

US STANDARD	US STANDARD (OUNCES)	METRIC (APPROXIMATE)
2 tablespoons	1 fl.oz.	30 mL
1/4 cup	2 fl.oz.	60 mL
1/2 cup	4 fl.oz.	120 mL
1 cup	8 fl.oz.	240 mL
1 1/2 cup	12 fl.oz.	355 mL
2 cups or 1 pint	16 fl.oz.	475 mL
4 cups or 1 quart	32 fl.oz.	1 L
1 gallon	128 fl.oz.	4 L

TEMPERATURES EQUIVALENTS

FAHRENHEIT(F)	CELSIUS(C) (APPROXIMATE)
225 °F	107 °C
250 °F	120 °C
275 °F	135 °C
300 °F	150 °C
325 °F	160 °C
350 °F	180 °C
375 °F	190 °C
400 °F	205 °C
425 °F	220 °C
450 °F	235 °C
475 °F	245 °C
500 °F	260 °C

WEIGHT EQUIVALENTS

US STANDARD	METRIC (APPROXIMATE)
1 ounce	28 g
2 ounces	57 g
5 ounces	142 g
10 ounces	284 g
15 ounces	425 g
16 ounces (1 pound)	455 g
1.5 pounds	680 g
2 pounds	907 g

Appendix 2: The Dirty Dozen and Clean Fifteen

The Environmental Working Group (EWG) is a nonprofit, nonpartisan organization dedicated to protecting human health and the environment Its mission is to empower people to live healthier lives in a healthier environment. This organization publishes an annual list of the twelve kinds of produce, in sequence, that have the highest amount of pesticide residue-the Dirty Dozen-as well as a list of the fifteen kinds of produce that have the least amount of pesticide residue-the Clean Fifteen.

THE DIRTY DOZEN

- The 2016 Dirty Dozen includes the following produce. These are considered among the year's most important produce to buy organic:

Strawberries	Spinach
Apples	Tomatoes
Nectarines	Bell peppers
Peaches	Cherry tomatoes
Celery	Cucumbers
Grapes	Kale/collard greens
Cherries	Hot peppers

- *The Dirty Dozen list contains two additional items kale/collard greens and hot peppers-because they tend to contain trace levels of highly hazardous pesticides.*

THE CLEAN FIFTEEN

- The least critical to buy organically are the Clean Fifteen list. The following are on the 2016 list:

Avocados	Papayas
Corn	Kiw
Pineapples	Eggplant
Cabbage	Honeydew
Sweet peas	Grapefruit
Onions	Cantaloupe
Asparagus	Cauliflower
Mangos	

- *Some of the sweet corn sold in the United States are made from genetically engineered (GE) seedstock. Buy organic varieties of these crops to avoid GE produce.*

Appendix 3: Recipes Index

A

Air Fryer Almond Flour Dinner Rolls 32
Air Fryer Butternut Squash and Ricotta Frittata 16
Air Fryer Pepper Egg Rings with Salsa 13
Air-Fried Blackened Red Snapper with Lemon 47
Air-Fried Caprese Eggplant Stacks 40
Air-Fried Crustless Spinach and Cheddar Pie 41
Air-Fried Eggplant Parmesan 41
Air-Fried Garlic Roasted Eggplant 35
Air-Fried Hake Gratin with Creamy Swiss Topping 46
Air-Fried Mushroom Zucchini Veggie Burgers 39
Air-Fried Pesto Chicken Parm 63
Air-Fried Salmon Spring Rolls with Fresh Herbs 45
Air-Fried Zucchini Boats with Tomatoes and Feta 31
Almond Butter Banana Blueberry Smoothie 14
Almond-Crusted Salmon with Honey Thyme Glaze 47
Anchovy Burrata Panini with Herbed Focaccia 81
Apple and Brown Rice Pudding 85
Aromatic Spiced Lamb Chops 57
Arugula Spinach Salad with Shaved Parmesan 73
Asian Swordfish 50
Asian-Style Hoisin Turkey Burgers 63
Asparagus Salad 73
Asparagus-Spinach Farro 20
Avgolemono 91
Avocado-Orange Fruit Salad 86

B

Bacalhau and Black-Eyed Pea Salad 77
Baked Harissa Shakshuka with Fresh Basil 17
Baked Ratatouille with Herbed Breadcrumbs and Goat Cheese 42
Baked Spinach Ricotta Bites with Basil 69
Baked Stuffed Eggplant with Caramelized Onions and Feta 32
Baked Tofu with Artichokes and Sun-Dried Tomatoes 40
Balsamic Cherry Ricotta with a Hint of Black Pepper 86
Balsamic Marinated Tofu with Basil and Oregano 39
Balsamic Pork Tenderloin 57
Balsamic Tomato Basil Chicken Thighs 61
Barbecue Chicken Pita Pizza 81
Beef Brisket with Onions 53
Bell Pepper Egg Rings with Avocado Salsa 11
Black Bean Salad with Corn and Tomato Relish 27
Black Chickpeas 25
Black Olive Toast with Herbed Hummus 15
Bowtie Pesto Pasta Salad with Spinach and Tomatoes 90
Braised Eggplant and Tomatoes 29
Braised Turkey Thighs with Fig Balsamic Sauce 59
Breakfast Quinoa with Figs and Walnuts 16
Buckwheat and Halloumi Bowl with Mint Dressing 23

C

Caponata (Sicilian Eggplant) 34
Caramelized Fennel and Sardines with Penne 48
Cauliflower and Carrot Skillet Hash 31
Cauliflower Baklava Breakfast Bowl 13
Cauliflower Crust Chicken Pizzas 60
Cauliflower Steaks with Olive Citrus Sauce 42
Cheese Stuffed Zucchini 38
Cheese-Stuffed Dates 69
Chicken and Goat Cheese Pizza 81
Chicken Artichoke Rice Bake 24
Chicken Avgolemono 59
Chicken Cutlets with Greek Salsa 62
Chicken in Mango Chutney 61
Chicken Skewers 64
Chicken with Artichokes 62
Chickpea and Green Bean Salad with Herbs and Mushrooms 22
Chickpea Hash with Eggs 12
Chili Lime Cauliflower with Cilantro 29
Chili-Spiced Beans 22
Chocolate Hazelnut Energy Truffles 86
Cinnamon Grilled Peaches with Honey Yogurt 85
Citrus and Spice Chicken 61
Citrus Avocado Salad 73
Citrus Nectarine Spinach-Arugula Salad 73
Citrus Shrimp Ceviche Salad with Avocado 49
Citrus-Infused Melon Salad 66
Classic Caprese Salad with Oregano Drizzle 72
Classic Mozzarella Basil Margherita Pizza 79
Cod and Cauliflower Chowder 45
Cod with Lemon Parsley Pistou 44
Cod with Tomatoes and Garlic 47
Cod with Warm Tabbouleh Salad 51

Creamy Blueberry Panna Cotta 85

Creamy Chickpea Sauce with Whole-Wheat Fusilli 39

Creamy Ginger-Lime Peanut Sauce 94

Creamy Pesto Shrimp with Zucchini Noodles 49

Crispy Five-Spice Air-Fried Chicken Wings 68

Crispy Green Beans 34

Crispy Lemon-Pepper Air-Fried Drumsticks 68

Crispy Pork and Beef Egg Rolls 56

Crispy Pork Milanese with Lemon and Parsley 53

Cube Steak Roll-Ups 57

D

Date and Honey Almond Milk Ice Cream 84

Dijon Salmon Niçoise with Chive Vinaigrette 66

Dill Salmon Salad Wraps 80

Dried Fruit Compote 84

E

Eggs Poached in Moroccan Tomato Sauce 38

F

Farro Salad with Tomatoes and Olives 20

Fava and Garbanzo Bean Fūl 23

Fava Bean Purée with Sautéed Chicory 41

Five-Spice Roasted Sweet Potatoes 31

Flank Steak and Blue Cheese Wraps 54

Freekeh Pilaf with Walnuts and Spiced Yogurt 35

French Green Lentils with Swiss Chard and Almonds 25

Fresh Figs with Chocolate Sauce 87

Fresh Stuffed Cucumbers with Avocado and Tomato 31

Fried Zucchini Salad 34

Fruited Chicken Salad 74

G

Garden Salad with Sardine Fillets 76

Garlic-Parmesan Crispy Baby Potatoes 36

Garlic-Rosemary Infused Olive Oil 94

Golden Spinach Puff Pastry Pie 15

Greek Egg and Tomato Scramble 12

Greek Potato Salad 75

Greek Spaghetti with Meat Sauce 91

Greek Street Tacos 68

Greek Yogurt Parfait with Granola 16

Greens Chips with Curried Yogurt Sauce 67

Grilled Eggplant Mozzarella Stacks 39

Grilled Fruit Skewers with Honey Vanilla Labneh 84

Grilled Kefta 53

Grilled Stone Fruit 85

Grilled Stone Fruit with Honey Whipped Ricotta 87

H

Halibut in Parchment with Zucchini, Shallots, and Herbs 50

Harissa Yogurt Chicken Thighs 60

Heart-Healthy Nut and Fruit Trail Mix 69

Hearts of Palm Salad with Avocado and Yellow Tomatoes 76

Hearty Three-Bean Vegan Chili 23

Herb-Crusted Parmesan Filet Mignon 55

Herbed Dijon Lamb Chops 56

Herbed Garlic Chicken with Wine Sauce and Couscous 61

Herbed Lamb Steaks 56

Herbed Lima Beans 24

Herbed Tuna Bocadillo with Piquillo Peppers 80

Herb-Infused Steamed Artichokes with Lemon Garlic Dip 67

Honey Roasted Plums with Nutty Crumble and Yogurt 86

Honey-Grilled Pineapple and Watermelon 85

Hummus Cucumber Basil Sandwiches 81

I

Iced Coffee with Almond and Cinnamon Twist 15

Instant Pot Almond Date Oatmeal 14

Instant Pot Buckwheat Porridge with Balsamic Berries 12

Instant Pot Cilantro Lime Brown Rice 21

Instant Pot Creamy Yellow Lentil Soup 24

Instant Pot Farro Breakfast Bowl with Maple and Mixed Fruit 14

Instant Pot Farro Mushroom Risotto 20

Instant Pot Lemon Garlic Brown Rice Pilaf 20

Instant Pot Polenta with Arugula, Figs, and Blue Cheese 19

K

Kale and Cannellini Bean Pizza 80

L

Lamb Stew 54

Lebanese Baba Ghanoush 32

Lemon Almond Pistachio Biscotti 84

Lemon Garlic Shrimp Fettuccine 92

Lemon Herb Chermoula Sauce 96

Lemon Pesto Salmon 46

Lemon-Dijon Shrimp Endive Salad	75
Lemon-Garlic Cabbage and Carrot Slaw	75
Lemony Quinoa Salad with Zucchini, Mint, and Pistachios	74
Lentils with Artichoke, Tomato, and Feta	19
Lentils with Cilantro and Lime	21
Light and Lemony Olive Oil Cupcakes	87

M

Maltese Sun-Dried Tomato Mushroom Vinaigrette	94
Manchego Crackers	68
Marinated Greek Veggie Salad with Goat Cheese	76
Mascarpone-Stuffed Dates with Toasted Pecans	69
Mediterranean Beef Pita Wraps	56
Mediterranean Fish Stew	49
Mediterranean Fruit Bulgur Breakfast Bowl	12
Mediterranean Greek Salad with Lemon-Oregano Dressing	72
Mediterranean Muesli and Breakfast Bowl	13
Mediterranean Pita Pizza with Feta and Olives	70
Mediterranean Roasted Chickpeas with Tomatoes and Feta	38
Mediterranean Salad with Bulgur	72
Mediterranean Tomato Rice with Fresh Herbs	19
Mediterranean Tuna and Olive Salad	76
Moroccan Braised Halibut with Cinnamon and Capers	47
Moroccan Chicken Stew with Green Olives and Couscous	62
Moroccan Lamb with White Beans and Spices	24
Moroccan Red Lentil and Pumpkin Stew	42
Moroccan-Spiced Sea Bass with Chickpeas and Artichokes	51

N

No-Mayo Florence Tuna Salad	76
No-Mayo Tuna Salad Cucumber Bites	70

O

Olive Mint Vinaigrette	95
Olive Oil Poached Fish with Citrus Arugula Salad	48
Olive Oil Poached Tuna with Fresh Herbs	45
One-Pan Mushroom Pasta with Mascarpone	40
One-Pot Pork Loin Dinner	54
One-Pot Shrimp Fried Rice	48
Open-Faced Eggplant Parmesan Sandwich	80

P

Pan-Fried Pork Chops with Peppers and Onions	55
Parchment-Baked Halibut with Fennel and Carrot Medley	49

Parsley-Mint Sauce	96
Pasta E Fagioli with Rosemary and Parmesan	22
Peach and Tomato Summer Salad	74
Peaches Poached in Rose Water	87
Penne with Tuna and Green Olives	90
Pesto Chicken English Muffin Pizzas	82
Pesto-Stuffed Cucumber Boats	70
Pistachio Quinoa Salad with Pomegranate Citrus Vinaigrette	75
Pistachio-Crusted Whitefish	47
Poached Apricots and Pistachios with Greek Yogurt	88
Power Peach Smoothie Bowl	13
Pumpkin Spice Greek Yogurt Parfait	17
Pumpkin-Ricotta Cheesecake	88

Q

Quick Almond Flour Sandwich Bread	95
Quick Garlic Mushrooms	67
Quinoa with Almonds and Cranberries	41
Quinoa with Kale, Carrots, and Walnuts	26

R

Radish Chips	31
Ras Al Hanout Lamb Flatbread with Pine Nuts and Mint	79
Red Pepper Chimichurri	95
Red Wine Braised Short Ribs	54
Refreshing Cucumber Lime Popsicles	85
Roast Pork Tenderloin	55
Roast Pork Tenderloin with Cherry Balsamic Reduction	53
Roasted Broccoli with Tahini Yogurt Sauce	35
Roasted Cauliflower Arugula Salad with Pomegranate and Pine Nuts	77
Roasted Cauliflower Salad with Tahini-Yogurt Dressing	77
Roasted Fennel with Za'atar	32
Roasted Harissa	96
Roasted Lemon Chicken with Artichokes and Crispy Kale	64
Roasted Vegetable Bocadillo with Romesco Sauce	79
Roasted Vegetables with Lemon Tahini Dressing	30
Rotini Pasta in Red Wine Marinara Sauce	92
Rotini with Walnut Pesto, Peas, and Cherry Tomatoes	90

S

Salmon with Broccoli Rabe, White Beans, and Garlic Chips	46
Salmon with Wild Rice and Citrus Mint Salad	44
Sautéed Garlic Prawns with Tomatoes and Fresh Basil	46
Sautéed Mushroom, Onion, and Pecorino Romano Panini	82
Savory Butternut Squash and Apples	30

Savory Cottage Cheese Breakfast Bowl 17
Seafood Paella 44
Seasoned Steamed Crab 50
Sesame Carrots and Sugar Snap Peas 33
Sicilian-Style Roasted Cauliflower with Capers, Currants, and Crispy Breadcrumbs 33
Simple Tri-Color Lentil Salad 21
Skillet Bulgur with Kale and Tomatoes 25
Slow Cooker Mediterranean Chicken Fried Rice 21
Slow Cooker Root Vegetable Hash with Plums 29
Slow Cooker Spicy Creamer Potatoes 33
Slow Cooker White Beans with Kale 23
Slow-Cooked Brown Onion Masala Base 94
Slow-Cooked Mediterranean Pork with Olives 57
Smoky Sausage Patties 14
South Indian Sambar with Mixed Vegetables 27
South of the Coast Sweet Potato Toast 11
Southern Italian Seafood Stew in Tomato Broth 50
Spanish Home Fries with Spicy Tomato Sauce 70
Spanish Tortilla with Potatoes and Peppers 11
Spiced Lamb Couscous with Vegetables and Herbs 55
Spicy Buffalo Chicken Cheese Bites 59
Spicy Lemon Broccoli Pasta Salad 90
Spicy Roasted Potatoes 66
Spinach and Feta Frittata 15
Spinach, Sun-Dried Tomato, and Feta Egg Wraps 17
Steamed River Trout with Fresh Herb Sauce 45
Strawberry Vanilla Collagen Smoothie 17
Stuffed Artichokes 29
Stuffed Cucumber Cups 70
Sumac-Spiced Pita Bread Salad 74
Sumac-Spiced Red Lentil Dip 66
Sweet and Crispy Roasted Pearl Onions 30
Sweet Potato Gorgonzola Veggie Burgers 30

T

Tangy Asparagus and Broccoli 41
Tex-Mex Chicken Roll-Ups 59

Three-Cheese Zucchini Boats 38
Tirokafteri (Spicy Feta and Yogurt Dip) 68
Tomato Caper Sicilian Salad 73
Tomato Stewed Okra with Cilantro 33
Tossed Green Mediterranean Salad 72
Tuna Croquettes 67
Turkey Breast in Yogurt Sauce 60
Turkey Meatloaf 63
Turkish Poached Eggs with Spiced Yogurt 16

V

Vegetable Pita Sandwiches 81
Vegetarian Dinner Loaf 26
Vinaigrette 95

W

Warm Bulgur Wheat Breakfast with Apples and Almonds 13
Warm Fava Beans with Whole-Wheat Pita 14
Warm Mediterranean Farro Bowl with Chickpeas and Artichokes 40
White Bean Dip with Garlic and Herbs 95
Whole-Wheat Capellini with Sardines, Olives, and Manchego 91
Whole-Wheat Puttanesca Spaghetti 91
Wild Cod Oreganata 51
Wilted Kale Salad 74

Z

Za'atar Chickpeas and Chicken 25
Zesty Cucumber Yogurt Dressing 96
Zesty Mint Walnut Pesto 96
Zucchini Marinara Chicken Bake 60
Zucchini Noodles Pomodoro 36
Zucchini Ribbons with Lemon Ricotta and Fresh Herbs 34

Made in United States
North Haven, CT
07 March 2025

66558372R00059